MY CITY WAS GONE

ALSO BY DENNIS LOVE

Blind Faith

MY CITY WAS GONE

One American Town's Toxic Secret,
Its Angry Band of Locals, and
a $700 Million Day in Court

DENNIS LOVE

WILLIAM MORROW
An Imprint of HarperCollins*Publishers*

Grateful acknowledgment is made to reprint lines from "Darkness on the Edge of Town" by Bruce Springsteen. Copyright © 1978 Bruce Springsteen (ASCAP). Reprinted by permission. International copyright secured. All rights reserved.

MY CITY WAS GONE. Copyright © 2006 by Dennis Love. All rights reserved. Printed in the United States of America. No part of this book may be used or reproduced in any manner whatsoever without written permission except in the case of brief quotations embodied in critical articles and reviews. For information address HarperCollins Publishers, 10 East 53rd Street, New York, NY 10022.

HarperCollins books may be purchased for educational, business, or sales promotional use. For information please write: Special Markets Department, HarperCollins Publishers, 10 East 53rd Street, New York, NY 10022.

FIRST EDITION

Designed by Susan Yang

Library of Congress Cataloging-in-Publication Data

Love, Dennis, 1954–
    My city was gone : one American town's toxic secret, its angry band of locals, and a $700 million day in court / Dennis Love.—1st ed.
        p. cm.
    ISBN-13: 978-0-06-058550-1
    ISBN-10: 0-06-058550-1
    1. Polychlorinated biphenyls—Environmental aspects—Alabama—Anniston.
    2. Monsanto Company—Trials, litigation, etc. I. Title.

TD427.P65L68 2006
363.738'4—dc22   2006043304

06 07 08 09 10   NMSG/QWF   10 9 8 7 6 5 4 3 2 1

Everybody's got a secret, son
Something that they just can't face
Some folks spend their whole lives trying to keep it
They carry it with them every step that they take
Till some day they just cut it loose
Cut it loose or let it drag 'em down
Where no one asks any questions
Or looks too long in your face
In the darkness on the edge of town
—BRUCE SPRINGSTEEN

Without chemicals, life itself would be impossible.
—FROM A 1977 AD CAMPAIGN FOR THE MONSANTO CORPORATION

CONTENTS

PROLOGUE

Highway 202 veers west from Anniston, Alabama, population 24,000, as if it suddenly just decided to get the hell out of town. Past the dog-eared Greyhound station on the left—still notorious for its role in a shocking racial incident in 1961—and a Winn-Dixie grocery store on the right, the road climbs a slight grade until it reaches an overpass that straddles the railroad tracks that run north and south through the city, clearly demarcating Anniston's West from its East Side. Stop your car, look back over your right shoulder, and you'll be confronted with the most detailed panorama the city has to offer: a foreground of grimy warehouses, foundries, and pockmarked working-class neighbor-hoods smudged with time and neglect, which dissolve to the turn-of-the-century facades of Noble Street, which in turn fade to marginally newer and shinier edifices of commerce, all framed by the soft back-drop of the pine-and-hardwood-dappled Appalachian foothills that have embraced Anniston for all of its 120-plus years.

Decidedly more romantic views of the city are available. From the wide decks and verandas of the eighty-year-old stone mansions that dot the "mountain" over on the East Side, where the old money lives along the winding avenues above the country club, Anniston emerges through the blue southern haze as some idyllic, foliage-dense hamlet—a quaint collection of church steeples, courthouse spires, and modest office buildings, a place where it would seem that life is serene and good and has been so for many, many years. And so it has, mostly, for anyone with a veranda view.

Yet it can be difficult to see with clarity from that fuzzy remove; things present themselves with more precision down on 202, from that perch above the railroad trestle. Continue your drive out toward the city limit, delving deeper into the blue-collar heart of the West Side, and you'll come upon the old Monsanto chemical plant, now spun off as Solutia, a primary anchor of Anniston's industrial profile since the 1930s. Take a right on Clydesdale Avenue, past the old Mars Hill Baptist Church and acres of barren, fenced-off land on the right and a clump of tattered homes and businesses on the left, past a desolate intersection and an incongruous-seeming office of the U.S. Environmental Protection Agency, and you'll finally come to McCord's Supermarket—a mom-and-pop grocery, now closed, a fixture of this close-knit neighborhood for decades. Inside, if you've picked the right day, you'll find Shirley McCord herself, a wizened, sharp-eyed little woman, in her seventies now, who, with some help from her friends and former customers, keeps watch over The List.

Smile and ask nicely and Shirley McCord will disappear back into her cluttered warren of an office and then reemerge with a sheaf of wrinkled notebook paper that, over time, has grown to seventeen pages. It is a roster, arduously written in her own hand, of acquaintances who have died in the last twenty-five years or so, with the cause of death noted in the margin beside each name. The vast majority list "cancer."

"We always thought it was strange," Shirley McCord says. "We lost so many loved ones to cancer. All kinds of cancers, nasty ones. But now it all makes sense."

The story has finally been cobbled together here in Anniston, my hometown, where I spent most of my first thirty years before I abruptly decided, much like Highway 202, to hang west toward wherever it was that the sun settled into the far hills every day. I left as that story slowly began to bubble up from the depths and finally thrashed to the surface, revealing itself like some craggy, prehistoric, deep-sea monster grown huge by aeons of bottom-feeding in the dark shadows of the ocean floor—a two-headed monster at that. As it turns out, Anniston—created from whole cloth to serve exclusively at the pleasure of commerce, a Reconstruction-era "model city" envisioned by its profiteering yet starry-eyed founders as a Utopian centerpiece of the Industrial Age—instead became the victim of a staggering, even historic, environmental double whammy brought on by the harsh, consumptive legacy of its long-standing paternal influences, the twin gods of industry and national defense.

Part of the story involves a case of insidious industrial pollution, covered up for generations, that led to years of litigation over the conduct of the Monsanto Chemical Corporation and eventually involved superlawyers like Johnnie Cochran and Jere Beasley, culminating in the largest legal settlement of its kind in U.S. history—dwarfing the famous Erin Brockovich case, the previous champion. The rest of the tale centers on the dense legacy of the Cold War and how Anniston came to be the site where a vast cache of lethal chemical weapons was left to atrophy and leak until they were deemed too dangerous to move, prompting the Army's decision to build a billion-dollar incinerator of debatable environmental integrity a very short drive down 202 from Shirley McCord's grocery.

This was the Anniston to which I returned in 2003, not the

bustling, prosperous, cultured, proud, sometimes even arrogantly superior New South city of my youth, but a place roiled and divided by acrimony, sprouting FOR SALE signs like mushrooms, hemorrhaging population and bad karma. Unrest proliferated, not only over the gargantuan lawsuits pressed by mostly black and poor West Siders against a longtime employer and civic player like Monsanto, but also by loud protests against the incinerator by high-profile local citizens and outsiders like Martin Luther King III. In a larger, symbolic sense, it was as if the working class of Anniston—weary of paying the wages of environmental sin of city fathers hidden away in their airy hillside lairs—"sick and tired," as the black preachers like to say, "of being sick and tired"—had finally risen up against the ruling class that had essentially had its way since the town's very inception.

Those of influence, of course, saw things much differently. These plaintiffs and protesters, in their view, were reckless rabble-rousers playing with fire. The legal judgments were not only creating a calamitous atmosphere for business but besmirching Anniston's reputation on heretofore unimaginable levels. (Everyone had seen, and cringed at, the city's treatment at the hands of *60 Minutes*.) And the thickening legal and political morass around the incinerator, by then ready to start "the burn," was seen by many as jeopardizing the presence in Calhoun County of the Army, its largest employer.

I returned to an Anniston where David Baker—a man who in his youth on the dauntingly hardscrabble West Side had watched his brother die of an inexplicable cancer, and had then spent thirty years in New York as a two-fisted union organizer before returning home—had become a folk hero, a sort of African-American Robin Hood, by leading the fight to gather plaintiffs for the lawsuits that would make international headlines and bring relief to people who had never dreamed of challenging the powers-that-had-always-been.

I returned to an Anniston where old white classmates of mine had risen to positions of leadership, people like Mayor Chip Howell—his late father not only a successful real estate entrepreneur but a chief architect in the 1970s of Anniston's fragile racial tolerance—who now found himself saddled by default with the task of forging a political solution to the incinerator crisis and with the challenge of creating a consensus about how to manage the city's very survival.

I returned to an Anniston where the U.S. government, in an unprecedented decision, distributed gas masks en masse to the mostly low-income residents within the "red zone" immediately surrounding the incinerator site; where my parents have set aside a special "panic room" in their home, to be sheeted in Army-issued plastic, in case of a real-life disaster not unlike the fictional "airborne toxic event" described in Don DeLillo's *White Noise*; where the funereal test wail of the community-wide incinerator warning system stops people in their tracks a few times each month; where Donald Stewart, the liberal, intense, prickly local attorney and former U.S. senator who first sued Solutia/Monsanto (and made tens of millions) is still harangued on Noble Street; where Joel Laird, the conscientious and God-fearing circuit judge who presided over Stewart's case, can be seen driving about town in his to-the-nines replica of the black-and-white squad car that patrolled Mayberry in *The Andy Griffith Show*; where people still talk about the time Johnnie Cochran came to town to "listen" to folks about Monsanto and PCBs and wound up speaking passionately to a crowd of five thousand that had materialized from nothing other than pure word of mouth, surely the largest assemblage ever in Anniston that didn't involve a televangelist or a football.

And I returned to an Anniston where my own past, present, and future had patiently waited for nearly twenty years while I pinballed across the country, finally running out of continent in California, that hypnotic, mythical place where every misfit and misanthrope worth his salt ends up after a while. California—especially Los Angeles—is a wonderful place to hide, the perfect getaway scheme, lousy with dreamers and posers of every stripe, which meant I fit in beautifully. But I could never escape Anniston—the one constant in my life, the place that attached itself to me like some ghostly barnacle and, for good or ill, never let go. So I came back, at last, back to the inevitable dissolution that time inflicts on family, friends, place, and memory.

I came back to tell Anniston's story and, along the way, to figure out mine—to look for hope and healing where I could find it, but also to confront the very real possibility that my hometown was being destroyed by the very forces that created it, that my city was gone.

CHAPTER ONE

GROUND ZERO

David Baker had fled Anniston all those years ago with a wad of ill-gotten cash in his pocket and the police on his tail, although at the time the cops didn't exactly know it was David they were looking for. There had been trouble in Anniston, real honest-to-God trouble, with black-against-white melees in broad daylight and, on both sides of town, the vengeful yellow flash of shotgun fire into houses from passing cars under the gauze of darkness. Things were crazy-tense, live-wire electric, black folks on the West Side guarding their homes with guns locked and loaded, venal good old boys joyriding through once-forbidden parts of town leaving an arrogant trail of spent beer cans and shotgun shells, carloads of young, angry, and bad-intentioned black men making their own incursions through parts of the city likewise once forbidden to them. Boundaries had been ruptured—not only the invisible yet universally agreed-upon geographic boundaries that had maintained Anniston's racial pecking order for as long as anyone could remember, but the boundaries of civil restraint as well. Everything had been brought to a great agitated boil, and David had not been uninvolved.

Then, as if by heavenly decree, David found money in his hand not rightfully his but intended for him all the same. It was a fateful sign in big block letters that the day had come to make tracks and waste no time in doing so. The tracks led to New York City, where David would spend the middle chunk of his life as a union organizer in the thick of chaos that demanded every molecule of skill and gumption he possessed; where he would fall in and out of love and back again; where he would shoot a man in self-defense; where he would come of age and become a fully realized piece of work. It was a dazzling, swashbuckling, all-consuming ride, one that after twenty-five years left him crisp at his core and thinking of home. New York had burned through tougher men than David Baker, and there was no shame in admitting it. He was done.

Or so he believed.

No, he was done, and sure of it, so he retreated back to Anniston with his union pension and time on his side, still a relatively young man, not yet fifty. The town razed by turmoil and animosity in his rearview mirror so long ago now appeared at peace with itself. He lazed around the West Side, enjoyed lunch at his mother's table, had a few every now and then with his running buddies from the old days. The guys were still around; fatter, uglier, but still there, mostly. A few—maybe more than a few—had already gone on to their rewards, long before their time, but wasn't that the way of the world? It made you appreciate what you had in the here and now. Here, now, away from New York, back in Anniston, David could breathe deeply, clear his head, look around, and give thanks for the simple pleasure of walking the ground upon which he was born and raised, among people he remembered and loved and who remembered and loved him. Sometimes he thought of New York and felt an emptiness, but nobody said the transition would be seamless. David figured it was the same for the retired ballplayer, his body broken and unable to continue but still haunted by the game-day thrill of competing, of kicking the other guy's can into oblivion, of *mattering*. It would take a while for the cheers to stop ringing in your ears, for the adrenaline to stop pumping. But it did, soon enough.

Then David took a job.

The cosmos holds many mysteries. One of the more intriguing ones, in retrospect, is why fate would conspire to see to it that David Baker, of all people, would be hired to help remove contaminated soil from property owned by the Monsanto Corporation on the West Side of Anniston, Alabama. Most men, especially struggling, poorly educated ones grateful just to have a job, are content to collect their paychecks and keep any questions to themselves. Go-along-to-get-along still carries a powerful resonance, particularly for a black man in the Deep South. But while David Baker may have been educated on the margins and was struggling in his own way, he had devoted a career a quarter of a century long to asking questions, to challenging authority, to twirling the dials on his bullshit detector until it reached peak operating efficiency. And the more time he spent on the Monsanto job, the more his bullshit detector screamed bloody damned murder.

David began to ask questions. Quietly at first, because that's the way you start. *What is this soil contaminated with? PCBs? What are those?* The questions led to other questions, and some very revealing answers. David began to look around at his hometown with new eyes, and what he saw disturbed him greatly. People young and old had been dying on this side of town of cruel and ghastly illnesses for as long as David could recall. His own brother had passed away at seventeen from a combination of maladies so hideously lethal that his doctors could barely describe them. People had always shaken their heads on the West Side and said, *Must be something in the water around here.*

What if there really was?

David's old instincts roared back at him. He began to call meetings. The first humble gathering consisted of himself and three others in a church basement. But David knew how to build momentum: you created it yourself, by the sheer dint of doing. He talked and hustled and politicked and browbeat and backslapped, and the meetings got bigger, and soon it seemed that "Monsanto" was on everyone's lips. Suddenly the puzzle pieces seemed to fly together. There were rumblings about a lawsuit filed against Monsanto by a black church situated across the road from the venerable fenced-off plant, while Monsanto attempted to purchase whole blocks of property surrounding the plant. David began to put together a coalition of people interested in PCBs and in what was happening to their community. David got laid off from his job at Monsanto; he didn't care. The old New York juices were flowing again, just like in the days of glory, when every day seemed like game day.

David Baker was *back,* baby, all the way back, ready to lead a fight that he now realized he had trained a lifetime for. It would be a fight that would make his New York years seem positively tame.

Well, Chip Howell said to himself, you wanted to be mayor, and so you are. Now buck up and *do your job.*

And his job, at the moment, consisted of deciding if he wanted to make a lot of people very angry in order to do the Right Thing. If it was indeed the Right Thing, and there was no way to know that. Only time and history and the telling of it would settle that, probably long after he was dead and gone. Unless, of course, the worst-case scenario played out—the "unthinkable," as some folks around town referred to it—in which case he most likely would be lynched immediately on Noble Street, a lusty throng of his fellow citizens (the ones who had survived) cheering his abrupt and dangling passage from this world into the next.

Chip sat in his City Hall office and mused over it all one more time. It was funny, really, what a nutty, unpredictable, bizarre job this could be. He had essentially been born to it, he knew that, and because he had been prepared and molded and readied to be mayor practically his entire life, he had mostly known what to expect. He had known that there would be people who would sprinkle his path with rose petals because he was mayor, and that there would be people who wouldn't even look him in the eye for the same reason. He had known that there would be times when the job was downright exhilarating, and times when it would be absolutely exasperating. He had known that in the course of doing his job he would probably lose some friends and make some new ones. He had expected that his golf game would probably suffer, which was no small thing, but he ran anyway.

But there were some things he didn't anticipate, some lessons he had to learn on the fly. One was: Never show up anywhere— anywhere—unprepared to make some impromptu remarks, or to lead the gathering in prayer. Even if he was merely sticking his head into some meeting or another for a minute or two, just to get a sense of what was going on, be it the planning commission or the PTA or the downtown booster club, he would invariably be spotted and given the floor. "Mister Mayor, would you say a few words?" Or "Chip, would you give thanks?" He didn't mind it, just hadn't realized that that little ritual was part of the bargain of being mayor.

There was something else he hadn't expected: that he would be making a decision that could literally mean life or death for tens of thousands of people. Oddly enough, if he did what he considered to be the Right Thing—if he stepped in and greased the skids to allow the incinerator to start "the burn"—an infinitesimal possibility existed that the whole thing could go haywire and send a billowing cloud of death over the city, like in some hokey made-for-TV disaster movie. Chip didn't believe that would happen in a million years, but it *was* possible. Crazier things had happened. That was the short-term worst case. The long-term worst case was that the incinerator wouldn't be as efficient as the Army claimed and that small amounts of lethal poison would be emitted from the incinerator's stacks, causing untold cumulative effects on the surrounding population, effects that might not be known for generations. Again, not the remotest chance of that happening, to Chip's mind—he had studied the science until his eyes virtually screamed—but yes, it *could* happen. Something, anything, could go wrong, and there would be a scapegoat hunt for the ages, and who do you suppose would be scapegoat number one? The mayor who made it all happen, of course.

He could easily dodge the entire matter, let the problem resolve itself on the natural. But that wasn't Chip's style, for one thing. For another, doing nothing in this instance carried its own set of perils. A noisy protest campaign against the incinerator had taken its toll, and the Calhoun County Commission, among others, had begun to insist on safety measures that to many observers were redundant, if not beyond the pale. The Army was getting more upset by the day— its billion-dollar baby just standing there, monolithic and inactive, like a magnificent racehorse kept in the stable, while the process dragged on. Chip's very real fear was that a continuing delay would begin to threaten the existence of the region's largest employer, the Anniston Army Depot. Who was to say that the Department of

Defense wouldn't put the depot on its 2005 base closures list out of pure spite? To Chip, who had helplessly watched the shuttering of Anniston's other long-standing military base, Fort McClellan, the odds of the Anniston Army Depot winding up in mothballs seemed much greater than the odds of the incinerator going up in highly toxic smoke. But who could know for sure?

Do your job.

If he provided political cover for the Army—and he had conjured up a strategy that he believed would do that very thing—he would incur the wrath of the county commission, local activists, and a sizable number of others who were interested in seeing the burn delayed or canceled outright. He would be on the hook if anything went awry, and he would have to live with the potentially devastating aftermath. If he did nothing, he might very well seal the fate of the Anniston Army Depot, his city's most important economic force.

Do your job.

Chip couldn't imagine that any of the mayors in the long and colorful history of the city he loved, the city that he had lived away from only to attend college, had ever held its fate in their hands as gingerly as he did at that moment.

Do your job.

Chip reached for the phone.

David Baker left Anniston as a young man and returned only after many years. Chip Howell never really left, tied to the place by destiny as well as heritage. For my part, I fell somewhere in between, hanging in until I was thirty, absorbing every last drop, then leaving in such a rush that I hardly looked back. I had been reluctant to leave, but I had also learned early on that Anniston was a place you could leave but never truly escape—it would follow you to the ends of the earth, lightly tethered, never really letting you go, and there was comfort in that.

My earliest memory of Anniston is of sitting astride my red-and-white tricycle at the top of the hill on Thirtieth Street, gathering my courage, staring down at the houses far below. Ours was one of them, a tiny frame house in the midst of a middling neighborhood filled with families whose breadwinners worked at the pipe foundries and textile mills that gave Anniston its rough-hewn identity in the late 1950s. But I didn't know anything about that then; I knew that my father worked at a grocery store, that my mother stayed home with me, and that the portal to the great outside world was the steep hill that soared from our short driveway to what seemed like the clouds.

I meant to conquer that hill. I knew that from that hill you could see the big four-lane boulevard, Quintard Avenue, that ran along the side of another, much larger hill and down into the center of town, with its mesmerizing stream of traffic. I knew that from that vantage point you could see Lee's Drive-In, the popular teen hangout in those days, from which hopped-up Chevys and Fords driven by bourbon-swilling hoods roared out onto Quintard like so many Robert Mitchums in so many pale-life reenactments of *Thunder Road*. I knew that from atop that hill you could see virtually everything anyone could possibly want to see or comprehend, and I craved the thrill.

And so, behind my mother's back and, as I well knew, against her wishes, I pedaled my tricycle down to the end of the driveway, turned right, and began to labor up the hill. At some point I dismounted to walk the trike the rest of the way up, pushing toward the summit. It couldn't have taken more than a few minutes, but I was four years old and it was as if I were scaling some foreign peak, the minutes seeping past like hours. (One of the odd mathematical realities of life is how much faster time expires the older you get. A year of life at age four represents fully 25 percent of your existence; at age fifty, a mere 2 percent. At age four, a year is a great, massive, marvelous, meandering entity, an epoch. At fifty, a year is a fleeting blur, flitting by like some buzzing, careless, unaware, short-lived insect whose sole intention is to furiously reproduce itself before the lights go out forever.)

I made the crest of the hill, turned the trike around, remounted, and gazed upon the world. It was all there: the teeming four-lane; the drive-in, its parking lot vacant in the harsh afternoon sun; the congealed assortment of frame houses that, with a few variations, looked exactly like mine; on the horizon, blue hills. I singled out our house, last on the left at the end of the street far below, down there among the rank-and-file earthlings. I felt a kind of weightlessness, some sort of highly flammable blend of exhilaration and fear, of *freedom*. I visualized my mother puttering innocently at home, not yet attuned to the telling clue of the odd stillness that had fallen, unaware of the craggy heights her fugitive, mountain-goat son had scaled. It seemed like I spent an eternity up there, encoding the view, squinting at the distant landmarks of my life then, a young prince among eagles. But I knew I had to return soon or risk discovery. And I knew the time had come to reward myself for my fearless climb, to launch out into the thin air and glide back toward home.

Like an Olympic jump-skier slipping down the chute, I shoved off, slowly. But merciless gravity took hold almost instantly, and as the trike began to hurtle downward I immediately realized that I had both underestimated the savage incline of the hill and overestimated my ability to control my ride at such a sustained speed. I hunched over and gripped the handlebars for dear life; the pedals spun viciously, hammering my bare feet out of the way. My heels groped for the pavement to no avail. Deafening air rushed past my ears at hurricane force. Things were happening at warp speed and in slow motion all at once, the big front wheel wobbling crazily from the stress, houses and driveways and parked cars zip-floating by, the trike beginning to buck and weave like some angry, snorting rodeo beast determined to send me flying and then gore me for my brazen trouble. The handlebars finally began to wrest themselves from my clenched grip, and the trike began to career wildly from side to side but somehow stayed upright, with me still on it. The bottom of the hill surged up at me like a fist; to my left somewhere I was vaguely aware of the clicking, frame-by-frame image of my mother exploding from our front door like a woman on fire, arms gyrating as if to ward off the flames, reaching out to hurl some metaphysical road-block in my path. And then, suddenly, the hill seemed to level out, the momentum of the trike seemed to slow, and I was tumbling along the asphalt for what seemed like days. I remember coming out of a trance, my mother picking me off the pavement, holding my head in her hands, imploring me to tell her I was okay. And I was, except, I noticed dreamily, for ten bloody stubs that had replaced my toes, evidence of my unconscious attempt to slow the wicked descent of the tricycle as it burned into the atmosphere back toward the planet's surface.

My mother—now assured that I had not been too seriously injured—launched into an epic, well-deserved ass-chewing, but I was hardly listening. I had stolen away on a reckless venture, had observed the unknown world from a mythical plain, and had survived the dangerous ride home, slathered in blood and glory. I couldn't wait to do it again, and again.

CHAPTER TWO

UNDERCURRENT

David Baker graduated from Wellborn High School in one day.

Well, four hours, really; just one morning is all he lasted. So much for trying to follow in big sister's shoes, sister Janice, who was already enrolled there and destined to be the first black female to wear the cap and gown at Wellborn. But Janice was always better at taking crap than David ever was, so that pretty much explained that.

David had never wanted to go to Wellborn in the first place. It was 1966, after all, and it was still rough, brother, *extremely* rough, as far as he was concerned. Everything about the place felt wrong, didn't fit. Even the name—*Wellborn*—didn't fit. Wasn't anybody who went to that school who was born well. Just a bunch of rednecks and niggers, in David's view, with rednecks outnumbering the niggers about fifty to one. And those white boys weren't shy about demonstrating what the lay of the land was, just in case anybody unfortunate enough to have black skin wasn't clear on the situation. And the situation was this: *We don't want you here, so watch your ass.* And you know what? David understood that, he really did.

Didn't even take it personally, to be honest with you. He wasn't going to back down if anybody challenged him—be sure about that—but he wasn't one of these people who necessarily went *looking* for it. No use in it. He'd seen too many things happen growing up on the West Side to go searching around for trouble to get into. Hell, Kenny Adams, the most notorious nigger-hater in town, shot Albert Satcher one day right in the gut for absolutely no reason in the world. Kenny got five years, and was proud to serve. You never knew when some crazy white boy was gonna go off.

David liked to think of himself as a path-of-least-resistance guy, and he was convinced that it was a beautiful and very practical philosophy. He knew in his heart that not *every* white kid at Wellborn wanted to try to whip his butt just because he was black. But most of them did, so why go around calling here-kitty-kitty in the lion's den? They just weren't ready to commune with black folks yet, and maybe the truth of it was that black folks weren't ready to get up with them either. All of which was fine, just fine, with David Baker. He didn't have anything against white kids; he played with them all the time when he was little. David still remembered the time he and a little white buddy of his, Mark Burgess, were playing out in the field when Dinky Adams and this little white gang of his started throwing rocks at them. You know, *Get outta here nigger* and all that. And Mark and David just started throwing rocks right back at 'em, side by side, making them run. Mark and David felt like they had won the Battle of Midway or something. Back then, you might be black and he might be white, but both of you were poor, so you were in the same leaking boat bailing bilgewater like your life depended on it, which it did.

But with all that said, David would be happy to go to Calhoun County Training School over in the next district in Hobson City,

3909395

where it was 100 percent black, the living was easy, and everybody got along great.

Except . . . Mama had this thing. Maybe Wellborn wasn't ready for the Baker kids, but the Baker kids were *damn* sure ready for Wellborn, in her mind. There was better schooling at Wellborn, she knew that, and her kids could use it. Maybe if David, who had always been a good boy and smart, got a decent high school diploma he could do something other than work in the pipe shop at M&H Valve like his daddy his whole life. Wasn't anything wrong with working in the shops, it was honorable work and the pay was good, but it seemed to take something out of a man, wrung the life out of him somehow. Mr. Baker had done well at M&H, had been the first black man to be allowed to pour the molds—he was proud of that. It was hot, hard work, but Bake had hung with it and made himself a place there and kept food on the table at home. Not that he was perfect; he was bad to fool around some, Mama knew that for a fact, and on Saturday night he was gonna drink gin and get drunk with his cronies, no matter what anybody said. But Sunday morning, you could count on it, Bake would be up bright and early and with the family at church, singing hymns with that deep, resonant voice of his. He was a provider and a churchgoing man, and Mama could live with that. But David could see for himself the chronic weariness that his daddy carried around with him, the pipe shop man's burden, and the toll it took on his body through the years. David wasn't anxious to live that way, and he understood that you had to have a high school diploma to have a chance to do something a little better with your life.

But Mama wasn't hearing anything about County Training. "You're gonna go over there to Wellborn with your sister, and that's that," she told David. "Besides, some of your friends are gonna be there too: Jerome Hawkins, for one, some of the Satcher boys, Tip Bagley. So it's not like it's gonna be you against the world." She kept at it, and at it, and *at* it. "All right, Mama, all *right*," David finally said, crumbling. Lord God, that woman could talk a dog up a tree when she got her mind set on something.

But he wasn't surprised by her resolve—David had seen it before. Mama was quiet, and sweet, with a gentle smile that could light up creation. She wasn't any troublemaker, that was for sure. But she had inner strength, or fortitude, or whatever you wanted to call it. It ran in the family. Her father, Ellecanaan Dunson, was a heck of a man, a country preacher down around Roanoke in Randolph County, where both sides of David's family were from. (There were so many Bakers down there they had one little community everybody called Bakerville. David's relatives still owned land in Randolph County and always told him he could have some of it one day if he wanted to live on it. But David knew enough to know he wasn't going to build any house down there in the middle of those woods. He was a city boy, and the city was where he planned to stay.) Granddaddy Dunson was an upright man, brought his children up by the Bible and by not sparing the rod, either. And his son James, David's uncle . . . well, he was a family legend.

David had heard the story a thousand times and never tired of it. Uncle James had been a soldier during World War II in Europe. One day he went up a hill with 230 men, and only about 30 of them came down. About 15 of those were captured by the Germans, including James, and about 5 of those died during the first week in the POW camp. The Germans kept James and some of the others in a pen next to a cage where they kept some of their guard dogs. They fed the dogs every day, but they only fed the prisoners a couple of times a week. They were all starving to death, for real; James watched several of his fellow prisoners die right in front of him. And he had no reason to believe that he was going to get out of there alive himself.

Sometimes, when they fed the dogs, James and some of the other POWS would try to reach into the cage to steal the food. But the dogs were ferocious and would just as soon tear your arm from its socket as look at you, especially if you were trying to take their sustenance. James finally gave up on that; he might starve to death, but he wasn't going to lose a hand and bleed to death either, trying to take some slop out of a dog's dish.

The night came when James knew he was on the brink of death. He was having visions that transported him to other places. He saw the world as it truly was, not only a place of cruelty and suffering but also one of love and happiness; he could see into the heavens and see the good Lord in all his radiant finery, beckoning him home. He wanted to go, was ready to go. *Take me, God.* Then he was presented with another vision. It was of his mother, sitting in her favorite chair in Roanoke. He could see her just as plain as day. Her hair was long and silky and she was rocking in that chair, smiling and saying something to him. And at that moment James knew that he wasn't going to die, that he would fight to live, because his mother was saying so.

The visions stopped, and James entered back into the earthly world, back into the stink and mire and suffering. He saw that the dogs had been fed, that there was food in the trough in the next cage. Desperate now, even though one of the guard dogs lay right there watching him, James reached into the cage to take a handful of food from the trough.

And the dog *moved aside.*

The dog, the same dog James had seen rip flesh from the others, let James eat. After that day, the dog never bothered James, always let him eat. It was what kept James alive, gave him a chance to get to the next day, and the next. It wasn't really a dog, James decided. It was an angel, sent by God.

What happened next, you couldn't make it up. The government had already paid a death benefit to the Dunsons. They had made their peace with God over it, as painful and unbelievable as it was to lose James. He had died a hero, they knew that, fighting for his country. In May 1945, a memorial service was held for James in his daddy's church, and it seemed like half of Roanoke was there. A marker was placed in the church cemetery. It was a sad, gorgeous spring day, and afterward everybody milled about outside the church, consoling the family as best they could. After a while a few people noticed a rail-thin boy walking up the road toward the church, but he was nobody they recognized so no one paid him much mind; but he got closer and somebody finally shouted out, "Praise God, it's James Dunson!" A wild near-panic broke out as people flocked around James, who weighed ninety pounds and looked like some withered, peanut-shell replica of the sinewy young man who had left for war three years before. James was mystified by the crowd; he first thought it was a homecoming reception that somehow had been arranged. "My son," the Reverend Dunson said, clutching James to his chest as tears fled down his cheeks, "we just buried you."

Turned out James had assumed that the Army would notify his family about his liberation from the POW camp, let them know that he was alive and would be home soon. No such notice came. While James was focused on getting well and getting home, his family had prepared for a proper send-off to the Promised Land.

Some years later James read in the newspaper about new benefits for former POWs. He drove down to Montgomery and presented himself to the clerk at the VA, told him why he was there. The white clerk looked at him and said, "You a damn liar. There weren't no nigger POWs in World War II." James nearly climbed through the counter window at him. It took him years to claim the benefits that were rightfully his—but he did, and he ended up legally adopting his grandchildren so they could be eligible for scholarships and go to college.

One other thing about James. David knew it; everybody who was ever around him knew it.

You did not mistreat a dog in his presence, or you answered to him.

That was the kind of cloth from which Mama was made. But she was plenty tough by her own lights; David had seen that for himself. She didn't back down from anybody, had proved that beyond any doubt back on Mother's Day in '61. As luck—or better put, as misfortune—would have it, on that Sunday, she and Bake had attended a funeral in the Bynum community west of town and were driving down Highway 202 going home. On the way, they rolled up on an amazing, terrifying sight—a Greyhound bus wrenched over to the side of the road, flames and black smoke cascading from it, black and white folks fleeing the burning vehicle. The bus was surrounded by a group of white men, men they recognized, laughing and carrying on. No one else was on the scene; the Bakers were the first to happen upon it. Bake didn't want to stop, and who could argue the point? These were dangerous white men up to absolutely no good, a glassy-eyed mob intent on inflicting serious damage on their fellow man. No, Bake didn't want to stop, wasn't going to—but Mama *made* him stop. Made him stop, and when he did she bolted from the car, crossed the road, and began to bang on the door of a house of a white woman who lived there. The door opened and Mama beseeched the home-owner to allow her to use the water hose in her front yard to spray water on the bus, to wash the acrid smoke and soot from the passengers' eyes, to give them something to drink, *anything*. Shamed, Bake left the car and made his way to the bus, guiding the coughing and wailing victims toward Mama, steering them from harm's way.

And then, soon enough, they got the hell out of there.

Back home, Mama wasn't sure at first what, exactly, they had seen out there, but by evening it seemed like the whole world knew. It was all over the TV: the Greyhound had been one of two buses full of "Freedom Riders" from up North, black folks and white folks riding together to try to integrate lunch counters and other facilities in the South. They had some luck in places like Charlotte and Nashville, but the people who were tracking their progress figured they would have a rougher time of it in the deeper South. On the way from Atlanta to Birmingham along U.S. 78—that pitiful excuse of a truck-clogged, speed-trapped, mostly two-lane highway that was the only major road between those two southern cities at the time—one of the buses had stopped at the Greyhound station near the intersection of Noble and Eighth streets. There had been some trouble there—a white crowd was there, rocking the buses, making threats, not letting any blacks get off. Someone slashed the tires on one of the buses. Finally the bus took off, with the mob in slow, heckling pursuit. The other bus had already reached Birmingham, where another mob waited and beat up many of the Freedom Riders at the downtown terminal there. The Anniston bus, flat tires flopping, was forced to pull over about three miles from the station, leading to the scene Mama happened upon.

There was quite an outcry, as you might imagine. The story was all over the *Anniston Star* the next afternoon, a big story, lots of pic-

tures, and a long editorial. Mama read the editorial with considerable interest:

> While that group of so-called "Freedom Riders" who were so
> badly mishandled by hoodlums yesterday in Birmingham and
> Anniston might have known that they were inviting trouble
> when they invaded the Deep South on their silly mission, this
> does not excuse our failure to uphold law and order.
>
> Both our city and county officials whose duty it becomes to
> uphold the law in the territories for which they are responsible
> learned of the outrages perpetrated in Birmingham and they
> should have summoned every policeman and deputy sheriff in
> the county to protect our own good name.
>
> Instead, however, not a single arrest was made by those who
> are in office for the protection of law and order and the civil
> rights of even the bus-riding nitwits who came South looking for
> trouble while they were within the realm of the law.
>
> Both the city and the county must know the names of a little
> band of scofflaws who have more than once in the last year or so
> thumbed their noses at the duly elected officials of the city and
> county whose duty it becomes to uphold law and order. . . .

Mama didn't agree with a lot of it—she personally admired the
Freedom Riders, was humbled by their crazy courage—but one thing
was for sure: everybody knew who burned that bus, even if they
weren't there. Who else but Kenny Adams and his gang? Adams was
notoriously racist, even by Anniston standards in those days, and
there wasn't a person in town, white or black, who couldn't have told
anyone who asked that Kenny's alibi should be the first one checked
out—as if Kenny would even bother with a cover story. Adams

owned a filling station at Tenth Street and Ware Avenue on the West Side and had a knack for making his sentiments clear, namely by the hand-painted NO NIGGERS sign he often affixed to the front of his business. (Sometimes, when people complained, Kenny would relent and post a WHITES ONLY sign.) That usually got his point across, but some folks didn't always get the message; once, according to neighborhood legend, a black would-be customer pulled in and asked for a fill-up. Kenny obliged by sticking the nozzle through the car window and soaking the back seat with regular. Then there was the infamous scene in Birmingham, when Nat King Cole became the first entertainer to break the color line at the city auditorium. Kenny and his henchmen drove over, bought tickets, and proceeded to pull King off the stage during his performance, another trick that made big headlines. One thing you had to admit about Kenny: he had a flair for public relations.

But Mama began to realize that this bus thing was something else, even for Kenny. There would be some heat over this particular prank. Kenny must have realized it too, because it wasn't long before word began to filter through the grapevine to Mama that some white folks were concerned about what—and who—she may have seen that afternoon. Then the anonymous phone calls began. And it wasn't too long before a white man knocked on the Bakers' door one afternoon, a man she didn't recognize. Bake wasn't home yet, but David was. Mama answered the door, and David heard the man say something about minding your own business. *You better mind your own business and get out my yard*, Mama said, and slammed the door in his face. She wasn't afraid; she was sputtering mad. David was in awe—she hadn't backed down one *inch*. It made him feel proud, like he had never felt before.

Did the police or the feds ever get around to asking Mama about what she saw? Of course not. They never even got close, probably

never even tried. And while Mama probably would have been willing to tell what she saw if asked, she wasn't stupid. She wasn't going
to traipse down to the police station and volunteer her testimony.
Everybody knew the cops turned a blind eye to Kenny and them
anyway, and to do something like that was a good way to get a load
of buckshot through your picture window in the middle of the
night. Incredibly, this time around, against outrageous odds, Kenny
and a few others ultimately would stand a semblance of trial for the
bus burning, only for the judge to enter a directed verdict for acquit-
tal. (The good old boys agreed: *That's more like it.*) As if anyone
would really throw the book at Kenny. But, by God, wasn't *nobody*
gonna tell Mama to mind her own business, and she proved it back
then in 1961.

So there wasn't much argument with Mama about going to
Wellborn, in the end. The first day of school arrived and David duti-
fully showed up, hoping for the best but ready for the worst. Right
off, Mr. Cassidy, the principal, pulled David, Jerome, Tip, and the
Satcher boys into his office. Mr. Cassidy was a short little tank of a
man, obese and bald, with bright pink skin. "You in a white folks'
school now," he told David and them, "so you have to stop talking
like a nigger. And stay off those back stairs, that's where everybody
gets in trouble. Any questions?"

David raised his hand. "I've got one, Mr. Cassidy."

"All right."

"Yes sir, just wondering. How does a nigger talk?"

So David and the principal didn't exactly start off as soul brothers. That was at eight o'clock; the fight started at noon, when classes
broke for lunch. David was going down the back stairs when his old
nemesis, Dinky Adams, kicked him in the butt from behind. They

scuffled and head-locked around just like the old days until a teacher broke it up and sent David to the principal's office. Mr. Cassidy was livid. "I thought I told you niggers to stay off those back stairs!" That tore it. David called Cassidy a big fat son of a bitch—shouldn't have, but that's what he did—and the principal grabbed his arm. David yanked it free and turned to see the vice principal emerging from the library. "Grab that nigger!" Cassidy yelled. Wasn't no way; David knew he was in for the ass-whupping of a lifetime if he let them. So David put his best O. J. Simpson juke on the vice principal, fled down the hall, out the front door, and sprinted home without stopping—four miles. If he'd had a stopwatch, it might have been a record.

He made it to his house on Cobb Avenue and collapsed in the front yard. Sitting in the shade of the front porch were David's father and his best buddy, Mr. Darius Thomas. Bake was working the afternoon shift then at M&H; Mr. Darius was on nights at U.S. Pipe, both of them killing time before they had to face the foundry-shop music. They stared at the crumpled figure on the lawn.

Bake called out, "David! What the hell's the matter with you? How come you not in school?"

David rose up, still laboring for breath, and saw the men sitting on the porch. "They—I—Dinky Adams—kicked me in the butt—"

He managed to spit it out, Bake and Mr. Darius getting madder and madder the more they heard. They finally got up and went inside, and reemerged a few minutes later with shotguns. "Whatch'all gonna do?" David asked, still gulping air.

"Sounds like it's open season on niggers over there," Bake replied as he squinted down the chamber of his weapon. "We gonna go get them other boys out of there before somebody gets hurt. And I might have a word with that fat-ass principal. Come on, Darius."

Right about then Mama pulled into the driveway, back from the store. "Move that car, woman!" Bake yelled. "We gotta go!"

Mama's eyes flitted between the shotguns and the faces of the agitated men who held them.

Bake again: "I said move that car out the way! Or gimme the keys and I'll do it myself."

And back and forth it went until Mama finally got the whole picture. She wouldn't budge. No way was she going to let these two wild men with blood in their eye leave the premises. No doubt in her mind, it'd be the last time she'd ever see either one of them without a price on their heads or a rope around their necks. No, she would stand her ground.

In a few minutes the situation had cooled. "You let me handle this," Mama told Bake. "Now I'm gonna fix some dinner so you can get on to work instead of being lynched by sundown. All right?"

The next morning, David enrolled at Calhoun County Training, where it was 100 percent black, the living was easy, and everybody got along great.

Little bro was an angel. That's what everybody said about him, and it was the truth. Three years younger than David, Terry Baker was very much like his big brother in many ways but different as night and day in others. They greatly resembled each other, more than most brothers, and he shared David's sharp sense of humor. But he didn't have David's robust athleticism and big, booming personality; he was smaller, quieter, more sensitive. David was a hell-raiser in high school who didn't mind running around, smoking, drinking a little wine and beer; Terry never touched liquor, never put a cigarette to his lips. He didn't disapprove of it necessarily, it just wasn't his bag.

Mama always said you can tell a lot about someone by the friends they keep. That went double for Terry. There was one kid in the neighborhood named Rogers Clark—everybody called him Head. Head was a smart, good-hearted boy who had a bizarre medical problem: a big sore on his leg that would never heal. It was a big, gaping, infected thing that not only was a horror to look at but stank like a corpse. Honestly, it was difficult to be in the same room with him. The other kids were cruel about it, of course, making fun of him and shunning him terribly. It was a devastating situation for Head; he felt like he was being persecuted for something he had no control over. Other than the sore, he was healthy. Like the other kids, he swam in Snow Creek, ran through the dusty fields behind the Monsanto plant. But Lord, that leg of his would smell.

Terry and Head became best friends. Terry was the only one who seemed to understand the emotional pain Head suffered from being ostracized by the others, and he was the only one who made any effort to adapt to Head's circumstances. Nobody except Terry was willing to ignore the stench and go into Head's house to play. Nobody except Terry took the time to get to know Head rather than just ridicule him or just flat-out avoid him. It was typical Terry. He had a big heart, was truly concerned for others. Mama wondered if he might turn out to be a minister, like his Granddaddy Dunson.

But it was the strangest thing: About the time Terry got to high school, he started getting sick. No one knew exactly when his illness started to become apparent, because it was so slow and gradual. Soon, however, it was clear that he had asthma or something like it because it seemed like he was always laboring to breathe, struggling to take in air. And headaches—killer headaches, the crippling kind that put him in bed for days at a time. "Migraines," the doctor said. "Migraines and asthma. He'll just have to deal with it best he can."

But Terry didn't get better, he got worse, and nobody seemed to be able to do anything about it. Finally he got so sick they put him in the hospital, where they performed a million tests—and the truth came out. He had a large brain tumor, and that wasn't all: his heart was enlarged, caused by hardening of the arteries. Either condition was bad enough to kill him, the doctors said, and would. So odd and tragic, the doctors kept saying, and hard to explain in a person so young. But awful as it was, these things happened, they said. Sometimes there was no figuring out God's plan.

Terry died the April he was seventeen. The autopsy found his heart was the size of a half-gallon bucket. There was a sad, twisted irony about it all, David thought: Terry, who always had a heart as big as open country with room for everyone, even poor, ostracized Head, died because his heart was literally too large. They mourned him terribly, and laid him to rest on a fresh windswept afternoon in a West Side cemetery, with undertaker and family friend Russell "Tombstone" Williams handling the arrangements. Granddaddy Dunson delivered a searing eulogy, one that spoke of the tortuous conflict between God's will and the inescapable pain of human loss. On this day, no emaciated miracle came walking up the road.

Back at the house, Mama must have brought out every picture ever taken of Terry. His grinning likeness was everywhere, on every wall and counter and table. David found an old school picture, one of those small ones, and slipped it in his billfold. He would always carry Terry with him, he told himself, in his billfold and in his heart. He didn't understand what had happened, *how* it had happened, why God would choose to take someone so young and good. David wasn't much for praying, but at that moment he closed his eyes and asked God to help him see the reason, help him sort through the grief and bewilderment and mystery of it all. It doesn't have to be today, David prayed, just someday. Someday.

Something weird was going on, that was clear, even to Chip Howell and the rest of his second-grade class at Tenth Street Elementary School. Come to think of it, things had been strange, off-kilter, for a couple of days now. Much tiptoeing around by Mrs. Williams and the other teachers; nervous, furtive, whispered conferences; drawn looks exchanged. And the kids were beginning to pick up on it instinctually, in the way that birds gather and grow quiet and seem to know tornado weather is coming even though the sun is still shining in a cloudless blue sky, or the way dogs begin to pace in advance of earthquakes. Something gets in the air, and you can smell it—even if it's 1962 and you are only in the second grade, and all you routinely worry about is whether you'll be allowed to stay up late enough Friday night to watch *77 Sunset Strip*, or if the cafeteria will have enough chocolate milk to go around at lunch.

Finally it was time to go home, the bell about to ring, and the classroom filled with the static of shoes shuffling on linoleum and books being shoved into satchels, all those going-home sounds, when something unusual happened. "Children," said Mrs. Williams, standing up from behind her desk. "Children—I need your attention." The class fell silent. *Was she crying?* "I want you to know something," she said in a trembling voice. "If anything happens, I want you to know that I loved you all very much."

Huh?

Then the bell, and Chip and the rest of Mrs. Williams's second-grade class scattered out into a neighborhood, town, country, and world that seemed much less glued together than it had been not so long before. He didn't know why, but Chip Howell felt like crying too, just like Mrs. Williams. It was weird, like the entire day had been.

Chip kept puzzling over it when he got home. He was a smart kid, smarter than most, and already someone his classmates looked to as a leader. They looked to Chip because he was sharp and likable, number one, but also because Chip always seemed to know the ropes, seemed to know what school and its surrounding swirl was all about, seemed to know what to do when nobody else did. And yet now something had happened, *was* happening, but he didn't get it. So he decided he would ask his dad. His dad would know, and he would tell Chip the truth, straight-out, because that's what he always did. No sugarcoating. If a relative was very sick, Hoyt Howell didn't spare Chip or his older sister Cheryl the bad news. He told them, straight-out. In Hoyt's house, you learned early not to ask if you really didn't want to know.

You wouldn't know it from being around him—he was a man of substantial charm and good humor—but Hoyt Howell's life had been full of unrelenting reality. He had grown up poor out in the country, damned poor, and had been the first member of his family to graduate from high school. He married his sweetheart, and told her the truth: *I can't promise you that our life together will be a fairy tale, but I promise you I'll work as hard as I'm able to make it one.* They moved from the desolate and ragged beauty of Cherokee County, thirty miles south to Anniston, the seat of Calhoun County, nestled in the foothills, where pipe foundries rumbled and spewed on the West Side of town and just about any able-bodied man could get work if he was willing to sweat and strain and withstand the foul air and triple-digit heat emanating from the great furnaces. Hoyt was willing and went to work doing manual labor at M&H Valve. He began to sell real estate on the side; he was smart, with dark good looks and a way with people, and Anniston was growing. He began to make his way around town, finally went in with a partner in his own firm. Before it was all over, Hoyt Howell would be a successful man—but not because he ever pretended he was anything but a poor kid from Cherokee County, or that he didn't have to work his tail off to get wherever it was he was destined to go, or that the world wasn't the way it really was. And so if any of his beloved children wanted to know something—his children who would have a childhood and a life far different from his, either that or he would die trying to make it that way—if they asked him something, he would do his best to level with them, give them the knowledge they wanted, for good or ill, and then help them deal with the consequences.

(One of Chip's earliest memories was of a Sunday morning at the Wilmer Avenue Baptist Church, the congregation filing out after worship service. Chip, without really looking, reached up and took his father's hand. They were out the front door and halfway down the sidewalk before Chip looked up and realized he had taken the hand of a perfect stranger . . . and, startled, spun around to see his father, bemused, watching from the church steps, seeing just how far his son would go before figuring it out. It was classic Hoyt: *Go ahead, make your own way, but I'm here if you need me. Right here.*)

And so young Chip Howell, precocious anyway, knew he would get a straight answer from his father about Mrs. Williams. At dinner that evening, he asked—and Hoyt, gently but honestly, gave Chip an answer he would remember for the rest of his life, one that would permanently shape his perception of his hometown and, in turn, propel him some forty years later to engineer a decision that he believed would erase a terrifying Anniston legacy.

The Anniston that surrounded Chip Howell during his childhood was a place of conspicuous comforts and pleasures. By the time Chip was old enough to attend school in the early 1960s, Hoyt had moved his family away from the working-class neighborhood along the northernmost stretches of Noble Street and built a large brick house, in the ranch-colonial hybrid style then popular in the South, near the crest of the "mountain" that overlooks downtown from the east. Chip and his sister Cheryl, two years older, came along somewhat later in life for Hoyt and Edith; their first child, Linda, was born in 1941 and was already attending a private college in Virginia. The Howells weren't members of the Anniston Country Club quite yet, but soon would be, under the auspices of Ralph Callahan, an executive at the *Anniston Star,* a formidable entrepreneur and a Hoyt mentor. Chip and Cheryl never really experienced the blue-collar phase of Hoyt's ascension from the poorhouse days in Cherokee County, although Hoyt talked frequently about the family's origins and often took his children to visit their grandparents and other relatives in Cherokee County. But the Howells of Anniston were prospering nicely by the 1960s, and Chip's earliest images of his father were of a polished businessman, hip-deep in the development of his growing city. He had even started playing *golf,* for God's sake, then still a mostly elitist game, usually in a foursome with Callahan and some others. Not that Hoyt was terribly good at it—his son would become the golfer of the family, one of the best in the state, in fact. (Hence Chip. Hoyt W. Howell Jr. was a chip off the old block as the name usually implies, but anyone who witnessed Chip's short game on the golf course from an early age understood that he was aptly named in that respect as well.) Hoyt learned to play golf for business, though he came to enjoy it. Chip, who learned the game and its etiquette caddying for his dad—it was passed down to him as an honorable gentleman's pursuit; unseemly displays like club-throwing were unconscionable—would play golf purely for pleasure. That said much about Hoyt's personal ambitions for his family. The man who built a career upon refining the standard of living for the town in which he had invested his life meant to do the same at home.

Chip's earliest specific memory of Noble Street was of the first purchase he ever made there with his "own" money, saved from his allowance: a pair of fire-engine-red Gold Cup socks, which, of course, were swift (or "swooft," in the local parlance) when matched with a glistening pair of penny loafers. He attended movies with his friends at the venerable Calhoun and Ritz theaters on Noble. He sat on Santa's lap at the Sears store on north Noble, very near the "white" and "colored" water fountains in the hardware department, and told the Great One what he wanted for Christmas. He lunged for candy thrown by Santa from his sleigh during the annual Christmas parade down Noble. Anniston was a neat, sensible, compact entity. Noble Street was its center, its heart, and young Chip Howell relished that.

Tenth Street Elementary School was a short, steep, two-minute ride down to the foot of the mountain from Chip's house. The school was a teeming focal point of the East Side, pulling kids not only from the mountain but from the hilly, all-white neighborhoods that bordered it to the west. Those neighborhoods were full of children, hundreds of them, Boomers raised on doorstep milk, Sunday school, and Dr. Spock, bright, well-dressed products of a newly minted middle class that, like Chip, was a generation removed from the agrarian and pipe-shop economy that had sustained their parents. Everyone knew everyone. Chip, sharp-eyed and smart, with dark hair, good looks, and an easy humor inherited from Hoyt, was a class favorite. Small but quick, he played tailback on the school's peewee football team and one year scored on a long run from scrimmage to help Tenth Street win the city championship. Afternoons and weekends were spent trooping through the woods that blanketed the hillsides; later, much of that time was spent on the public golf course above Kilby Terrace (named for Depression-era steel magnate Thomas Kilby, the only Annistonian ever elected governor) that sat atop "the hill" east of downtown. ("The hill" was not to be confused with "the mountain," where the well-to-do lived. The hill was middle class by Anniston standards, separated from the mountain by Tenth Street, the city's primary east-west artery. If you told someone you played golf "on the hill" that afternoon, he knew exactly what you meant. If you added that later you were going to a party "on the mountain," he knew exactly what that meant too.)

Summers were glorious, languorous affairs. Fall was for football on crisp afternoons, the brief winters for family gatherings and holiday celebrations. On the rare occasions that it snowed enough to close the schools and the more treacherous roads, Tenth Street mountain became a winter theme park, with Chip and dozens of others spinning down the incline on waxed boards, garbage can lids, anything approximating a sled. Nobody owned a sled, because it never snowed enough for it to occur to an Anniston kid to want one; it would have been like an Eskimo longing for a surfboard. The only kid who seemed to actually own a sled was Dean Papageorge, whose father was the manager of the Monsanto plant and who had moved to Anniston from corporate headquarters in St. Louis, where it snowed plenty and sleds were a standard component of a youngster's winter arsenal. When it snowed, kids queued up as if at a carnival concession stand to hurtle downhill on Dean's sled. Winter or summer, rain or shine, Chip Howell's Anniston was about as pleasant as pleasant can be.

Not that there wasn't some dark intrigue from time to time. Most of the East Side kids knew that on the far side of the mountain range that framed every day of their lives was the Fort, a vast, mysterious compound that might as well have been on Mars for all they saw or heard about it. Some of the bolder, more reckless kids occasionally organized clandestine missions up and over the hill, through the fence, and onto the military reservation. They returned with discarded, unexploded ordnance as well as stories of helicopters clattering overhead and glimpses of the "Vietnam Village," a stand of thatched-roof huts and jungle vegetation used for training exercises. (Many Anniston kids collected the ordnance that was easily found on the Fort's artillery range. That practice reached its tragic apex when one teenager told his friends he was going to blow up a prominent fire tower on Mount Cheaha; no one took him seriously until the hoard of explosives he carried to the base of Horseblock Tower one day detonated prematurely and killed him.)

Largely, however, for Chip and his peers Anniston was a thriving yet bucolic place, cozy and unthreatening yet rife with can-do-ism and opportunity. It was also, in a view Hoyt held and passed down to his son, a town with a very unusual characteristic for the South at that time: a soul. Anniston was a place where an up-and-coming businessman like Hoyt Howell could write a guest article about the need to "declare war" on substandard housing in the city, as he did in 1956, and see it displayed across the top of the front page of the *Anniston Star.* Sure there was a small profit motive, but mostly Hoyt had seen how poor working folks—not unlike the economically oppressed people he had grown up among—lived in the dilapidated and deteriorating pipe-shop neighborhoods and mill villages on the West Side, and thought it shameful. Surely there was something people of resources and goodwill could do about it. Hoyt got a coalition together, Callahan and some others, and improvements were made. As Chip grew into consciousness, his father shared his feelings about these and many other things, trying to pass along not only a zest for the good life that a town like Anniston offered its fortunate sons but a sense of social responsibility. Hoyt always liked to joke about his three abiding rules to live by: (1) the 18th green at the Vestavia Hills Country Club in Birmingham always breaks uphill; (2) never lie, that way you don't have to remember what you said;

and (3) pay your civic rent. He would smile as he ticked them off, but that smile masked serious intent. Early on, Chip Howell came to believe that Anniston was a place to be enjoyed, appreciated, preserved, and protected.

On that evening in October 1962, on the day that Mrs. Williams tearfully bade her second graders good-bye, Hoyt explained to Chip over dinner that Anniston, Alabama, was a town with a bull's-eye on its back. There is a foreign country, he said, the Soviet Union, with which our country doesn't get along. The Soviets don't believe in freedom like America does; the Soviet Union feels threatened by America, and America feels threatened by the Soviets. Because of this ill will, both countries have built great armies and manufactured vast stores of weapons, some of them powerful enough to destroy the world. And right here in Anniston, Hoyt said, are two of the most important military centers in the United States: Fort McClellan, where thousands of soldiers are stationed, men who would be some of the first called into action in case of war; and the Anniston Army Depot, where hundreds of thousands of bombs and missiles and tanks and other weapons are salted away, also in case of war. The combination of Fort McClellan and the Depot makes Anniston a vitally significant place in the world—and a dangerous place. If the United States is ever attacked by long-range Soviet missiles, Hoyt told Chip, it's very possible that Anniston will be one of the main targets.

Now something has happened, he went on. There is an island country only ninety miles from the southern tip of Florida—not all that far from here—called Cuba, ruled by a dictator named Castro. Castro doesn't believe in freedom and is very friendly with the leaders of the Soviet Union. So friendly that the Soviets secretly shipped some very deadly weapons to Cuba and have hidden them there, to make it easier to attack our country. But President Kennedy is a very smart man and has discovered the weapons in Cuba. He has told the Soviet leaders that unless they remove the weapons from Cuba we will be forced to attack *them*. But we don't know if the Soviets will do what President Kennedy says, or whether we'll be able to stop them in time if they decide to attack us. We don't know where those missiles might land if they launch them . . . so we're waiting, and praying. We're praying that President Kennedy can work everything out. We're praying that we'll all be okay and we won't have to go to war with the Soviet Union, and that here in Anniston we'll be safe.

Chip chewed on all this for a moment. Then why do we live in Anniston, he finally asked, if it's so dangerous?

We live here because this is home, Hoyt replied. We live here because in America we can live where we want to live. We have to trust that the Army will protect us. They protect *us,* and we must support *them.* We can't just turn tail and run. That would be like admitting we're scared. And we're *not* scared. God will take care of us, no matter what happens. Okay, son?

All right, Chip said, and that was the end of it. A few days later, the Soviet Union backed down, and the relief that flooded everywhere seemed tangible and real enough to pick up and examine. But for years to come, Chip Howell carried with him a mental home movie of his family and friends going about their lives in Anniston, day in and day out, laboring at school and work, all the while with big yellow-and-black bull's-eyes painted on their backs, marked for life.

If David Baker's innocence about Anniston—such as it was—ended on his first day of high school in 1965, and if Chip Howell's ended when he quizzed his father about the Cuban Missile Crisis, then my own peculiarly insular Anniston reverie was traumatically interrupted on a Friday evening in December 1969. I was fifteen; school had been dismissed that afternoon for the holidays, and I was lounging in pajamas on the couch in the den watching *Judd for the Defense.* My father had just come home from work, having closed down the IGA supermarket he managed and partially owned in nearby Oxford, the small town just south of Anniston. As was his custom after a long day, he immediately jumped in the shower. My mother busied herself in the kitchen with a late dinner for Dad. My younger brother, Barry, seven, had already gone to bed.

The front doorbell sounded through the small house, which was odd; it was nine o'clock, long past decent visiting hours. Still immersed in *Judd,* I heard my mother pad into the living room to see which neighbor had come calling so late. Then I heard two things: the violent jangle of the decorative Christmas bells on the front door, and Mom calling out something unintelligible. *What?* I left the couch and headed down the hallway and into the living room, where two men in suits and porkpie hats stood with handguns trained on my mother and then on me.

"Where is he?" one of them grunted, meaning Dad, but my mother and I were speechless. The man heard the shower running, figured it out, and burst into the bathroom where he ripped back the shower curtain and thrust the gun in on my startled father. "Get out," he said, and my father, dripping-wet naked, did so. The man took Dad into the bedroom, told him to get dressed, and explained what was going to happen: everyone was going to get into a car and drive to my father's store, where he was going to empty the safe. "All right, all right," I remember Dad saying. "There's no need to do anything drastic. No need." Within reach in his closet was a loaded revolver, but he decided to heed his own advice. My brother was rousted from his bed—the commotion had awakened him, but he had played possum—and soon the four of us were wedged into the front seat of our tiny Rambler American, Dad driving, the two gunmen in back.

It was the most surreal car ride of my life. The two men reeked of whiskey and fear. They were clearly very nervous, which in turn frightened me deeply. They talked as if they had watched far too many gangster movies, constantly asking Dad if he was going to try to be a "hero." My father—scared but, I could tell, incensed at the sheer gall of these men—kept calm, kept reassuring them that he had no intention of doing anything except cooperating. One of the men directed a number of pointed questions at me: How old was I? Where did I go to school? Did I make good grades?

"You must be proud of your boys," he finally said to my father.

"I sure am," Dad replied.

"I'd sure hate to see anything happen because you decided to be a hero. You're not gonna be a hero, are you?"

"No sir."

I reeled at it all, this horrifying true-crime U-turn that my Christmas holidays had suddenly taken. It seemed very possible that these jokers could actually *kill us*. Somehow I had faith that they wouldn't, but that was based more on denial than clarity. They weren't wearing masks or making any other attempt to obscure their faces, save the hats—was that because they weren't going to let us live long enough to testify against them? Even at a vacuous fifteen, I had seen enough of Robert Stack in *The Untouchables* to know that kidnapping was a federal crime. The penalty would be severe, and J. Edgar Hoover's FBI would be pursuing this investigation, as opposed to the local waffle-house boys, who, if their reputation was to be believed, had trouble enough making cases for petty shoplifting.

It had never occurred to me that something like this could happen in Anniston, *my* Anniston. We lived in Golden Springs, essentially Anniston's first suburb, still within the city limits but located in the first valley beyond the "mountain." It was a perfect place for a kid to spend his bike-riding years. A patchwork of new streets had been carved out of the red clay and pine stands and cow pastures and broom sage there, and we lived in a new, three-bedroom, 1300-square-foot brick ranch purchased for $17,000. I attended the new Golden Springs Elementary School (so new it was even air-conditioned, a Jesus miracle in the Deep South in the 1960s). We were among the founding members of the new Golden Springs Baptist Church. We drank fountain Cokes and got prescriptions filled at the new Golden Springs Pharmacy in the new Golden Springs Shopping Center, which also featured a cleaners and a modest grocery. Golden Springs was its own little squared-away self-sufficient universe, isolated and secure, almost womblike, and for my parents it represented a certain sense of Having Arrived, or at least of Getting There.

My father had grown up in the Depression-era countryside outside the little town of Piedmont, Alabama, about twenty-five miles north of Anniston, which in turn was about twenty miles south of Centre, the seat of Cherokee County where Hoyt Howell had grown up poor. Dad had married his high school sweetheart—Virginia Price, who grew up near the Georgia state line in tiny Esom Hill, Georgia, and whose parents had both died by the time she was eighteen. Neither my mother nor my father grew up poor in the sense of poverty-stricken, but they were raised in hard times that tested them early in life. Both families owned some farm property; both my parents remember picking cotton as young children. My father worked at a hamburger stand from the age of twelve to earn money to buy his own shoes, and by high school he was managing the grill at the local pool hall, where he learned everything one needed to know about human nature. My mother, by her own admission, didn't stick her head out of the door until she was eighteen and on her own. The world they knew then was one of small communities, large families (Dad was one of seven kids, Mom one of five), and much love. But it was also a world full of "pure meanness," where stark violence was common and everyone trod carefully. Piedmont had always been a lawless, Deadwood sort of place, percolating with extortionists and whiskey runners and gambling rings, all of which was only exacerbated in the years after World War II when its GIs returned home with money in their pockets and trouble in mind. My father watched his brothers and many others in Piedmont get into brutal fights on a regular basis, more or less for sport; in a hamburger hop parking lot, he once saw his most volatile brother, Jack, taunt a pistol-wielding antagonist to shoot. After church one Sunday, a prominent moonshiner politely but clearly threatened to kill my mother's father if he kept chopping up the stills he found on his property. (He took the threat seriously and started looking the other way.)

Like many of their generation, my parents were set on the notion that they would raise their family in a more genteel, even sterile environment. After a four-year Navy tour, during which I was born in Norfolk, Virginia, we moved back south—first to Atlanta, where my father started out as a stock clerk for the Kroger supermarket chain, and then a couple years later to Anniston, where Dad had been promoted to manage a Kroger store. Our first home in Anniston was a small rental in a working-class neighborhood north of downtown; though neither of us remember it, Chip Howell and I first met in a Sunbeams class at the Wilmer Avenue Baptist Church there. We then moved a couple of miles farther north to a roomier place in Blue Mountain, a small village that surrounded an old textile mill. My brother was born when I was eight, and very soon after that we finally made the move to Golden Springs in 1962, where the Loves got down to the serious business of trying suburbia on for size.

It is impossible to exaggerate the profoundly protected nature of my existence throughout these years. I was shielded from virtually anything that was sad, disturbing, or worrisome, save *Old Yeller*. I wasn't told until many years later that my parents had lost another son three days after his premature birth when I was four. (I hadn't even fathomed that my mother was pregnant.) I was seven when Kenny Adams's mob burned the Freedom Riders' bus on the outskirts of town, prompting Anniston datelines around the world; I heard nothing. The Cuban Missile Crisis? No idea it even happened. Until President Kennedy was assassinated in 1963—a world-altering event that even my mother couldn't hide from my blinkered field of vision—I lived in a virtual bubble, a 24-7 real-life news blackout.

That changed some in 1965 when Dad was transferred back to Atlanta to manage the largest Kroger store in the South. Atlanta was a big, hustling city by then, and my parents were wary. While my father worked seventy hours a week, my mother taught at an elementary school several miles away from the house we had rented. Rather than attend the neighborhood schools, my brother and I were enrolled where my mother taught and rode to school with her every morning, an emasculating experience for a seventh-grader like me. The kids on my block always resented this somehow, viewing my absence as rejection, and I was taunted and threatened whenever I ventured out among them. I had had too many friends to count in Anniston, and Golden Springs had been my own personal sprawling playground over which I had ruled like a prince; now I found myself trapped in some weird no-man's-land, an eleven-year-old loner who didn't live among the kids at school and didn't go to school with the kids at home. This bad chemistry came to a head on Halloween. Rather than letting me go trick-or-treating with the locals, my mother insisted I stay home and give out candy. Soon enough the gang of my would-be friends came to the door, hooting and braying. I dolefully and parsimoniously handed out the goods, embarrassed that I wasn't out spreading terror alongside them; finally, Johnny Finley, the neighborhood alpha dog, bowled past me and simply took the *entire stash* of candy from the living room table. Humiliated, I turned out the porch light and didn't tell my mother a thing.

When my father was given an opportunity to buy into and manage a new IGA store and return to Anniston, the decision was an easy one. Atlanta was too big, too fast, too rough, and in truth, as far as many white families like ours were concerned, becoming too black too quickly. Anniston shimmered in our collective memory like some romantic dream of a golden age. After less than a year in Atlanta, we moved back to Golden Springs, back into the same house we had left behind. (My parents had wisely rented the place out instead of selling.) Nothing had changed. We resumed our friendships, our routines, our lives. I was back in the Anniston cocoon—the ultimate comfort zone, assiduously and lovingly constructed, so far as I knew, for me and me alone.

To have strangers with guns burst in on this placid, paint-by-numbers scene, then, like some comic-book panel come to life, was beyond comprehension for me. My parents knew better. They had seen enough of the bare-fisted landscape that surrounded our little enclave to know of the lurking malice out there, papered over, perhaps, ignored out of wishful thinking but not forgotten. It must have been their worst horror fully realized to find themselves shoehorned with their two sheltered sons at gunpoint into the front seat of the family car, taking a portentous ride from Golden Springs into the unknown.

When we reached the store, one of the men accompanied my father while he unlocked the front door. His partner stayed behind in the car with Mom, Barry, and me. They returned a few minutes later with the gunman carrying a grocery bag, and it was clear that he was upset. The cause soon became clear: as Dad had known all along, there wasn't much money in the safe. Each evening before closing he made a night drop at the bank; he only left enough cash behind in the store to open up with the next morning. As we began the drive back to Golden Springs, the two kidnappers foraged through the bag and quietly but tersely fought with each other. They had less than a hundred dollars in cash, plus a stack of personal checks made out to the store—worthless to them. Essentially they had committed a federal crime for squat, and they were ticked. My father patiently explained the bank deposit procedure, hoping to deflect any suspicion that he was holding out.

Back home, the men made us lie facedown on a bedroom floor— a terrifying moment. *This is it*, I thought. *Execution-style.* But they simply tied our hands behind our backs and left. My brother was the first to wriggle loose from his bonds; soon we were all free, and before long our street was awash with revolving patrol-car lights and craning neighbors. We pieced things together. The men had probably followed Dad home. My mother had opened the front door only because she mistook one of the men for a store employee. We all seemed to be handling things pretty well. My mother seemed especially strong. We had weathered a great crisis together, and were glad to be alive.

The *Anniston Star* arrived the next afternoon, and "Local Grocer, Family Kidnapped" was front-page news. The article featured a grinning mug shot of my father, some innocuous Civitan Club file photo. "Why would they have a picture of him *smiling* like that?" Mom said, hysteria creeping into her voice. "Why is he *smiling*?" She burst into tears, finally breaking down. We were all traumatized more than we knew.

Despite the best efforts of my mother and father, despite the paternalistic barriers that had been erected to ensure an upbringing unruffled by outside influences, my shrink-wrapped existence had been dramatically pierced. Soon things would return more or less to normal, of course; the lid was clamped down more tightly than ever, and for me pretty much stayed that way until college. But the kidnapping had left me with the germinating realization that Anniston was part of a larger, more threatening (and more fascinating) world, hardly immune from a gallery of dark and complex dangers that I couldn't even begin to understand.

Much later, as my knowledge of Anniston's extraordinary history expanded, I realized that my own particular road-to-Damascus experience—like the revelatory experiences of others like David Baker and Chip Howell—was a metaphor for the city at large. Anniston had been built upon a basic bargain: its creators would assume the risk and responsibility of ensuring its prosperity; all its don't-worry-be-happy people had to do was put in a hard life's work and trust said creators to keep the problematic, less wieldy outside world at arm's length, if not further. It was a bargain that held together for a long time, but not forever.

CHAPTER THREE

A TEST-TUBE TOWN

The city of Anniston, Alabama, did not have the luxury of natural evolution. From its inception in the years after the Civil War, it was the product of a sort of divine civic creationism; the town didn't crawl from the sea and gradually adapt to its environment but instead was manufactured on the spot, virtually from thin air. Anniston wasn't an accidental occurrence, owing its existence to the bend of a river, perhaps, or a dusty crossroads of rutted pig trails and cattle-cart paths, and almost randomly morphing over time from trading post to settlement to center of commerce. From the start, Anniston was no mere notion but a fully formed *idea,* one anchored on the familiar foundations of ego and money but with special emphasis placed on the principle of a benevolent but all-powerful corporate ruling class.

As an adventuresome young man of means in Cornwall, England, in the early nineteenth century, James Noble dreamed of moving to America and making his own fortune in the burgeoning iron ore industry. In 1837 Noble, with his wife and growing brood of children in tow, relocated to Reading, Pennsylvania, where he spent several successful years as an executive with the Reading Railroad Company. But he remained enamored of the iron business, and he ultimately left the railroad to start his own foundry. It was as a newly minted industrialist that he returned to England in 1851 to attend the Crystal Palace Exhibition, where he caught a vivid glimpse of the future: examples of high-quality iron ore from the southeastern United States.

Noble returned to Pennsylvania and, despite a fraying national political climate exacerbated by the Kansas-Nebraska Act, began to plot a strategy to establish a beachhead in the still-virginal South, underpopulated and brimming with untapped natural resources. Finally, with the aid of his six sons who were coming of age, the decision was made to move to Rome, Georgia, located about forty miles west of Atlanta, and launch a new ironworks there.

It was hardly a smooth trip, according to family legend. When he boarded the train for Rome, Noble carried with him a carpetbag that contained his entire cash reserves, about four thousand dollars. At Augusta, Georgia, Noble realized the bag was missing. The conductor implicated two well-dressed men who had boarded the train the previous evening in North Carolina. Noble had the men detained, but they were quickly released when it was determined the suspects were U.S. Secretary of War Jefferson Davis, later president of the Confederacy, and his aide. Years later a priest wrote the Noble family to report that he had given last rites to a train conductor who confessed on his deathbed that he had stolen the money.

Despite that omen, the Nobles prospered in Rome. During these years before the war, Samuel Noble emerged as the most gifted and dynamic son of the clan, the son who most passionately shared his father's ardor for the business of milling iron, and who gradually came to be recognized as the ambitious, charismatic, high-energy head of the family. Under his guidance, Noble Brothers and

Company distinguished itself as one of the preeminent ironworks in the United States, and the family ledgers showed consistent profits.

The onset of the Civil War, however, changed everything. The historical and anecdotal record is vague about the family's political views, particularly regarding slavery; nonetheless, the family had cast its lot by heading South and now had little choice but to throw in with the Confederate effort. Through the friendship of Jefferson Davis—a relationship that dated back to the star-crossed train trip years before—the Nobles obtained contracts to manufacture Confederate cannons and rifle bullets. After a disastrous fire shut down the ironworks in 1862, the family obtained another Confederate contract to build a new furnace in Cherokee County, Alabama, which they named Cornwall.

By then, however, the opportunistic Sam Noble had gauged the prevailing winds. English by birth, Yankee by upbringing, and Southern by his father's business ambitions, Noble was in a position not only to objectively foretell how the conflict would end but also to build unorthodox networks to make money during a war when the old ways of doing business had been eradicated outright. When he was captured by federal troops in Tennessee during an expedition in search of supplies for the Cornwall furnace and exiled back to Pennsylvania, Noble set about reinforcing his political and financial relationships in the North. He met with bankers in New York and was even granted an audience with President Lincoln. According to one account, Lincoln and Noble "talked about the future of the nation, the importance of restoring prosperity, and the part that Southern mineral wealth and cotton would play in rebuilding the country." Later it would become apparent that their conversation had been much more expansive. When Noble returned to the South during the last months of the war, he operated as a broker between Southern cotton planters and Northern markets. A postwar congressional investigation found that Noble was at the center of a cadre of

Southern businessmen who sold cotton not only for money but in exchange for "necessary articles to sustain the Rebel armies," to an extent that "surpasses belief." A federal treasury agent who solicited Southern cotton contracts, Hanson Risley, testified that Sam Noble— whose family had manufactured rifle bullets that took Yankee lives on the battlefield—had approached him bearing a letter of introduction from President Lincoln.

When the war ended, the Nobles dove back into their iron ventures with a pent-up vengeance. With fresh capital from Northern investors, the family reopened the Rome ironworks and manufactured pig iron at the Cornwall furnace in Alabama. But Sam Noble was restless; he had an innovative business model in mind, and the family's current holdings were constraining him. By 1869 he had convinced the family to sell the Rome works and abandon the Cornwall furnace, which had deteriorated greatly and had already depleted the limited resources in that area. It was around this time that Sam Noble and his father began to search for the site of a new furnace, and soon found themselves perched on horseback atop a heavily forested Alabama mountain range near the Choccolocco Valley, some forty miles southwest of the Cornwall furnace, gazing down at a lovely, pocket-shaped expanse surrounded by beautiful rolling foothills.

It seemed a perfect location. The nearby ruins of another Confederacy-financed foundry operation, the Oxford furnace, attested to the abundance of hematite ores in the area. There was only one drawback: it was in the middle of nowhere. Nothing existed to provide support and sustenance to the type of enterprise Noble had in mind. They would need stores. They would need people. They would need, in short, everything.

All right, Sam Noble decided. We won't just build a furnace. We'll build the whole damned *town*.

———

Again with the help of Northern investors, Noble began to purchase chunks of land adjacent to the small settlement of Oxford, which consisted of little save a tiny railroad platform and a small, last-rate hotel that preyed on weary travelers without other options. By 1871 he had amassed the real estate portfolio he needed to stage what by then had become an all-consuming vision of a Reconstruction-era industrial Utopia. He pictured a private company town, complete with quaint cottages for foundry workers lined up along a perfect grid of squared-away streets, with a main avenue set aside for commerce, and another, broader boulevard designed for the grander residences of Noble family members, company officers, and the rest of the elite who surely would invest and settle there. His remaining problem, as always, was capital. Sam Noble had always been extraordinarily deft in attracting Northern investors to his various enterprises. This was especially true in the aftermath of the war, when Northern venture capitalists were eager to grab a profitable foothold in the defeated, remolding, resource-saturated South. Noble had managed to gather the money he needed to buy the land for his Alabama dream, and it was a good start. But the Noble family had endured a long series of economic calamities; their ledgers, while improving, were still rather slim in the context of the bold plan he meant to undertake. Sam Noble needed more money, much more, to fully implement his notion of a lavishly outfitted foundry underpinned by a thriving, made-from-scratch city. And he would find it— not in the North, but in Charleston, in the form of Daniel Tyler, a controversial, seventy-three-year-old retired Union general, whose surname would become synonymous with Noble's in the history of the drawing-board city that glimmered in his mind's eye.

Tyler, born in 1799 of distinguished bloodlines in Windham County, Connecticut, seemed almost preordained for a life of leadership. His father had been the adjutant of his regiment at the Battle of Bunker Hill; his mother was the oldest granddaughter of Jonathan Edwards and a first cousin of Aaron Burr. Young Daniel studied civil engineering and graduated from West Point in 1819, and after a decade in the army—during which he gained expertise in artillery and ordnance—he attended the French Artillery School of Practice at Metz. There the ambitious Tyler translated into English the manual of the latest French artillery system, which he believed to be superior to American methods. He also collected drawings and other information at a personal expense of two thousand dollars. The French methods were ultimately instituted by the U.S. Army, but Tyler was only partially reimbursed for his expenses and didn't receive an anticipated promotion. Tyler, already carrying the reputation of a maverick, allowed his resentment to fester.

A few years later Tyler's promotion to captain was finally arranged, only to be vetoed by President Andrew Jackson. Fed up, First Lieutenant Tyler resigned from the Army in May 1834. His old commanding officer tried to persuade him to change his mind, but he would have none of it. "I have lost all ambition to be connected with the service where politics and prejudice ruled," Tyler wrote in a letter, "and where the fact that a man was not born in the South was a bar to promotion."

Tyler then set about the business of making money. He moved to Pennsylvania, prospered in the iron and coal business, and specialized in revitalizing struggling railroads. One of his railroads, the Macon and Atlanta (reorganized by Tyler in 1844 into the Macon and Western), prompted Tyler to spend four years in the Deep

South. There he gained an appreciation for the enormous business potential of the region's abundant natural resources, but was also disturbed by the growing animosity of Southerners toward the federal government. He would later write that he had "been a careful observer of the political movements of the South, and after [a] six months stay was convinced that . . . the political changes going on from day to day would in less than 10 years result in a disruption of the Union." Tyler ultimately left the Macon and Western, explaining that he wanted to educate his sons north of "Mason and Dixon's line." The South, he said, was teaching its children "to hate the Union and despise the North."

In 1860, with the outbreak of the war he had long anticipated, Tyler offered his services to General Winfield Scott in Washington. But Secretary of War Simon Cameron was not on good terms with Tyler and objected to his age, then sixty-two. Failing to secure a commission in Washington, Tyler instead accepted an invitation from the governor of Connecticut to take command of that state's first regiment. By May 1861 he headed a brigade and received the corresponding rank of brigadier general.

Characteristically, Tyler again landed in trouble with his superiors. He served as commander of the largest of General Irvin McDowell's five divisions at the first Battle of Bull Run, a major Confederate victory. McDowell claimed afterward that Tyler had exceeded orders and was guilty of "undistinguished troop handling." But according to at least one Civil War historian, the disagreement between Tyler and McDowell stemmed from Tyler's push to attack the Rebel troops upon their first encounter at Bull Run, while the North still held an advantage; instead, McDowell waffled for four days, allowing the Confederates to retrench.

By August 1861 Tyler had been mustered out of service and returned to Connecticut to help recruit and equip volunteers.

Before long, however, he was back in active service with a commission from General Scott in the United States Volunteers and served with the Army of the Mississippi in the siege of Corinth. He also commanded troops in Baltimore and then became commander of the District of Delaware. But in 1864, with the war winding down, and grieving from the death of his wife, he resigned from the Army for good.

After the war Tyler, still hale as he approached seventy, traveled widely in the United States, Cuba, and Europe, and had recently returned from abroad when he decided to visit his eldest son, Alfred, in Charleston. It was there in Alfred's business office in 1872 that General Tyler, already scheming to establish a commercial foothold in the rapidly reconstructing South, by sheer chance happened to meet a charismatic businessman from Georgia who had come calling to discuss a business venture in Alabama. Samuel Noble and Daniel Tyler instantly bonded—Tyler to Noble's infectious salesmanship and detailed knowledge of iron markets and the southern mineral deposits that had long intrigued him, and Noble to Tyler's disciplined bearing, forthright business savvy, and well-documented track record as a successful investor and industrialist. Noble shared his plans for a private industrial town in the Alabama foothills with the older Tyler, whose background in civil engineering enabled him to envision Noble's burgeoning dream. Sensing that he might have found his long-sought-after partner, Noble invited Tyler to accompany him to inspect the town site with his own eyes. Tyler accepted.

Ten days later Tyler arrived by train in Rome, where Noble boarded, and together they traveled to the forlorn train station at Oxford, Alabama. There they rented horses and spent three days traveling the countryside, with Noble showing Tyler his land holdings and sketching out his scheme for a new town. Noble marveled not only at Tyler's ability to ride tirelessly at age seventy-three but at his business acumen. They spent their evenings at the threadbare Oxford hotel, where Tyler was forced to instruct the staff on the proper method of preparing his tea. The pair talked long into the night, and their newly formed bond strengthened. Tyler saw that Noble was a canny visionary who knew the intricacies of iron ore and its manufacture; Noble saw that Tyler was an analytical, decisive, big-picture mentor with a substantial balance sheet. It seemed clear they could do business together.

The Noble and Tyler families convened in Charleston on April 29, 1872, and drew up an incorporation document that created the Woodstock Iron Company. The name was borrowed from an English village near Oxford, England, much as the new concern was adjacent to Oxford, Alabama. The name also paid homage to the ample supplies of timber that would feed the Woodstock furnaces. The amount of capital stock was set at $75,000, with each family receiving 375 shares valued at $100 per share.

And thus did a Brit and a Connecticut Yankee come to a lush, undisturbed corner of Alabama to build a dream-draped outpost for the smoky fires of the Industrial Revolution.

By the time seven-year-old Chip Howell was trying to get his head around the Cuban Missile Crisis and David Baker was engaged in rock-throwing battles with Dinky Adams, Anniston—so named upon its incorporation in 1873 in honor of Alfred Tyler's wife, Annie ("Annie's Town")—had evolved into a city of nearly 30,000 souls and was still trading on the mystique of its highly unusual conception in the bubbling recesses of Sam Noble's effervescent dreams. Even Annistonians as young as Chip—the white ones, anyway—had been given a rudimentary knowledge in school, if not at home, of the town's unique origins and had been imbued with the sense that Anniston was simply more special than any other city in Alabama, or at least more special than any other Alabama town its size. After all, it was an outsider, the great Atlanta newspaperman Henry Grady, who had given Anniston the nickname that became its proud slogan: "The Model City."

Anniston was, first of all, the focal point of a beautiful natural setting; Sam Noble had chosen well. The town rested in the shadows of the lovely Appalachian foothills, only a short crow's flight from Mount Cheaha, at 2,407 feet the highest point in the state. In spring, ancient dogwoods and azaleas bloomed gloriously; in fall, the surrounding hills exploded into magnificent color. In summer, Anniston exulted in the shade of thousands of water oaks planted at Noble's behest in the town's early years. Even amid its mild winters, Anniston held a distinctive physical beauty.

The town's manmade features were just as impressive. The streets of Anniston had been laid out in a sensible grid, with numbered streets running east and west and avenues running north and south that bore a variety of names from the Noble and Tyler families, as well as those of various investors, residents, and other friends and benefactors of the city. Noble Street, the primary commercial boulevard, was a thriving corridor that in the 1960s still featured many of its original Victorian-era facades. Two blocks to the east was Quintard Avenue (named for the Nobles' New York banker), a four-lane thoroughfare graced by a wide, grass-and-tree-lined median; a fine statue of Samuel Noble, erected in 1895, was poised at the busy intersection of Eleventh Street and Quintard, while many of the Victorian mansions built by early well-heeled residents still stood along either side of the avenue. At Tenth and Quintard stood Grace Episcopal Church, the town's oldest, a Gothic cut-stone and cedar edifice that served as the site of General Tyler's funeral in 1882. An equally impressive structure, the Parker Memorial Baptist Church, took up the east side of Quintard between Twelfth and Thirteenth streets. Meanwhile, over on the West Side stood one of the most beautiful structures in the state, St. Michael and All Angels Episcopal Church, a gift from the Nobles to the working people of the city. For the Romanesque building the Nobles chose a twelve-acre site near the conglomeration of new coke furnaces and pipe shops that had sprung to life there, and envisioned a priest to work among the poor and an infirmary where a sisterhood could attend the sick and injured. A ninety-five-foot tower housed twelve bells, each named for a member of the Noble family. The altar was carved from a twelve-and-a-half-foot slab of Carrara marble, while the reredos was of alabaster standing twenty-six and a half feet tall and featuring heads of the archangels Gabriel, Michael, and Rafael, surrounded by seven other angels. Shipbuilders constructed the ceiling, and Bavarian wood carvers fashioned angels' heads on the end of each trussed Gothic arch. The church was completed in 1897 at a cost of some $125,000, not only a symbol of the founders' patriarchal attitudes toward the working class of the city but a testament to the snow-balling financial success that the Nobles and Tylers enjoyed thanks to their Alabama venture.

Indeed, with iron in great demand and selling at the fantastic price of $52 a ton in 1872, the Woodstock Iron Company got off to an outstanding start, showing profits of some eighty-seven thousand dollars in its first year. The Panic of 1873, however, ultimately hammered down the price of iron to $18, and many foundries across the country were shuttered. But Sam Noble's vaunted salesmanship, his ability to root out new markets, and the renowned quality of his pig iron kept the Woodstock furnace operating during the ensuing depression. The founders later diversified, opening Anniston's first textile mill, which operated for more than a century, and nurturing a budding soil-pipe industry that began shortly after the town went public in 1882. Those concerns, along with the sale of real estate to investors and speculators, kept the founding families in excellent financial condition long after the Woodstock Iron Company was shut down in the 1890s.

In the 1960s, Anniston's leaders were still touting their city as an industrial powerhouse—among other things, it was known as the "Soil Pipe Capital of the World"—and as a symbol of municipal progress, much as its founders had from the town's beginning. Sam Noble's relentless salesmanship hadn't been confined to the much-sought-after pig iron that the Woodstock foundries produced; he was a tireless promoter of Anniston itself, and he seemed to have a gift for gleaning the kind of publicity for the town that money couldn't buy. "From a rugged landscape," sang the *New York Times* in 1881, "there sprang, as if by magic, beauty, order and prosperity." Story after story made mention of the town's Utopian beginnings, the "brilliant common sense" behind the Woodstock Iron Company and its surrounding town, its modern, cast-iron-pipe water system, reputed to be among the best in America, its innovative use of electricity for streetlights, streetcars, and other practical purposes, its high wages (its workers earned 80 cents to $1 a day, compared with the going rate of 50 to 60 cents a day in most parts of the South). The *Atlanta Constitution* in 1882 published a widely circulated story headlined "Anniston, the Wonderful Alabama Town," which extolled the many virtues of the town and its founders, especially Sam Noble, all of which added up, in the paper's histrionic opinion, to "the most remarkable chapter of American enterprise and success in our remembrance." Noble was grandly quoted about the company's philosophy of reinvesting its profits into the company and the town: "Instead of dissipating our earnings in dividends, we have concentrated them here. . . . These reinvestments were judiciously made, and every dollar was made to do its best." As historian Grace Hooten Gates put it, "Anniston's projected image was one of a perfectly planned town in a naturally endowed location with beneficent proprietors." (Not everyone was so accepting of the rivers of praise flowing from Anniston, however. Gates noted that one Augusta newspaperman returned home from a tour to report that in Anniston, "every bunch of sassafras is a mighty forest, every frog pond a sylvan lake, every waterfall a second Tallulah, every ridge of rocks a coal mine . . . and every man a liar.")

That civic hubris was still very much in evidence nearly a century later. In the early 1960s, Anniston was still an impressive industrial player, even if by then its roots in iron manufacturing were but a history lesson. The explanation for the demise of its core industry was simple: the timber stocks that fueled the furnaces had been spent. The producers of iron and, later, steel had largely converted to coal as fuel, a development that strongly propelled the development of Birmingham, "the Pittsburgh of the South," sixty miles to the west of Anniston and adjacent to a wealth of coal fields in west-central Alabama. At that juncture, however, pipe makers had largely taken over in Anniston, building foundries on the West Side to take advantage of the ample working-class labor that already resided there. Industries of other stripes had set up shop in Anniston as well, most notably the Monsanto Chemical Corporation, which purchased the locally owned Swann Chemical Company in the 1930s.

And then there was the military, layered over Anniston's twentieth-century industrial profile like heavy gauze. By the time Hoyt Howell provided Chip with the broad strokes of its presence in his hometown, the Army had established a sixty-year-old legacy there. It began with an encampment northeast of Anniston during the Spanish-American War, when the Army saw that the hilly terrain formed a perfect backdrop for artillery training. The War Department formally established

Camp McClellan in 1917, named in honor of Major General George B. McClellan, general-in-chief of the Union Army in 1861 and 1862 and later governor of New Jersey. Some locals thought it insulting to name a Southern fort for a Yankee general, but there was a thematic logic to the choice. The much-revered McClellan was credited with the quick training and mobilization of the Army of the Potomac during the Civil War, and from its inception Camp McClellan's mandate was to quickly and efficiently mobilize and train the modern generations of Army recruits. One month after Camp McClellan's commission, the newly activated 29th National Guard Division from the mid-Atlantic states arrived in Anniston; two months later, there were more than twenty-seven thousand men training there. The 29th packed off to France in the summer of 1918 and suffered some six thousand casualties in the Meuse-Argonne offensive.

Camp McClellan was formally named a permanent post in 1929, with its designation changed to Fort McClellan. The installation quickly became a military powerhouse. The Army estimates that more than five hundred thousand soldiers trained at McClellan during World War II; the most famous may have been the 27th Division from New York, which arrived in Anniston in November 1940 and was deployed overseas twelve days after the Japanese attacked Pearl Harbor. The 27th fought across the Marshall and Gilbert Islands, Saipan, Guam, and the Philippines and later took up occupational duty in Japan. In 1943 the Fort also became a POW camp for three thousand German and Italian soldiers. (Murals painted by prisoners depicting scenes from their homelands are preserved in Remington Hall, the site of the old officers' club; a memorial service is held annually at a cemetery on the property, where twenty-six German and three Italian POWs are interred.)

In 1947, however, Fort McClellan was placed on inactive status, with only a small maintenance crew on post. On a tour of the fort shortly after the end of World War II, General Dwight D. Eisenhower had presaged its fate: "You have a gem of a little fort here," he said, "but sometimes we have to sell our gems to buy meat and bread." The closing of Fort McClellan hit Anniston like a thunderbolt. For all the muttered complaint common among town residents about the pervasive (and sometimes unruly) presence of GIs, the economic impact of the base was inescapably apparent. Harry M. Ayers, publisher of the *Anniston Star,* a retired Army colonel himself, was particularly disturbed and began an aggressive campaign to have the fort reopened. A shrewd, respected, and supremely well-connected man, "the Colonel," as he was known around town, began to pull strings. He traveled to Washington to meet with Secretary of Defense Louis Johnson, who was an old American Legion mate of Ayers's. Johnson's deputy, Mark Selva, was from Selma, Alabama, and a close friend of Ayers's dating back to their fraternity days. The Colonel's lobbying was effective—he received a call from Johnson a few months later informing him that McClellan would soon be reopened. In 1950 the facility was recommissioned as a National Guard training center. Its long-term status was assured in the next few years with the arrival of the Chemical Corps and the Women's Army Corps Center. In 1962 the Army's Combat Developments Command Chemical Biological-Radiological Agency was also transferred to Fort McClellan, for reasons that would later become clear.

And yet Fort McClellan was only part of the military presence in Anniston. The other half of the Army equation there—and, inarguably, by far the most important half—was the Anniston Army Depot. The "munitions dump," as it was called in its earliest days, was authorized by Congress in 1940 with a twelve-million-dollar appropriation for a facility on a 15,000-acre site at a Southern Railroad stop about eight miles from downtown Anniston in the old Bynum community. Construction began on five hundred ammunition storage igloos of reinforced concrete in February 1941; my grandfather, Wheeler Love, helped build them. The first ammunition shipments to the Depot began later that year. By the mid-1950s, the Depot's mission had been expanded to include the overhaul, repair, and modification of tanks and other combat vehicles, as well as antiaircraft and mobile artillery.

Although Fort McClellan had a monumental impact on the economic well-being of Anniston, its influence and role within Anniston and the surrounding area paled in comparison with those of the Depot. Fort McClellan was largely a self-contained enterprise; it had its own housing, PX, schools, churches, recreational facilities (including a movie theater and one of the finest golf courses in the state), and other amenities. Anniston benefited from the Fort primarily in the retail sector that surrounded the installation, and from military retirees and some active personnel who bought or rented homes in the community at large. The Depot's impact was far more discernible. At its peak it had some six thousand local civilians on its payroll—good government jobs with lots of overtime—in a town of only thirty thousand residents and in a county of less than a hundred thousand. Figure in the tens of millions of dollars each year spent on contracts with Anniston-area satellite-defense-related industries, and the significance of the Depot seemed almost overwhelming.

Anniston's leaders fully understood and appreciated the value of the military's presence. To that end, they worked diligently to keep the lines of communication open with officials at both facilities; for many years, the most prestigious posting within the Anniston Chamber of Commerce was the chairmanship of the military affairs committee. Colonel Ayers himself held the position for many years, then was succeeded by Ralph Callahan, Ayers's consigliere at the *Star*, who was if anything more canny in the ways of local empire-building than Ayers himself.

Therefore much civic pride—not to mention economic value—
was associated with the Fort and the Depot. Yet there was a black lin-
ing to this silver cloud, a murky Cold War underpinning that the
people of Anniston probably could have, even should have, seen for
themselves had they thought about it much. By the early 1960s, the
rules of engagement among international foes like the United States
and the Soviet Union had changed. Sure, everyone understood that
the United States needed well-trained and well-equipped soldiers;
that would never change, and that mission was what the Fort and the
Depot were all about. It was nothing less than Anniston being asked
to fulfill its patriotic duty. With Anniston, like the rest of the Deep
South, an adamantly jingoistic place, that request was happily
obliged. If ancillary economic privileges came with that responsibility, well, wasn't there some divine justice in that? What had changed,
of course, was the nuclear component of the global geopolitics.
Missile silos on the high plains and situation-room bunkers in Omaha
and all the other trappings of the Atomic Age weren't as 007-ized in
the popular culture as they are today, but the man and woman on the
street—in Anniston and elsewhere—on some level understood the
principle of deterrence, of how nuclear saber-rattling was the best
strategy going to keep the shoe-pounding Commies at bay.

But somewhere in there, between the conventional forces arrayed
around Anniston and the ballistic missiles that simmered in some
Nebraska cornfield, was a quiet, mysterious middle—another, much
more shadowy category of weapons. They were nasty, lethal, cruel,
and suffering-inflicting, un-American really. But the enemy had
them, so we had to have them too, in the name of deterrence. Their
very existence was, for the most part, classified; certainly their location was top secret, not to mention a hot potato among military and
intelligence insiders saddled with the decision of where to put them.
In the middle of nowhere was the most desirable option, and places

like the Utah desert, an isolated corner of Colorado, rural Oregon, and darkest Arkansas worked perfectly. The West, with its empty, unpopulated voids, was an easy call. If anything went wrong, precious few people would be endangered. The East Coast, however, posed issues. Political risks had to be taken into account. Where would the weapons have the best chance of remaining a well-kept secret? Where were people circumspect, where did they respect privacy and authority? And, God forbid, if the worst happened, where would a disaster be most survivable politically? Where should the shooting-gallery targets be when Soviet ICBMs started raining down like flaming arrows onto a wagon train in a John Wayne Western? The choices that eventually were made were instructive: the depots near Lexington, Kentucky, and Anniston, Alabama, were located in two of the least-educated areas of America.

Anniston, especially, made beautiful sense. Its very origins were rooted in adherence to a paternalistic power structure that treated its workers well but made it clear from the beginning how the show was being run, and by whom. Anniston had an established history of looking the other way when it came to the doings of its various sugar daddies, corporate and military, who had passed out paychecks to the masses for so long. The classic case was Monsanto, which several times a week around dusk emitted a pervasive rotten-egg stench from its stacks that wilted noses for miles. The stink offended even the acclimated locals and was virtually fatal for visitors, who would invariably gag and ask their hosts what the *hell* that was. "Smells like money, don't it?" was the popular reply, and it was pretty much left at that. And so it was when the first secretive shipments began to arrive at the Anniston Army Depot in 1963. Certainly an exclusive, trusted handful of civilians who worked at the Depot knew the score; but the situation being classified, it definitely wasn't anything they discussed out of school. These were people who were happy to have their jobs, and tended not to ask questions anyway. Uncle Sam, just like the corporate paymasters, knew what he was doing. Didn't he always?

It followed that the white middle and upper classes that populated the East Side—the old-money scions, doctors, lawyers, small business owners, corporate managers transferred in from out of state—saw Anniston in the early 1960s as an exquisitely ordered place. The fortunate ones who lived on the mountain still sent their children to the venerable Anniston High School or the newly founded and private Donoho School. The blue-collar working class was safely stashed away over on the West Side, near the pipe shops and other grease-monkey enterprises, their children attending Wellborn High School and its feeder school Mechanicsville Elementary School (where my mother taught for a few years and where I attended first grade). The Negroes kept to themselves for the most part in their two well-demarcated neighborhoods west of Noble Street out along Fifteenth Street and south of downtown along Leighton Avenue. Okay, there had been some racial trouble—what else was new?—when Kenny Adams and his gang of West Side rednecks had burned that Freedom Riders bus on the western outskirts of town. That had been embarrassing, but some of the white preachers and black preachers got together and figured something out, kept things together.

Anniston, for those with any sort of city view on the East Side, was still a place of immense promise. And for the next twenty-five years, the town would more or less go about the business of fulfilling that promise, at least to all appearances. When racial turmoil broke out once again in 1970, a coalition of black and white citizens, with Hoyt Howell in the key role, worked to keep the city calm. Another coalition, this one made up of social mavens and other culturally aware East Siders, founded an annual Shakespeare festival that attracted stage actors from New York and was favorably reviewed in the *New York Times*. When the economic malaise of the 1970s began to drain jobs from Anniston's industrial base, a consortium of businessmen raised a million dollars—an enormous figure for the time and place—to finance an industrial park. Its natural history museum began to get national notice. Its social event of the year, the Reveler's Ball, attracted social luminaries from across the South and beyond. In the 1980s, town leaders put together a dog-and-pony show worthy of Sam Noble himself in a successful bid to have Anniston designated an "All American City." Anniston, it seemed, had once again managed to reinforce the notion that it was a special, unique place, truly "The Model City."

"Anniston is a different animal, that's for sure," Birmingham ad executive Jim Townsend told *Anniston Star* reporter Dennis Love in 1983, on the occasion of the newspaper's one hundredth anniversary.

The Anniston metropolitan area stands out like a sore thumb. You have to take so many things into account. You have an amazing amount of millionaires there for a town that size. The middle class is very upwardly mobile and culturally aware . . . it's the damndest place in the world for a Shakespeare company and a top-rate museum. There is a distinctive diversity within the black community—two different centers on the south and west sides of town. You have a very large military segment that adds to the mix. There's a big university to the north in Jacksonville. Finally, at the root of it all, you start to find the people who resemble the people you find everywhere else—the blue collar group and other working class segments who depend on the state of the economy for their livelihoods. Usually you aim your strategy at that group and figure the others will take care of themselves. But not in Anniston. It's a tough sell.

Anniston luxuriated in its self-perceived, contrary wonderfulness—at least, those in a position to enjoy it did. But a number of very expensive bills were about to come due for The Model City. Very stealthily, far beneath the civic radar, a furious siege was building in this "little gem" of a town in the picturesque Alabama hills. Its lovingly cultivated history was about to melt down like so much Woodstock pig iron.

It was the fall of 1966, and a team of biological researchers from Mississippi State University trooped to the edge of Snow Creek in Anniston, downstream from Monsanto's West Side facility. Monsanto had hired biology professor Denzel Ferguson to conduct a series of confidential water-quality tests, and Ferguson in turn had brought along a cadre of graduate assistants to help. Among them was George Murphy, a promising student who was eager to participate. Monsanto had dumped waste into the creek for decades, and the word was that a debate was taking place within the company over levels of industrial coolants called polychlorinated biphenyls, or PCBs, in the water. Murphy was intrigued and was anxious to see what the tests would determine.

The team carried tanks containing twenty-five bluegill fish. The fish were divided among the researchers, who were dispatched to various junctures along the creek. Murphy watched as one fish was placed in a cloth container and dipped in the water—and was shocked by what he witnessed. Within ten seconds, blood started spurting from the gills of the fish and its skin started wilting off like a blister. The fish almost immediately lost equilibrium and died within three and a half minutes. *My God,* Murphy thought, *it's like they were dunked in battery acid.*

The results were similar for the other fish. The team concluded that the problem was the "extremely toxic" wastewater flowing directly from the Monsanto plant into Snow Creek, and then into the larger Choccolocco Creek, where other "die-offs" were noted. A report was compiled that said the outflow "would probably kill fish when diluted 1,000 times or so." The study further warned, "Since this is a surface stream that passes through residential areas, it may represent a potential source of danger to children." The report urged Monsanto to clean up Snow Creek and to stop dumping untreated waste there. The findings were delivered to Monsanto. Ferguson, Murphy, and the others waited for news of the company's action in response to the alarming findings. And waited, and waited, and waited.

CHAPTER FOUR

THE TRAIL LEFT BEHIND

The first time he wrote it off as an accident, as a pleasant little error in his favor. When it happened again the very next week, it was an unmistakable sign, a message from the Great Beyond.

David Baker was eighteen years old, recently graduated from Calhoun County Training, and following in his father's footsteps— that is, working like a sweating dog at M&H Valve. *Just temporary,* he kept telling himself, but who knew for sure? All of Mama's warnings about the value of a good education seemed to be coming home to roost. County Training had been a good experience for him—he had loved it there. Wonderful classmates, teachers who cared. Even so, David knew as well as anyone that he probably wasn't getting the kind of education he needed or deserved; Training was an all-black school in Hobson City, the first all-black incorporated town in the country, so the deck was stacked from the very beginning. In the late 1960s, black schools in the South were the ignored stepchildren of the public education system, and anybody who didn't admit that was just fooling himself. David suspected as much, and his mother certainly knew, which is why she had insisted David go to Wellborn High School in the first place. But the Dinky Adams business had taken care of that. Still, bottom line, David wasn't any scholar anyway. He was plenty smart, and he did what he had to do bookwise to get by, but he wasn't college material even if he could have afforded to go. High school, for David, was that last fleeting phase of youth and glory when you mostly concentrated on ripping around hellbent on chasing girls and good times, enjoying each day as it came and for what it was: that final lungful of freedom before you had to exhale and go out into the world to get about the grim business of being a man.

David had grown tall and strapping, well over six feet. He had played center on the Training basketball team and could light up the scoreboard, and he didn't mind telling you he could either. (His nickname was "Puddin'," because his game was so smooth.) They had some decent teams and even beat Cobb, Anniston's powerful all-black school, one roiling night at the Training gym in Hobson City. That had been one hell of an evening—David had flung in a wild buzzer-beater for the win, and when the refs let the shot stand, the fight that broke out in the stands and spread to the floor was even better than the game. (The refs' decision was just icing; there was going to be a fight no matter what.) Training didn't just win the game but the fight too, in David's opinion anyway, and the team emerged bloody, delirious, and on top of the world. Every so often David would run into some of his old teammates on the street or in a club somewhere on the West Side, and they would always, *always,* talk about that night, the night they beat the mighty Cobb Panthers.

Not that everything was rosy during those days, even with the basketball team. David's senior year, right before the county tournament, the coach was riding the team hard, running them to death. Everyone was banged up and hurting but giving all they had as best they could, and Coach was *still* on them. Then, the day before the tournament, Coach called for a 6 A.M. practice—unprecedented, and strictly out of spite, the way the team saw it. Nobody could believe it. The buses didn't even run that early, for God's sake. David tried to plead their case, but Coach cut him off at the knees. The team was livid, David most of all. According to the latest information he had, Lincoln had freed the slaves—a long damn time ago, in fact. This was cruel and unusual punishment for sure.

So . . . David called a strike. He got the team together after Coach was gone, stated his case, held a vote. No one showed for practice the next morning, and by the time school started later that day Coach was prowling the halls, snorting mad, like some wounded bull. He pulled the players from their classes, marched them to the gym, and demanded to know what the hell was going on. David spoke for the team, his words echoing around the hollow gym. He explained that the players had worked hard all year, given every ounce of effort they had, done everything Coach had asked them to do. But to demand that they gather for a crack-of-dawn practice the day before the county tournament, when they were beat up from a long, tough season and needing their rest more than ever, well, that just smacked of disrespect. They deserved better treatment than that, David went on, and wouldn't practice or play until they got it. Coach looked like he might spontaneously combust, absolutely *burst* from the inside out, but he kept the lid on. Okay, he growled, practice this afternoon at the usual time, and no more of this crap.

And that was the end of it, except that Training lost in the first round of the tournament anyway, after all that. No matter. David felt like the team had stood up for themselves against unreasonable, even abusive, authority. It was true what they said: There was power in numbers. If you signed up enough people to the cause, you could even make *Coach* back up and listen. That was something else the guys always talked about later on when they bumped into each other in the clubs, over wine and amid the thunderclouds of smoke from the double-o's: the time Puddin' had the audacity to call a strike right before the tournament. *Damn, boy, Coach wanted to strangle every last one of us. . . .*

Glory times. David thought about those days a lot while he was hitting the clock at M&H, sinking into the heat and labor and ever-revolving sameness of foundry life. The money was decent—about 150 bucks a week, plus overtime—so there was nothing to complain about in that department. It was the monotony, the dead-end feel of the job that gnawed at him. It didn't seem right or fair that a young man not even old enough to vote should already have wrung the sweet part from his life, that his best days were already behind him. But as far as what to do about it, he had no idea. David had some relatives in New York, folks who would put him up for a while if he decided to make that leap, but he would need a stake for the trip and for pocket money once he got there. Saving that kind of money was a slow go, and what if it didn't work out up there? There was no guarantee the foundry would hire him back. No matter how desultory it might have been at M&H, he was damn lucky to have the job—and he knew it. He wasn't going anywhere, unless a miracle happened.

The first hint came one Friday when David tore open his pay envelope and found an extra $75 in his check, or about half again as much as it should have been. It was like striking gold when you weren't even panning the river. David quarreled with himself for about three seconds over whether he should do the right thing and bring the overage to the attention of the boss, but who was he to argue with fate? Finder's keepers, etc. God knows they probably owed it to him anyway, as hard as he worked. In any case, he wasn't going to lie awake at night and feel guilty about it. The money was his.

The next payday arrived. David tore open his envelope and was confronted with a check for nearly $1,200. For one of the precious few times in his life, David Baker was speechless. This was beginning to enter the realm of divine intervention. He had two months' pay right there in his foundry-calloused hands. *Somebody's trying to tell me something,* David thought to himself. Then something else occurred to him: *Free at last, free at last, thank God Almighty I'm free at last.*

It wasn't such a bad time to get out of town.

Blacks and whites were virtually at war in Anniston in 1970. The racial peace that had been hastily patched together with spit and baling wire after the bus burning in 1961 had collapsed. The numbers of black students at traditionally white Anniston schools were rapidly increasing as more African-American families took advantage of the Freedom of Choice policy that had been instituted by the federal courts. There had been some nasty fights between black and white kids at Wellborn High School. Blacks were becoming more militant at Anniston High as well. Finally, in an episode that would have huge short- and long-term ramifications, a riot erupted at the Anniston High homecoming parade. Upset that the homecoming court on display was all white, blacks started throwing rocks at the parading cars and floats, one of them striking the homecoming queen. One thing led to another, and soon a violent fight of terrifying proportions had broken out. (Trouble clearly had been anticipated: several of the white combatants were armed with bats, chains, and other makeshift weapons that had been hidden from view.) Police finally broke up the melee and the participants all fled for the hills. But an anarchic weekend would follow, one that would presage a paradigm shift. The Last Homecoming Parade, as it came to be known, was to become the pivotal chapter in the history of Anniston High School, and arguably in the history of the city itself. For it was the parade, and the tumultuous weekend that followed it, that convinced white Anniston that black Anniston could no longer be "contained"; it was the parade that convinced white Anniston that its children were no longer "safe" in a school system that was, year by year, becoming more integrated; it was the parade that, once and for all, began the exodus into adjoining places like Oxford, Saks, and the aptly named White Plains. Those closely held attitudes, along with the scrapping of Freedom of Choice in 1973 and the advent of forced integration in southern schools, would radically transform Anniston into a different place.

The night after the homecoming riot, nineteen rifle bullets were fired into the West Anniston home of the Reverend John Nettles, a charismatic and polarizing black leader who had marched with the late Martin Luther King Jr. and was the president of the local chapter of the Southern Christian Leadership Conference. No one was hurt, but word spread quickly through the black neighborhoods, and within an hour a self-appointed, heavily armed militia of black citizens had massed in the street outside the Nettles home to prevent another attack. Inevitably, some of the more revenge-minded took it upon themselves to commandeer a few cars and go looking for trouble. David went along and, as he would admit many years later, did some things he shouldn't have done. (It was common knowledge in Anniston that weekend that several houses on both sides of town were shot into and many interracial fights occurred, all of which were downplayed by police in an attempt to stem further trouble and by city officials who, as always, were consumed by their obsession with Anniston's public image.)

It was very soon after that tense weekend that some one thousand dollars' worth of manna from heaven appeared in David

Baker's paycheck. He didn't wait around long. He cashed the check, bought a used car from Sunny King Ford down on South Quintard, and, like so many generations of his African-American brethren before him, headed north.

About the time that David Baker aimed his freshly purchased automobile toward New York City, an intriguing article appeared in the *Anniston Star*. Stripped across the top of the front page and headlined "Chemicals Above Acceptable Amounts," the story by staff writer Judy Johnson reported that recent analyses by the Food and Drug Administration "showed catfish from Choccolocco Creek with more than 50 times the acceptable level of a chemical substance and carp from Logan Martin Lake with almost eight times the acceptable amount of the same material."

That chemical substance, the story explained, was PCBs— polychlorinated biphenyls, members of a general chemical group known as chlorinated hydrocarbons. (*Phenyls* are benzene rings connected to other compounds.) PCBs were contained in a manmade fluid, brand-named Aroclors, which because of its outstanding characteristics as an electrical insulator was prevalent throughout the world in everyday products from paint to newsprint. Aroclors had but one American manufacturer: the Monsanto Chemical Corporation. The substance was primarily produced at the location where it had been initially developed in the 1920s: Monsanto's Anniston plant.

PCBs had recently been in the news. About six months before the *Star* article appeared, Democratic New York congressman William F. Ryan held a press conference to detail his alarm over growing evidence that pointed to PCBs as an environmental hazard. The problem with PCBs, Ryan said, was that like DDT—another Monsanto product— PCBs were not biodegradable. Instead, the substance built up in the food chain, with animals at the top of the chain carrying concentrations in their flesh at a much higher level than was detectable in the environment. Ryan went on to charge that PCBs threatened the reproductive cycles of birds and was suspected of being harmful to animals and humans. Ryan further claimed that PCBs, when ingested, could cause "nausea, rapid breathing, loss of weight and a lowered red blood cell count. More serious results are the deterioration of the kidneys, jaundice and atrophy of the liver."

Johnson, a prim and circumspect *Star* veteran known for her dogged investigative work, had noted Ryan's assertions and begun to make some phone calls. She knew that Monsanto had manufactured PCBs in Anniston for decades and wondered if there was reason for local environmental concern. "The environment" in 1970 was still a relatively trendy notion, certainly in a backwater like Anniston; the U.S. Environmental Protection Agency had not even been created yet. Still, mainly because of the hostile smells that frequently swarmed from Monsanto's stacks and enveloped the town, Johnson knew that the plant was the subject of considerable urban legend about what, exactly, went on there. It was as good an excuse as any to start asking around.

Finally, a source at the FDA passed along to Johnson the results of a preliminary survey of the levels of various impurities in the flesh of fish in Alabama streams and other waterways. The data were disquieting. Catfish samples from Choccolocco Creek, Anniston's primary water supply and long considered one of the most plentiful and high-quality water sources in the Southeast, showed PCB levels as high as 277 parts per million; the FDA's "acceptable tolerance level" was only 5 parts per million. Results for carp taken from Logan Martin Lake, a massive reservoir located about thirty miles downstream from Anniston, were also sky-high, although not as high as those found nearer to Anniston in the Choccolocco. Johnson began to write her story, and put in calls to Monsanto and to the Alabama Water Improvement Commission, or AWIC, the state agency formed in 1947 to protect Alabama's plentiful array of rivers and tributaries.

"I can't get alarmed about the PCB question," said Joe Crockett, a high-ranking official with AWIC. "There's not enough evidence to be alarmed." He went on to say that Monsanto itself had brought the PCB issue to his attention. "They had been very concerned about it," Crockett told Johnson. "They're trying to control any loss of PCBs at their Anniston works. We are satisfied they are doing a very effective job." Gene Jessee, then Monsanto's Anniston plant manager, gave Johnson a tour of the facility and explained that the company's understanding of the effects of PCBs on the environment was "in its infancy." "We've just scratched the surface on know-how about the product," Jessee said of the compound that Monsanto had produced for some thirty-five years. "It has been a slow process because of the ability to identify the materials and the lack of sophisticated analysis equipment." Nonetheless, Jessee added emphatically, "We made sure no major quantities of PCBs leave the plant." As for the FDA test results from Choccolocco Creek and Logan Martin Lake, the plant manager was skeptical; he said Monsanto's own lab had been unable to produce "consistent" measurements of PCB levels. "I don't know whether these [FDA] results are repetitive results," he said.

In any case, Jessee told Johnson, "I don't see cause for worry from a public health standpoint. I do see that as a responsible company we have an obligation to minimize the possibility of gross quantities of the materials leaving the plant." Johnson also quoted an unnamed Monsanto official: "People are trying to find out what effect PCBs have on living organisms. We can't find any documented evidence at this point. People are looking at it, but they can't find any documented results of effects from environmental contact." The bottom line, according to AWIC's Crockett, was that no action was planned as a result of the FDA findings. "I can't say that they would necessarily require action," he said. "The value of PCB in my opinion is something that has yet to be decided."

Johnson's story prompted little public reaction, and essentially went away. The following week, a memo was routed from the Anniston plant to Monsanto's corporate headquarters in St. Louis:

> *The* Anniston Star *somehow obtained figures from the FDA which showed unusually high levels of PCB in fish samples taken from Choccolocco Creek. A* Star *reporter contacted the Anniston plant for comments on the data and information about our PCB production operations there. Public relations prepared replies to specific questions.*
>
> *Plant management convinced the reporter to visit the plant for a firsthand view of what the plant was doing to eliminate PCB escape to the environment. A factual front-page feature appeared in the* Star's *Sunday, November 22, edition reflecting the value of cooperating with news media planning PCB stories.*
>
> *Quoting both plant management and the Alabama Water Improvement Commission, the feature emphasized the PCB problem was relatively new, was being solved by Monsanto and, at this point, was no cause for public alarm.*

The Southern Manganese Corporation opened for business in West Anniston in 1917, its chief product being shell casings for artillery used during World War I. After the war, however, its founder and owner, Theodore Swann of Birmingham, began to shift the company's focus to the burgeoning chemical industry that was taking hold across the country. By 1925, when the plant's name was changed to the Swann Chemical Company, researchers were well on their way to making Swann the first site in the world to produce polychlorinated biphenyls, to be used in industrial coolants that came to be known by the brand name of Aroclors. These had gigantic potential in an era when the use of electrical equipment was revolutionizing not only American industry but the daily lives of ordinary Americans. Production of PCBs officially began in 1929 and immediately proved to be an immensely profitable venture, even amid the stock market crash of that year and the ensuing Great Depression.

In 1935 the Monsanto Chemical Corporation—recognizing the enormous value of the Swann-produced PCBs—bought the company at an undisclosed price. Whatever Monsanto paid for the Swann Chemical Company, it was money well spent. Already a wealthy multinational concern and battle-tested in the ways of large-scale marketing, Monsanto was singularly well positioned to make the utmost use of PCB technology. By the time Johnson's article appeared in the *Star* in 1970, Aroclors-related products were responsible for twenty-two million dollars in annual worldwide sales to clients such as Westinghouse, General Electric, and the U.S. Navy—and a very impressive ten million dollars in profits.

Long before then, however, some thirty years before Gene Jessee assured the *Star* that public health was not at risk and that, indeed, Monsanto's understanding of PCBs was only germinating, the company had begun to grapple with the negative, even deadly implications of PCB exposure. In a series of internal memorandums and other documents that would come to light years later, Monsanto showed itself to be keenly aware of the toxic effects of PCBs and aggressively working to keep that information under wraps so as not to affect the substantial profits that flowed from Aroclors products.

As early as 1937, a memo warned of "systemic toxic effects," including an "acne-form skin eruption," from exposure to PCBs. The following year, a researcher named Dr. Cecil Drinkard forwarded a study to Monsanto reporting that test animals exposed to PCBs developed liver damage. Drinkard published his findings in 1939 in the *Journal of Industrial Hygiene and Toxicology*. Eight years later, in response to an inquiry from one of its customers about possible liver damage to its workers from PCB exposure, Monsanto referred the customer to Drinkard's study and praised it as "the best published information about the toxicity of Aroclors vapors. . . . Based on our practical experience in the manufacture and sale of millions of pounds of Aroclors annually, the point that we would emphasize is that workers should not be exposed to Aroclors vapors and that the men working with Aroclors should observe 'good housekeeping' rules about keeping their clothing and skins free of the material and avoid ingestion of it."

A 1950 document outlining the use of Aroclors at the Anniston Monsanto plant and at the company's William G. Krummrich plant in Sauget, Illinois—the only other U.S. facility that produced PCBs—noted that "from the start of Aroclor manufacture at the Krummrich plant the operators have been supplied a clean change of clothes every day, and time has been allowed at the end of the shift for bathing. Operators are advised to wash hands and face before eating. The Anniston operators do not have the same issue of clean clothes. . . . At Anniston, no special protective clothing is provided for the Diphenyl and Aroclors operators. A daily change of clothing was provided in the past but this practice ceased before the war . . . the men are expected to take a bath, on their own time, at the end of the shift." One Aroclors manual reported that in the "early days of development," workers at the Anniston plant had developed chloracne and liver problems.

A 1952 memo regarding an agreement between Monsanto and

the U.S. Public Health Service about the labeling requirements for Aroclors revealed not only one disturbing use of the product during its inception period but also knowledge that deaths had resulted from exposure:

> *Back in 1938 or thereabouts, when the Aroclor applications were relatively few and the customers about equally few, there was indeed the prize application of using Aroclor 1254 as a chewing gum platisticizer. The wording of our label would not be compatible with this sort of thing.*
>
> *While the toxicity hazard of Aroclor's fumes is well established and should be thoroughly understood by all, yet, as we go along we find that we are always confronted with one violation or another, and indeed, regard keeping in touch with these things to be a major responsibility in the promotion of Aroclors.*
>
> *Referring to the few deaths and the relatively large number of acne or dermatitis cases arising during the war, in connection with fabricators of Navy cable coating materials using a mixture of Aroclors 4465 and Halowax, there are two things to keep in mind. One is that this combination of chlorinated hydrocarbons is more toxic than the chlorinated biphenyls or terphenyls alone; and secondly, in this program of operations, proper working facilities and cleanliness were overlooked. In fact, the workers' wives at home even acquired acne and dermatitis which was traced back to the halogenated hydrocarbon compounds.*
>
> *In light of the immediate above, it is interesting to keep in mind that we are currently selling at least two and one-half million pounds a year of, particularly, Aroclor 5460; but also some Aroclor 4465 for hot melt impregnation of asbestos wound wire, and also as impregnating agents used in the construction of Navy cable.*
>
> *In the past, when the toxicology of Aroclors may not have been*

particularly well understood, this factor certainly was a heavy load in the development of these products. The subject . . . is not the easiest one in the world to understand, but in view of the large stake that we now have in the rather widespread commercial use of Aroclors, we constantly strive to learn more about this subject of Aroclor toxicology and to safeguard against any possible hazards.

In 1955 Dr. J. W. Barrett, a Monsanto researcher stationed in London, suggested that further research be conducted into the toxic effects of Aroclors. He was countermanded in a memo from Dr. Emmet Kelly, a high-ranking official at Monsanto headquarters in St. Louis:

I don't know how you would get any particular advantage to doing more work. What is it that you want to prove? I believe your work should be directed towards finding out what the concentrations are of Aroclors during different operations whether it is industrial or painting. . . . MCC's position can be summarized in this fashion. We know Aroclors are toxic but the actual limit has not been precisely defined. It does not make much difference, it seems to me, because our main worry is what will happen if an individual develops any type of liver disease and gives a history of Aroclors exposure. I am sure the juries would not pay a great deal of attention to MACs (maximum allowable concentrations).

During the next few years, concern began to grow within Monsanto over a series of independent tests the Navy was conducting over Pydraul 150, an Aroclors product used in submarines. Despite the reality that Monsanto had long been aware that Aroclors fumes posed a variety of health issues in poorly ventilated spaces, the company appeared eager to convince the Navy, a vital customer, to discount its own studies and accept Monsanto's data at face value. In December 1956, Monsanto official Elmer P. Wheeler wrote:

Dr. Kelly and I have discussed Commander Siegel's position on Pydraul 150 with several of the people getting a copy of this memo. I believe there is general agreement among us here in St. Louis that this is about the last straw in our relationship with the Bureau of Medicine.

Without a knowledge of the details of the experiments [being conducted] for Siegel, we can only conclude from your description of the tests that Siegel is drawing conclusions from data obtained by exposures to animals which have no practical significance insofar as potential human exposure aboard a submarine is concerned. We can do nothing to influence the type of tests which he wants done. . . . Apparently we can do nothing about influencing his conclusions based on such tests.

Our only approach would appear to be to make all data which we have available to the Toxicological Committee of the National Research Council (which we have done) and let them decide about the validity of any conclusions which Siegel reaches based on a comparison of our data and the [Navy] data. At the moment none of us here feel like approaching Dr. Hodge's committee requesting an opinion from that group.

In the first place, I don't know if we at Monsanto could ethically make such a proposal to Dr. Hodge and secondly, I don't know how the Hodge committee could force any action out of Siegel if they wanted to. In the third place, of course, if we received a favorable recommendation from the committee over Siegel's objections, it would not improve our "friendly" relationship with him.

*Out of all of this it appears quite certain that we will not spend
one nickel to develop toxicity data on hydraulic fuels for the Navy.
We will continue to get information to satisfy ourselves that use of
our fluids is safe under any normal foreseeable conditions. This is
generally enough to satisfy our non-military customers.*

*If the Navy has interest in any of these fluids and wishes to accept
them toxicity wise on the information available, then they are welcome to do so. If the fluids are not acceptable on the basis of such
data, then perhaps we can save a lot of time and effort by advising
the Navy to look elsewhere for their requirements.*

A month later, Dr. Emmet Kelley reported on another meeting
during which Navy officials shared some of their Pydraul research
findings:

*Skin applications of Pydraul 150 caused the death in all of the rab-
bits tested. . . . The inhalation of 10 milligrams of Pydraul 150 per
cubic meter or approximately two tenths of a part of the Aroclor
component per million for 24 hours a day for 50 days caused definite
liver damage. No matter how we discussed the situation, it was
impossible to change their thinking that Pydraul 150 is just too toxic
for use on a submarine. It may be that such concentrations would
never be reached in the submarine but the Navy does not appear
willing to even put the material in a trial run to see if it will work.*

*It would appear, therefore, that we should discontinue to sell
Pydraul 150 for this particular application and try to develop a
hydraulic fluid without Aroclors as one of its components. . . .*

In 1958, as more accountable labeling laws were enacted across
the United States, the subject of Pydraul products was raised again
within Monsanto:

In order to comply with recent changes in labeling laws enacted by several state legislatures, the subject of correct labeling has been of great concern to us.

This situation was brought forcibly to our attention by a specific request from Socony Mobil that a caution stamp be affixed to all Pydraul which they purchase from Monsanto for resale. We believe the wording which they use on this stamp is not in the best interest of Pydraul sales, and is such that our competition could use to great advantage. . . .

It is our desire to comply with the necessary regulations, but to comply with the minimum and not to give any unnecessary information which could very well damage our sales position in the synthetic hydraulic fuel field.

Other Monsanto customers began to voice their concerns about the use of Aroclors products in the workplace. In a typical communication, the chief engineer of New York–based Hexagon Laboratories wrote to Emmet Kelly in 1961:

In reference to our recent telephone conversation, I would like to further discuss the incident wherein two of our plant personnel were exposed to hot Aroclor 1248 vapors generated by a broken pipe connection. For your information and records the two men developed symptoms of hepatitis as you predicted and were confined to a hospital for approximately two weeks.

In view of the above experience which has given me considerable concern I felt that the matter should be brought to your attention. Since we are dealing with a highly toxic material at high temperatures and since these failures cannot be prevented, it is felt that a more thorough and clearly written description of the hazards be described under Safety of Handling. Also the antidote or first aid treatment if any be included. I certainly would be interested in this information if available.

I trust that this matter will be given your serious consideration so that other or new users are fully aware of the problem. . . .

Despite Monsanto's efforts "to comply with the minimum" and despite mounting evidence of Aroclors toxicity, a letter in 1962 from Emmet Kelly to Dr. Marcus Key of the U.S. Public Health Service sought to downplay concerns:

As I told you on the telephone, our experience, and the experience of our customers over a period of nearly 25 years, has been singularly free of difficulties. . . . We have not in any case attempted to minimize potential hazards.

In 1965 an internal memo from Elmer Wheeler to Monsanto colleague Richard Davis discussed a festering situation with the Reliance Electric and Engineering Company of Cleveland:

As I told you on the telephone Mr. Haredos called me earlier this week quite disturbed as a result of my letter of August 27. This letter apparently alerted him somewhat to the potential toxic hazards of the use of Aroclor 1242 at elevated temperatures. He told me that the Monsanto literature furnished him had been more reassuring in terms of what problems might arise in their application. I guess what really shook him was when I mentioned that with temperatures greater than 150 [degrees] mechanical exhaust ventilation should be provided to remove vapors.

For the record Mr. Haredos' application involves the use of Aroclor 1242 as a coolant in electrical motors. . . . He told me there had been some complaints in mines where the motors were being used. He wasn't specific but I understood that the complaints were of odor and irritation. Whether or not the levels are actually irritating I don't know. It may be that the miners have just recognized that there is something in the air now that wasn't there before. Mr. Haredos went on to say that in his own plant hot Aroclors spills on the floor were common and that his own employees had complained of discomfort. I was brutally frank and told him that this had to stop before he killed somebody with liver or kidney damage—not because of a single exposure necessarily but only to emphasize that 8-hour daily exposure of this type would be completely unsafe. . . .

Eighteen months later, with news reports beginning to circulate in Europe, particularly in Sweden, about the possible widespread impact of PCBs on human health, Emmet Kelly issued a memo about rising concern within Monsanto:

We have had a rather extensive meeting, which included the St. Louis individuals receiving copies of this memorandum, on Aroclor in the air and in various fish and other living reservoirs. . . .

We are very worried about what is liable to happen in the states when the various technical and lay media pick up the subject. This is especially critical at this time because air pollution is getting a tremendous amount of publicity in the United States.

We have been receiving quite a few communications from our customers, but the most critical one is NCR [National Cash Register], who are very much involved with their carbonless carbon paper. . . .

The consensus in St. Louis is that while Monsanto would like to stay in the background in this problem, we don't see how we will be able to in the United States. We feel our customers, especially NCR, may ask us for some sort of data concerning the safety of these residues in humans. This obviously might be opening the door to an

*extensive and quite expensive toxicological/pharmacological investi-
gation. . . .*

Despite these concerns, the Monsanto board of directors in November 1967 by unanimous vote approved a $2.9 million expansion of its Aroclors program in Anniston and Sauget. A year later, internal memos began to circulate about the well-publicized discovery of PCBs in California wildlife. "It only seems a matter of time before the regulatory agencies will be looking down our throats," one memo warned. A consultant advised Monsanto to stop denying the problems and start cleaning up: "The evidence regarding PCB effects on environmental quality is sufficiently substantial, widespread and alarming to require immediate corrective action." A subsequent Monsanto memo suggested that "We should begin to protect ourselves."

In August 1969, Monsanto formed an Aroclors Ad Hoc Committee charged with assessing the PCB situation and making recommendations on how to protect the company's global Aroclors market. The committee issued its first report two months later, and listed its priorities:

1. Protect continued sales and profits of Aroclors;
2. Permit continued development of new uses and sales;
3. Protect the image of the Organic Division and the Corporation as members of the business community recognizing their responsibilities to prevent and/or control contamination of the global ecosystem.

The committee reported:

As the alarm concerning the contamination of the environment grows it is almost certain that a number of our customers and or their products will be incriminated. The company could be considered derelict, morally if not legally, if it fails to notify all customers of the potential implication.

"Subject is snowballing," one committee member wrote in his notes. "Where do we go from here?" Graphs were produced charting Aroclors profits versus liability over time, and committee members urged that studies be generated that might poke holes in government findings about PCBs.

Also in 1969, Monsanto found fish in an Anniston creek with 7,500 times the allowable PCB levels. A subsequent memo declared that "there is little object in going to expensive extremes in limiting discharges." Later that same year, the committee chairman reported that Monsanto's own tests on rats, chickens, and dogs "are exhibiting a greater degree of toxicity than we had anticipated." Fish test results were worse: "Doses which were believed to be OK produced 100 percent kill." The Monsanto consultant who conducted the tests was encouraged by the committee to produce friendlier results but replied, "We are very sorry that we can't paint a brighter picture at this time."

The consultant also found "ominous" concentrations of PCBs in the streams and sediment in and around Choccolocco Creek in Anniston. "It is apparent to us that there is a cause-and-effect relationship," he wrote. After discussing the report, the Aroclors committee proposed that Monsanto reduce PCB emissions in Anniston to "an absolute minimum," then struck out the word *absolute*.

By May 1970, with members of Congress calling for PCB hearings ("This would shut us down depending on what plants or animals they choose to find harmed," the committee had warned), Monsanto decided to inform the Alabama Water Improvement Commission that PCBs were entering Snow Creek. A May 7 memo reported on a meeting between three Monsanto officials and Joe Crockett of the AWIC in Montgomery:

Mr. Crockett and the AWIC staff were totally unaware of the published information regarding Aroclors. . . . Mr. Crockett was most appreciative of Monsanto's approach to the problem and the fact that Monsanto came to him. He alluded that our action would produce a situation that was beneficial to the protection of both Monsanto and AWIC positions. His recommendations were as follows: (1) Supply the AWIC with a general process description detailing potential loss sources. (2) Continue to develop information and as major items develop inform the AWIC. (3) Give no statements or publications which would bring the situation to the public's attention. . . .

In summary, Mr. Crockett was noticeably unexcited at our disclosure and all his remarks were directed toward a careful evaluation followed by actions as required by data. The full cooperation of the AWIC to reach the above objective on a confidential basis can be anticipated.

By August of the same year, the FDA had notified Monsanto of its findings of high levels of PCBs in fish downstream from its Anniston plant—the same study that would result in Judy Johnson's November article in the *Star*. A memo with the heading "CONFIDENTIAL— F.Y.I. AND DESTROY" noted:

Joe Crockett, Secretary of the Alabama Water Improvement Commission, will try to handle the problem quietly without release of information to the public at this time. He believes that the FDA will not [act] precipitately in this matter (he did not advise how the FWQA [Federal Water Quality Agency] might react). . . .

Ten days later, a memo to J. C. Landwehr of the Anniston plant from Jack T. Garrett of Monsanto's medical department revealed that Crockett was beginning to feel heat from federal authorities and that he had asked Monsanto to provide the AWIC with a paper trail regarding the company's PCB discharges:

> *[Crockett] suggested that our control program should be written up and submitted to the state as a report covering our past efforts, present status and our future plans in connection with limiting PCB in the Snow Creek effluent. . . .*
>
> *Crockett told me that if this PCB issue hits the Alabama press, the Alabama Water Improvement Commission would be forced to close Choccolocco Creek and the Logan-Martin Reservoir to commercial and sport fishing unless we can prove that the contamination level does not reach the reservoir. The State of Alabama has no choice but to follow the guide lines of the FDA which calls for no more than 5 ppm in fish.*

On September 18, 1970, two months before the *Star* article appeared, a "confidential" memo from corporate offices in St. Louis to an Anniston plant official expressed concern that PCB levels in Snow Creek were not improving, and wondered how to present that data to Crockett in a new report that was being prepared:

> *There is extreme reluctance to report even the relatively low emission figures because the information could be subpoenaed and used against us in legal actions. Obviously, having to report these gross losses multiplies, enormously, our problems because the figures would appear to indicate lack of control.*

In August 1971 Monsanto quietly ceased production of PCBs at its Anniston plant, shifting its entire Aroclors operation to the

Sauget plant. The federal government, faced with mounting evidence of the carcinogenic effects of PCBs, banned production of the compounds in 1977. There appears to be no instance in which Monsanto ever issued any public warning in Anniston (or elsewhere) about the widespread toxic effects of the some two million pounds of PCBs the company had dumped in Anniston's water and soil for some forty years, or any evidence that any such warning was ever considered.

CHAPTER FIVE

CONFRONTING THE HYDRA

By the time Chip Howell became mayor of Anniston in 2000, he had done his homework on chemical weapons. What he had learned was that he had learned more than he really wanted to know.

He had gleaned quite a bit before he ever cracked a book in earnest on the topic. Despite the secrecy that had draped the arrival of chemical weapons at the Anniston Army Depot in the early 1960s, the presence of those weapons had become fairly common knowledge around town by the time Chip entered high school. Too many civilians worked at the Depot to keep things hush-hush for very long. And just in case any doubters remained, a spectacle of an event occurred in 1970 that precisely demonstrated the strategic position held by Anniston, Alabama, in the midst of the Cold War.

In August of that year, a forty-six-car, half-mile-long munitions train pulled away from the rail yard at the Depot loaded with 305 steel and concrete vaults, each encased in quarter-inch-thick armor plating, each containing nerve gas rockets. The train also included a guard car and cars containing fire trucks and decontamination materials, a tank car holding twenty thousand gallons of water, and several empty flatcars spaced throughout to absorb shock should an accident occur. The munitions train was preceded by a twenty-one-car pilot train that carried armed personnel and sundry other equipment.

The mission at hand was simple. The cargo, consisting of chemical weapons deemed either surplus or too unsafe to remain at the Depot, was to be shipped some 660 miles to an ocean terminal in Sunny Point, North Carolina, where it would be loaded onto a Navy ship and sunk off the Atlantic coast. This disposal method—horrifying by contemporary standards—was then standard operating procedure that had been followed for years, albeit in much more discreet circumstances. No one knows how many of these shipments were made from Anniston and other storage sites around the United States, but it is safe to say that none received the attention accorded this particular exercise in 1970.

Word of the Anniston shipment and a concurrent one from the Blue Grass Depot in Kentucky had leaked long before from congressional sources and had resulted in a heated debate in Washington and elsewhere about the wisdom of transporting lethal chemical weapons by rail through unsuspecting metropolitan areas. ("I don't think that a problem with such potential cataclysmic effects on the population—whatever low probability that it may occur—should be one for the Army to decide," consumer advocate Ralph Nader said on the ABC program *Issues and Answers*.) Moreover, the dumping plan had drawn the attention of U Thant, then secretary general of the United Nations, who charged that the disposal in international waters violated a UN General Assembly resolution regarding pollution of the high seas. The U.S. State Department sought to discredit that claim, but the clamor surrounding the shipments had served to make the Army's plans front-page news. The days of unilateral decision-making by the Army regarding the disposition of chemical weapons had effectively come to an end.

The Army and a few politicians strove to assure the public that the situation was under control. Georgia governor Lester Maddox, a cartoonish, race-baiting icon never averse to sensational publicity, offered to ride atop the train as it rolled through his state toward the Carolinas to demonstrate his confidence in the Army's precautions. (The Army politely declined.) Other elected officials weren't as cooperative; Florida governor Claude Kirk and three Florida congressmen were prominent dissenting voices, appealing to Defense Secretary Melvin Laird to halt the dumping. The swirl surrounding the disposal served to put the Army into an uncharacteristically defensive mode. Before the Anniston train departed, Colonel Samuel M. Burney told the assembled media (its presence another striking contrast with disposals past) that the shipment was "safer than a load of coal." Asked to elaborate, Burney said, "Every bearing on this train has been inspected. On a coal train a bearing might burn out and dump the coal and you might get dirty." He added that Army chemical experts would be on board and that numerous mechanical gas leak detectors would be backed up by twelve rabbits and twelve pigeons, highly sensitive to gas. Detonation of a sixty-pound charge of dynamite would not be enough to rupture a vault, Burney said. And once the shipment reached its ultimate destination, the ocean would render the nerve agent harmless by dilution if the vaults ever cracked.

The Army offered a further consolation, one that was buried deep within most news accounts of the event, including a story published in the *Anniston Star* the day after the shipment left town: "Army spokesmen said similar shipments in the future will be unnecessary because the Army is developing a method of decomposing the gas at the military bases where it is stored." The nature of that "method" would not unfold for general consumption for nearly twenty years, but no matter. In 1970 the Army was conceding that it too could read the writing on the wall concerning the storage, handling, and elimination of chemical weapons.

The train left Anniston on schedule on August 10. Oddly, an air of festivity pervaded the city. Hundreds of curious residents crowded around the local train station and still more were strung along the rail route out of town. As the train slowly lumbered by, many onlookers brandished small American flags, and others waved as if the president were chugging through on some whistle-stop campaign tour. Many years later, people who were there seemed hard-pressed to explain the emotional outpouring on that day. It wasn't an expression of relief that the weapons were leaving the vicinity; everybody knew that there were plenty more left behind at the Depot. Besides, given their inherent trust in the military, Anniston folks were never terribly concerned about the safety of the weapons in the first place. The whole episode was just, well, damn it . . . *exciting,* a vivid reaffirmation of Anniston's role in the military universe.

Even Hercules cheated.

When confronted with the many-headed hydra, the superhero of Greek mythology flushed his nemesis from its den with fiery arrows dipped in pitch. After slaying the monster, he sliced open the carcass and bathed his arrows in its lethal venom for use against future foes; thus did mighty Hercules foreshadow the cruel innovations of modern warfare. Indeed, the word *toxic* is derived from the ancient Greek word *toxon,* meaning "arrow."

The Chinese were probably the first to use chemical weapons, sometime around the seventh century B.C., as a development from their early practice of fumigating dwellings to eradicate fleas. The Chinese held the philosophical view that all matter eventually morphed into a less tangible form, which prompted a significant interest in the study of vapors, which led to more sinister applications of smoke and gases. Historic Chinese writings contain hundreds of recipes for the production of poisonous or irritating smokes for war, and offer many accounts of their use. There was the lethal "soul-hunting fog" (arsenic) and the crippling "five-league fog" (created from a slow-burning gunpowder augmented by such exotic ingredients as wolf dung). The use of a riot control agent (finely powdered lime dispersed into the air) is described in a Chinese account of the suppression of a peasant revolt in A.D. 178. Delivery systems with such elegantly disarming names as the "poison fog magic smoke eruptor" can be found in very old Chinese Army artillery manuals.

These Chinese applications for noxious fumes were not lost on their European counterparts. In the fourth century B.C., Aeneas the Tactician's book on how to survive sieges devoted a section to chemically enhanced fires. Formulas for Chinese-style "fire lances" can be found in Biringuccio's 1540 treatise, *De La Pirotechnia*. In theory, chemical warfare was frowned upon in the West—the Greeks talked righteously of the "fair fight," while a panel of Roman jurists during the Renaissance declared, "*Armis bella non venenis gerl*" ("War is fought with weapons, not with poisons"). Yet those moralistic pronouncements did not deter the use of the horrific "Greek fire," a fabled incendiary weapon and early predecessor to napalm that was used to break the Muslim siege of Constantinople and to defend against subsequent attacks by the Russians. "The Greeks possess something like fire from the heavens," a Russian commander wrote. Nor did the unseemly nature of chemical warfare preclude the

Romans from ruthlessly poisoning the wells of their enemies. (Well-poisoning has become a dastardly and time-honored tradition of war. The practice occurred during the American Civil War, the Boer War in South Africa, and was reported in Turkish Kurdistan in the late 1990s.)

The role of such weapons diminished during the Renaissance, but Leonardo da Vinci ruminated that during marine warfare one might "throw poison in the form of powder on the galleys. Chalk, fine sulfide of arsenic, and powdered verdigris may be thrown among enemy ships by means of small mangonels, and all those who, as they breathe, inhale the powder into their lungs will become asphyxiated." This was hardly an original notion; barrels of blinding quicklime had been catapulted by the English onto French vessels during the mid-thirteenth century.

By the 1800s, more insidious applications of chemical weapons were debated but apparently were rarely used because of the taint of dishonor associated with them. An English stratagem during the Crimean War to smoke out the Russian garrison at Sebastopol with a lethal mixture of sulfur and coke was not executed. A suggestion to develop shells filled with chlorine to be used against Confederate troops in the Civil War was rejected by the Union leadership.

No such restraint was demonstrated by the Germans during World War I. This dispatch detailing a lethal and shocking chlorine attack was filed by Will Irwin, a war correspondent for the *New York Tribune,* on April 27, 1915:

The gaseous vapor which the Germans used against the French divisions near Ypres last Thursday, contrary to the rules of the Hague Convention, introduces a new element into warfare. The attack of last Thursday evening was preceded by a rising cloud of vapor, greenish gray and iridescent. That vapor settled to the ground like a swamp mist and drifted toward the French trenches on a brisk wind. Its effect on the French was a violent nausea and faintness, followed by an utter collapse. It is believed that the Germans, who charged in behind the vapor, met no resistance at all, the French at their front being virtually paralyzed.

. . . The work of sending out the vapor was done from the advanced German trenches. Men garbed in a dress resembling the harness of a diver and armed with retorts or generators about three feet high and connected with ordinary hose pipe turned the vapor loose toward the French lines. . . . The German troops, who followed up this advantage with a direct attack, held inspirators in their mouths, thus preventing them from being overcome by the fumes. . . .

Military historians have estimated that some five thousand soldiers were killed and another fifteen hundred were incapacitated in the attack at Ypres. This development caused a significant panic among the Allied forces arrayed against the Germans, which only increased a month later as the Germans employed an even deadlier mixture of chlorine and phosgene gas in an assault at the Russian front that piled up nine thousand casualties, including six thousand deaths.

By the end of the war, both sides were using massive amounts of gas-filled artillery shells, including the blockbuster agent mustard gas, which not only was toxic to the respiratory system but was a wicked blistering agent. Phosgene was spread from the air, causing huge concentrations of that chemical. The development of gas masks and other protective measures dramatically blunted chemical-related casualties in the latter stages of the war, but the losses were still hideous: an estimated 1.3 million deaths, many of those resulting from infectious diseases that developed in the aftermath of exposure. It is believed that fully 11 percent of Russian losses suffered during World War I resulted from chemical attacks.

The use of chemical weapons diminished dramatically during World War II in the European theater. The long, stationary sieges that made large numbers of troops vulnerable to chemical attack in World War I were replaced by swift, blitzkrieg-style fighting. The Allies also quickly established superiority in the air, which greatly reduced the Germans' opportunity to launch large-scale chemical offensives. Perhaps most importantly, by the Second World War the United States and its Allies were believed to have greatly increased their stores of chemical weapons, including sarin and other agents, which effectively served as a deterrent to the Germans' propensity for employing chemicals on the battlefield. (Historians have argued over whether the Allies actually had achieved equal footing with Germany in developing chemical weapons, but in this instance perception appears to have blended into reality.)

But it was the subsequent Cold War that proved to be the most influential development in the proliferation of chemical weapons. With the United States and its NATO allies on one side and the Soviet Union and the Warsaw Pact nations on the other, a chemical arms race began—a competition, again fueled by the concept of deterrence rather than real-world intentions, to out-research, out-develop, and out-produce the other side, to build deadlier chemical weapons and in greater numbers than ever before.

Both sides soon showed results from their revved-up chemical weapons programs. In 1973, during the Yom Kippur War, the Israelis intercepted devices indicating that the Soviets had made striking advances in their ability to wage chemical warfare. Those fears were confirmed during the Soviet war in Afghanistan from 1979 to 1983, when the Soviets experimented extensively with chemical weapons designed to be undetectable. The United States used Agent Orange and other defoliants aggressively and pervasively in Vietnam, prompting decades of controversy about the effects of those chemicals on the health of American soldiers, Vietnamese civilians, and their children.

The United States stashed millions of Agent-loaded rockets, land mines, bombs, and artillery shells at Army depots in Anniston; Tooele, Utah; Pueblo, Colorado; Pine Bluff, Arkansas; Newport, Indiana; Richmond, Kentucky; and Edgewood, Maryland. Of these, the Tooele and Anniston sites were the major players in terms of numbers of weapons stored, with Tooele a clear number one. So rapidly did the United States accumulate these weapons—and so quickly run out of places to store them—that production of binary chemical weapons was halted in 1968, although research continued. By 1987, with Iraqi dictator Saddam Hussein having built what was believed to be the third-largest chemical weapons stockpile in the world (and having shown his willingness to use it during the Iraq-Iran War), and with evidence of chemical-weapon advances in other parts of the world, the United States briefly resumed its production.

By the 1990s, with the Soviet Union diminished in power and the Cold War waning, the world at large began to become more attuned to the widespread presence and evolving dangers of chemical weapons. The Gulf War in 1990 exposed nearly seven hundred thousand U.S. troops and thousands of Coalition soldiers from other countries to the threat of Saddam's chemical arsenal; many years later, medical experts were still debating the root cause of symptoms experienced by Gulf War vets. A presidential advisory group reported in 1996 that stress was the likely culprit and that there was no "causal link" between exposure to toxins and multisymptom conditions—headaches, fatigue, numbness, diarrhea, cognitive impairment, and Lou Gehrig's disease among them—documented among veterans. That conclusion was challenged in 2004, when a federal panel of medical experts cited new scientific research on the effects of exposure to low levels of neurotoxins. Of particular concern, the panel reported, were soldiers who had been exposed to sarin when an Iraqi weapons depot was blown up by U.S. forces in 1991.

It suddenly seemed as if the world was festering with chemical weapons. As early as the 1980s, world leaders had struggled over what to do with the towering stockpiles of deteriorating chemical arms that had accumulated around the globe. And in Anniston, Chip Howell and many others were well aware that one of the most fearsome and fragile caches of chemical weapons in existence was molting away at the Army Depot—and there was a growing sense that a measly train shipment or two to the sea would not nearly rectify things.

That 1970 train shipment was but one component of Chip Howell's anecdotal education regarding Anniston and its history with chemical weapons. His formal education would begin years later, after he returned home from the University of Alabama, joined his father's business, and became involved in civic affairs and, inevitably, city politics. It was essentially a matter of predestination—Chip seemed to have been elected president of his class every year as far back as anyone could remember. At the University of Alabama, he pledged Sigma Nu, arguably the most political fraternity on a campus dominated by The Machine, a consortium of Greek organizations that had run student affairs and groomed prospects for real-world elective office since the early 1900s. He returned to Anniston after his college days in Tuscaloosa and seemed to slip effortlessly back into the rhythms of the place, as if there had never been any question that this was exactly what he was meant to do.

There were two distinct camps of young people in Anniston when Chip grew up there: one that yearned and longed and plotted for the day when they would finally slip the surly bonds and leave Anniston for a more cosmopolitan clime, be it Birmingham or Nashville or Mobile or New York or L.A.; and one that never even considered the notion that anywhere else would be a remotely suitable place to live. Chip was different in that he knew full well there were wonderful places out there in the lush world beyond Anniston in which to pursue life and its dreams. But Anniston was where his future had always lain before him, and so Anniston it would be. He married Carol Evans, his high school sweetheart, and set about the job of burrowing even more deeply into the challenge and responsibility of being a Howell in the town of his birth.

Under the tutelage of Hoyt Senior, Chip began to circulate among the institutions that were the touchstones of the Anniston business community: the chamber of commerce, the United Way, the Rotary Club, and, to a lesser extent, the Anniston Country Club. "The club," perched on a rolling swath of leafy acreage at the foot of the mountain, was where the city's white insiders gathered for shrimp salad lunches, for golf, for cards, for Friday afternoon drinks, far from where the middle and blue-collar classes boiled up against one another out on the front lines. Chip was very much at home in this insular setting, most especially on the golf course, where he continued to hone his game while he cultivated the relationships that are the core ingredient of every small-town businessman's recipe for civic success. (Yet golf was more than a mere hobby for Chip. He had been widely recognized as one of the best high school golfers in the state and later became a member of the very competitive and prestigious University of Alabama golf team, where his teammates included fellow Anniston product Jerry Pate, who as a PGA rookie in 1975 won the U.S. Open and went on to a successful pro career.) Chip mastered this aspect of networking so well that, years later, he would be privately derided by the vituperative attorney Donald Stewart as a "country club card room mayor."

But Chip Howell wasn't just a manifestation of Anniston's longstanding East Side power structure, although he certainly was that. His family's real estate and insurance businesses took him throughout the city, exposed him to every stratum of Anniston's social structure. He learned who was who on the West Side, knowledge that very few East Siders went to the trouble to acquire, and formed tenable relationships there. He was still Hoyt's son, which meant combining sound, conservative business principles with a social conscience. When Hoyt died in 1988—a deep shock not only to Chip and the rest of the Howell family but to the town Hoyt had tirelessly served for forty years—Chip was left with the family business and with the task of making his own way without Hoyt's counsel and support. Chip already knew what he would do: he meant to carry on his father's legacy, to continue his work on a larger, more ambitious, even more effective scale, be it commerce or city affairs. He began to map his life according to the way Hoyt had led his, except that he would do it bigger, better, *faster*. Hoyt was president of the chamber of commerce at age fifty; Chip aimed to capture the same post by thirty-nine (and did). Up and down the list of civic institutions that made Anniston tick, the formal and informal gatherings along Noble Street, at the chamber office, at football games, at city hall, at the country club, at the YMCA banquet hall, on the golf course, inside the civic engines that had always made the place rattle and hum, the son looked to outdo the father. It was competition, in the way that in one fashion or another all sons strive to escape the sprawling shadow cast by towering fathers who block out the sun, but it was also tribute. And in so doing, Chip Howell evolved into his own man, which meant that he saw the world—and his hometown—with his own set of discerning eyes.

What he saw in the 1980s and 1990s was a city much different from the one his father had gazed upon in the 1950s and 1960s. Hoyt and his contemporaries had presided over an Anniston that enjoyed two distinct and muscular economic forces: the soil pipe industry and the military. The city's economic stability seemed assured forever. By 2000 when Chip began to contemplate a run for mayor, he had seen the beginning of the inevitable decline of the pipe shops in the face of foreign competition. He had also borne witness to something that he and the rest of northeast Alabama had believed would never occur: the closing of venerable Fort McClellan, compliments of the federal government in the form of the Base Realignment and Closure Commission, or BRAC.

There was plenty of blame, finger-pointing, and woe-is-us-ism to go around in the aftermath of Fort McClellan's shuttering. This never would have happened, people muttered, if Bill Nichols were still alive and in Washington—Nichols being the Democratic congressman from nearby Sylacauga, the town that also listed among its famous progeny Jim Nabors, aka Gomer Pyle of Mayberry fame. Nichols, businesslike, crew cut, with a burly football build, walked with a tortured limp from a severe war wound suffered in Korea and was routinely returned to Washington every two years by his faithful constituents. His mounting seniority and gimlet-eyed methodology ultimately elevated him to chairman of the House Committee on Armed Services, where he guarded Anniston's military interests the way an eagle patrols a mountaintop. But Nichols's death in office in 1988 effectively ended Anniston's hands-off status in the halls of the

Capitol and the Pentagon, and it began to dawn on cold-blooded realists around town—Chip among them—that Fort McClellan's days just might be numbered.

There had been close calls during the BRAC rounds of 1991 and 1993, when the Department of Defense placed Fort McClellan on the "recommended closures" list it forwarded to the commission. In both instances, the commission removed Fort McClellan from the list. In 1995, however, the situation was reversed; the Department of Defense did not include Fort McClellan among its candidates for closure, but the commission decided to take the Red River Arsenal in Texas off the list and replace that site with Fort McClellan. A storm of indignant protest ensued, with McClellan's advocates charging that two Missourians on the commission were angling to transfer McClellan's chemical and military police schools to their state. Demands that the Missouri representatives recuse themselves due to conflict of interest were rebuffed. And so it was settled— McClellan would be closed. The chemical and MP operations would be reassigned to Fort Leonard Wood in Missouri. Bloody murder was alleged from the Alabama governor's office on down, but there was no Bill Nichols—or anyone like him—to make it right. Fort McClellan, a Calhoun County fixture for nearly a hundred years, was gone.

That decision was enough to scare the stuffing out of anyone who cared to ponder its potential ramifications for Anniston's future. Closure of the Fort was a savage blow, to be sure; it would, in many ways, require a redirection of the region's economic bloodstream. At the same time, however, despite the doomsday gloom that had suddenly pervaded the town, it wasn't a mortal loss. Chip and the other city fathers reminded themselves that Fort McClellan had always been a self-contained universe of sorts, its impact on Anniston and the surrounding area more peripheral than central. *This could be sur-*

vived. A deal could be worked out where the Army would turn over the massive property, some of the most desirable real estate in the region, to private and municipal development. A viable infrastructure was already in place: roads, charming homes that had housed the Army officers, churches, school campuses, a fine golf course and other recreational facilities, an airstrip, office complexes, a gorgeous officers' club, all on twenty thousand rolling acres of empty land, perfect for new housing, industry, shopping centers, what-have-you.

It didn't take someone with a real estate development background, like Chip, to picture the possibilities, but neither did it hurt. Central to the art of real estate, Hoyt always said, was the ability to channel a negative into a positive. Chip took to long, meandering drives throughout the Fort property and began to envision just how it all might come together. He began to see the closure of Fort McClellan as something that could radically transform Anniston's geographic and economic landscape. *Why not think big?* Of course, a thorough and costly environmental cleanup would be required; for starters, two toxic landfills capped for thirty years most likely posed significant hazards, and God only knew how much unexploded ordnance still littered the area. (Things apparently hadn't changed much in that regard since Chip was a kid. His wife, Carol, who had become a science teacher at their old alma mater Tenth Street Elementary School, had stared in disbelief one day when for show-and-tell a student lugged in a twenty-five-pound Air Force BDU-33 practice bomb he had recently found in the woods that buffered the school and Fort property. To add to the surreal scene, when Army officials investigated, they coincidentally spied a spent grenade fuse on the school playground. Then a fifth-grader told of some "Army stuff" he and a friend had seen in the woods behind the school playground; from his description, investigators deduced that the children had encountered two live hand grenades and machine gun ammunition. When the kids led them to the site, nothing was found—already carted off as souvenirs, it was presumed. "We can tell that the kids know more than they are telling us," an Army spokesman said at the time.)

The bottom line was that Anniston, despite the challenges involved, could very well turn the padlocking of Fort McClellan into an advantage, or at least a wash. It would take years, and much unpleasant negotiating with the Army over terms of the turnover and cleanup and a thousand other things, but someone like Chip Howell in 1999 could sit in his SUV on a quiet promontory somewhere on the Fort's back forty and take in the majestic sweep of glorious foliage and even more glorious potential, and envision how it all might work out for the good.

Which was fine, and there was much comfort to be gained from the thought. But there was another nagging fear: *If they can close Fort McClellan . . . who can say they won't close the Depot?*

A fretful notion indeed, and one that didn't lend itself to wonderful, visionary, alternative plan-B fix-its. Fort McClellan was one thing; the Anniston Army Depot was something else entirely. While there had been the occasional debate over the exact nature of the contribution the Fort made to the local economy—its impact was undoubtedly significant but often indistinct, leading one merchant to remark in the seventies that his method of gauging its economic influence was "by counting crew cuts at the Calhoun Theater on Saturday night"—there was no such quibbling when it came to the Depot, the Army's largest such facility. With more than six thousand workers and a $325 million payroll, it was by far the largest employer in the four-county region that loosely considered Anniston its traditional hub. Through contracts and other satellite operations, the livelihoods of thirteen thousand other families also depended on the Depot. A Jacksonville State

University study estimated the Depot's total stimulus to the area at $1.1 billion, or 11 percent of the local economy. There was no doubt: the Depot was the one critical, irreplaceable anchor that kept Anniston and dozens of surrounding communities from floating off into some uncharted economic sea. As Chip sat there in 1999, trying to make up his mind about running for mayor, he was already hearing rumors that another BRAC round would be launched after the 2000 presidential election, no matter who won the White House. And if the general angst had any validity, the early betting among insiders was that the Anniston Army Depot would be a prime target.

So the next mayor of Anniston would not only be charged with the task of salvaging Fort McClellan—the largest development in the town's history—but also with the challenge of making sure that the Depot wasn't declared extinct on his watch. And anyone who knew anything about the Depot's prospects for long-term viability understood that there was a forty-year-old problem at the facility that had to be dealt with sooner or later: tens of thousands of rotting chemical weapons that rested fitfully in concrete igloos on that military reservation in West Anniston. The next mayor would be thrust squarely into the middle of a marathon scrum between the federal government, local leaders, and environmentalists over how, exactly, those weapons would be eliminated. All this would be on the mayor's plate, not to mention the other projects and duties and responsibilities and rituals that would be required as well, ranging from the past-due refurbishing of Noble Street to, undoubtedly, early Sunday morning phone calls from parents wondering if their kid could be unarrested from the night before.

Chip decided he would do it. He would run for mayor, and win, and take it on: the Fort, the Depot, everything else, all of it. Chip would do it not simply for personal glory, although he liked thinking of himself as mayor, but because the stakes were high, and frankly, he wasn't sure that anyone else willing to do the job could do any better. Someone had to remove that yellow-and-black bull's-eye from Anniston's back. It might as well be him.

But, he thought, let the record show: Hoyt never had to deal with crap like *this*.

CHAPTER SIX

WARTS AND ALL

My means of escape from Anniston turned out to be the newspaper business, although at first I didn't quite recognize the transitory nature of the profession—or, for that matter, the urge building within me to break free from the people and places I had grown up with and loved dearly.

One of the most mystifying and disconcerting things I encountered once I entered college and then the working world was the bitterness with which so many people described their hometowns, their childhoods, and especially their high school years. *I couldn't wait to get out of there*, they would say. *It was horrid. No one understood me. My parents were insufferable. And high school—oh my God, high school—was the worst. It was primeval, insipid; the alienation was simply unbearable. . . .*

I would listen to these indictments in silence because I didn't know what the hell they were talking about. I didn't relate because, as I was forced to admit to myself, the simple truth was that I had loved growing up in Anniston, Alabama. I had especially enjoyed attending Anniston High School, alongside classmates I had known since elementary school, who enjoyed it just as much as I did. You mean people from other places didn't love hanging out with friends they had known for years and years? Didn't they love English with Mrs. Bagley, or someone like her, who surely must have encouraged them to write for their school paper too? Didn't they cherish the Bama Drive-In and watching movies like *Butch Cassidy and the Sundance Kid* and *Vanishing Point* about eleven times apiece? Didn't they love those gorgeous summer nights, ripping around the wooded, two-lane countryside in Mustangs and Novas and Impalas and Falcons, windows down to let the rich humid air rush in, *Get Your Ya-Yas Out!* bellowing from the eight-track, Marlboro Reds being smoked by the carton and Schlitz Malt Liquor consumed by the case? Didn't they have best friends like Roger Couch and Steve Mullendore? Didn't they have girlfriends like Donna Plummer and Becky Clark? Didn't they play football for the Anniston High Bulldogs and wear a tie and team-issued red blazer on game days and sit on the stage during the afternoon pep rally and feel the spine-chill while the student body cheered and stomped and implored them to beat the hell out of Oxford or Wellborn or Saks? Didn't they go to Anniston High basketball games and sit squarely amid the Bleacher Bums and yell themselves hoarse at the command of their fearless leader, Tubby Bass, who created more electric tumult and exuded more school spirit than a thousand short-skirted, megaphone-wielding cheerleaders ever could? Didn't they go to the prom in pastel tuxedoes and white shoes and stay out until dawn? Didn't they pass geometry—a prerequisite for any decent college—only because their teacher, Myrtle Holland, white-headed and nearing retirement and surely burned out, shamed and personally tutored them each morning before school on her own time because she simply wouldn't abide a failing grade from someone with a dim glimmer of potential, no matter how distracted and lackadaisical and utterly without clue or ambition they might have been? Didn't they well up with tears when Myrtle Holland hugged and praised them for the A they scored on their geometry final? Didn't they stand in the football stadium on graduation night and look around with great affection at the eager, shining, glad-to-be-alive people who stood with them, people with whom they had learned arithmetic and trick-or-treated and ridden bikes and celebrated birthdays and discovered the Beatles and gone camping and watched *The Man From U.N.C.L.E.* and, later on, with whom they had survived chemistry and wrecked cars and signed yearbooks and read *In Cold Blood* and built homecoming parade floats and seen *Play Misty for Me* and rooted for Alabama against Southern Cal and crammed for finals and made love? Didn't they look around at those people with whom they had shared their lives and think about the place that had nurtured them and allowed them to achieve and fail and triumph and learn things the hard way, and experience some sensation of gratitude and great fortune?

Well, didn't they?

No, as it turns out, they didn't. I was to learn—especially as I went to work for the *Anniston Star* and began to encounter people from beyond the South, people from money with Ivy League educations and a certain worldview—that one's upbringing was something to be overcome, repressed, or jettisoned outright. For this realization I was pathetically ill-prepared. How could I have been so stupid, so bereft of self-awareness, so impervious to depth and nuance, as to have grown up, of all mortifying things . . . satisfied?

It had never occurred to me to be miserable in my own skin, to scarcely endure the abject humiliation of my upbringing, to be harshly judgmental of where I was raised. I eventually came to understand that, for many people, the time and place for that inevitable coming-to-terms with the inexcusable moral vacuum of one's youth was college, that bubbling vat of people and ideas that, in theory, defy conventional wisdom and prompt malleable underclassmen to cast aside the shackles of their provincial and/or wickedly self-absorbed backgrounds, to reject old notions of self and place, and to instead embrace the New Way of Things, whatever that may be at any given time.

College didn't provide that experience for me. For me, the University of Alabama was essentially a more sophisticated version of Anniston High School, where more things remained the same than had changed. My best friend and I pledged the same fraternity and roomed together our first semester. My high school girlfriend attended Alabama and we continued to date for two years. People from Anniston—like, for example, Chip Howell—permeated the Greek system and campus politics. Far from being a catalyst for personal change, I found college instead to be a powerful argument for conformity. What were fraternities, after all, if not rigid social structures based on ideals and rules that in turn were based on tradition—tradition being defined as hewing to the way things had always been done? And once you conformed, then your mission became to regenerate, to convince still others to conform just as you had.

I pledged Theta Chi, and for the first two years fraternity life fit me like a glove. The guys were great, Alabama's football teams were in peak form, the beer flowed; I was just far enough way from home (about 120 miles) to feel mildly dangerous. For lack of a better idea I set out to be a lawyer, following what had been suggested to me as a prelaw curriculum. Some political science classes went along with that, and I sat through much high-minded discourse about the cogs and wheels of pre-Watergate democracy. But my real education, political and otherwise, was taking place back at the Theta Chi house. Theta Chi, I was to learn, was a prominent member of The Machine—a secret society made up of representatives from most of the Greek organizations on campus, essentially a fraternity of fraternities and some sororities, with roots dating back to the late 1800s. U.S. senators and governors and any number of corporate leaders and other movers and shakers had matriculated through The Machine over the years, honed their political skills and formed friendships and networks that stood them in good stead for the rest of their lives. The Machine met in secret at undisclosed locations and, we were told, operated with a set of initiation rites, mystic symbols, and loyalty oaths. The intrigue and prestige of belonging to the most elite organization on campus must have been entertainment enough for its chosen few, but the mission of The Machine was ruthlessly serious—to control all aspects of student government and, by extension, every facet of campus life at the University of Alabama.

All this swooping, megalomaniacal ambition struck me at first as ludicrous. Control what, exactly? This was *college,* after all, an alternate universe, not the actual one. College, it seemed to me, was a place where people played at being adults—most of them not really out on their own just yet, but in possession of exactly enough rope to hang themselves with if they chose. That was how I viewed The Machine at first—as a bunch of frat guys ("politicos," we called them) harmlessly and pointlessly playing at being politicians. How wrong I was. What I came to see was that by assembling a slate of candidates that year after year dominated the elections for the Student Government Association, The Machine put itself in a position to cherry-pick the occupants of virtually every student position of consequence at the University of Alabama. And that mattered because classroom performance in a great many instances was not the only determinant of success after graduation; extracurricular activities played a great part as well. For someone looking to find work with the best law firms or top corporations or what-have-you, the value of festooning his résumé with the sort of bling that, say, being SGA vice president provided was incalculable. Who was the more attractive applicant: the guy with the 4.0 who looked as if he holed up in his dorm room for four years, eschewing showers and the outside world, or the well-rounded-seeming chap whose grades weren't bulletproof but who chaired some committees and held some elective offices and did some towel-snapping with his fellow man along the way? And why, the politicos mused, should some GDI (God damn independent) gain that potential benefit instead of some dues-paying Machine guy over at the Sigma Chi house?

And so Election Day would roll around, the politicos would hand out the mimeographed copies of the Machine slate, and a couple of thousand brothers would swarm out of Fraternity Row and descend like ravens upon the polling places about campus, flapping and cawing and picking the process to pieces. They voted not just once but as many times as they could get away with, taking advantage of a diversion staged here or a Machine-friendly poll worker there who could be counted on to look the other way. Guys swaggered back to the house boasting of having voted five, ten, twenty times. It made Richard Daly's Chicago look like a church service. It was anarchy of a sort, except that it was employed in the service of the status quo, of keeping power where it had always been and the favors flowing to the people to whom the favors had always flowed. And, in the beginning at least, it didn't bother me much at all. I viewed it as sport, and it just so happened that the Greeks in this particular realm of play had a decided and long-standing home-field advantage.

But there was a venal side to this Machine groupthink, and soon enough I began to witness it with new eyes. Prodded by a journalism teacher—the sacrifices (i.e., grades) required to get into law school were starting to seem too daunting to someone as undisciplined as me, so I had begun to hedge my bets, curriculumwise—I started writing for the school newspaper, the *Crimson White*. For the first time, I was exposed to students who thought that Vietnam was an abomination, that Nixon was evil, that Neil Young's "Alabama" on the *Harvest* album was right on, that good Colombian was at least as interesting as draft beer, and that the Machine stranglehold on campus affairs wasn't necessarily something to be accepted without protest. They were smart, edgy, fascinating people, many of them from out of state and immune to the peculiar insularity that had been the hallmark of Alabama as a university, state, and people for as long as there had been an Alabama. They influenced me, and as I moved up through the ranks of the paper I began to drift away from the Greek-centric life of my first two years on campus. Mine wasn't a total conversion—the anti-Greek malice that prevailed among most of my cohorts at the *Crimson White* sometimes seemed, in its own way, just as pigheaded as the anti-independent condescension of my fraternity brothers. So, even though I had moved off-campus and spent ever-larger chunks of time with the newspaper staff, I remained a member in good standing at Theta Chi and ate dinner there several times each week, viewing myself as an odd and happy hybrid nurtured in the university hothouse.

Then I was forced to choose.

By my senior year I had made sports editor. It was a fabulous dream come true. As a lifelong Alabama football fan I now had entrée to hang around the legendary coach Paul "Bear" Bryant, who in the mid-1970s was presiding over some of his most talented and powerful teams. Bryant had made his nut back in the 1960s with two national championships at Alabama when he played the role of the fiery, hard-core, in-your-face leader of a hardy band of overachieving white boys. By the time I came along he had morphed into an aloof icon, the master manipulator of a teeming, crimson-clad army, sending waves of players, black and white, onto the field like the choreographer of some lavish big-budget Hollywood musical. I was totally intimidated by the man. His daily custom, after watching the highly ritualized team practices from a custom-made tower that gave him the stony, distant, dictatorial air of Brezhnev on the reviewing stand in Red Square, was to repair to a small interview room with the press. There he would talk about who had looked good in practice, who was injured, and, in the disingenuous, self-deprecating way that fooled no one, about the fearsome respect he harbored for next Saturday's opponent and how Alabama didn't have a chance in hell of winning the game because he was doing such a poor job of coaching these unfortunate kids who had signed on to play for such a bedraggled football program. (Then, invariably, Alabama would go out and thoroughly dismantle said opponent, and afterward Bryant would only talk about how lucky they had been to win.) In those after-practice sessions he would smoke Chesterfields and glare at the reporters with a crinkled visage that looked as if it was chiseled from marble.

I never, not once, requested a one-on-one interview. It would have been like requesting a sit-down with God—that is, the scary, creepy, bush-burning, flood-invoking, Old Testament God. I simply hid behind the professional sportswriters, scribbled my notes, and then stole away into the gathering darkness, content once again merely to have breathed the same secondhand-smoke-befouled air as the Great Man. To be sports editor, for me, was the equivalent of that SGA office, that extracurricular plum that might convince some distracted editor somewhere that I was that well-rounded chap whose grades weren't exactly bulletproof (bullet-riddled was more like it) but had plunged into the fecund college mix and come out of it marginally qualified and hirable, albeit reeking slightly of pot and attention deficit disorder.

Among the perks of the job was considerable cachet with my fraternity brothers. Because a mug shot appeared above my column twice a week, I was "somebody" on campus and thus my opinions suddenly carried heft. I didn't mind that development at all. And for a long while I convinced myself that I was that rarest of campus creatures, one who circulated effortlessly between the Greek world and its sworn enemies (i.e., everyone else). Barriers didn't apply to me. I was special and unique. After all, wasn't I from Anniston?

I was wrong, of course. No one plays the field forever, and before I left Tuscaloosa for good I was forced to choose decisively between the power structure and the rebels—no wriggle room allowed. As sports editor I was automatically granted a seat on the paper's editorial board, which meant nothing 364 days of the year. Yet on that 365th day it mattered because it meant I was required to cast a vote to help determine which candidates for SGA office would receive the endorsement of the *Crimson White*. Most important was the endorsement for the post of SGA president—the ultimate plum, the quintessential résumé bling, the single most prestigious gun-handle notch an Alabama student could acquire.

Precious little drama was usually involved in the endorsement process. Machine candidates had won the presidential election in an uninterrupted line that seemed to stretch back into reverse infinity. (Even George Wallace had been unable to break that trend when he attended Alabama. The man who would burn his imprimatur on the state like no other, save Bear Bryant, was forced to settle for the presidency of the Cotillion Club, a minor-league social organization that no longer existed by the time I got to the university.) The *Crimson*

White had not maintained a strict anti-Machine bias throughout its history. Back in the days before the countercultural types gained control, the top editors at the paper were the same fraternity men and sorority women who held the other positions of influence on campus. Even when the paper ceased to be just another Machine tool, Machine candidates more often than not captured the paper's endorsement simply because—by virtue of experience gained in campus affairs, resulting from the self-perpetuating powers of appointment of the fraternity kingmakers—they were often the most qualified for the job.

Not so this particular year. The Machine candidate in 1975 was Fat Joe Williamson, a rotund, unctuous politico from Fort Payne, a small textile and farming center in the vast, scenic, hilly nowhere of northern Alabama, a town that would later become internationally famous as the home of the country music group Alabama. Joe had paid his dues in the Machine tradition—volunteer grunt work as a freshman, then appointed to a homecoming committee here or a yearbook staff there, then getting the nod for a Senate seat to prime the pump for a presidential bid. (No one could ever explain how one specific person ever won the Machine nomination for president. Sometimes it was just his fraternity's turn; sometimes through sheer dint of coalition-building and force of personality, it became obvious that a certain someone was The Next Guy.) Williamson was by no means a flawless candidate—he wasn't universally liked in the Greek world and had the reputation of being a shady deal-maker, not necessarily to be trusted. But it was a down year for Machine talent, Joe had clout, and so the story went that the politicos got together, held their noses, and anointed Williamson for the job. It wasn't as if he could *lose.*

But Williamson's opponent was no inconsequential dorm rat. Cleo Thomas—brilliant, charismatic, popular, hardworking, charac-

ter above reproach—was the real deal in every way. Anyone who
knew anything about state politics saw Cleo as an absolute comer, a
young man who, if he chose to get into the game, could be a governor
or a senator one day; he was that good. That people spoke of Cleo in
such fawning terms in the mid-1970s in Alabama was even more
impressive when you factored into the equation that he was black—
and if elected would be the first African-American to hold the SGA
presidency at the University of Alabama, an achievement that no
doubt would attract national attention. And he was from Anniston,
always a hotbed of young political talent, and I knew him well.

Once this matchup took shape I knew immediately that I was on
the spot. Cleo was, to my mind, by far the most qualified candidate,
but it wasn't going to be that simple. I still had ties to the fraternity—and by extension the Machine—and I knew that pressure
would be applied on me to cast my vote for Fat Joe. It started right
away. I was approached by a couple of Machine types, to whom I
was polite but noncommittal, and then finally by a couple of Theta
Chis known to drink deeply of the Machine Kool-Aid. I fought them
off with some mumbled doublespeak—"Don't worry about it, I'll
do the right thing," or something equally evasive—but I knew in my
heart that the correct vote was for Cleo. I had already watched
Governor George Wallace come to the Alabama campus and personally place the crown upon the head of the school's first black
homecoming queen. The issue of race was shifting a bit in Alabama
in slow, incremental drips, and Cleo's election would make yet
another small but positive statement about that process. But it
wasn't even about that, at its root. Statements aside, I had no doubt
that Cleo was simply the better man for the job by a mile. So why
was I struggling with this so much? Why did I feel guilty about voting against the Machine?

Because I was a spineless product of my Darwinist environment, was all I could figure. The herd instinct still bubbled in my blood. The fraternity had taken me in, given me instant friends and a ready-made social life on campus. Its members had inculcated in me the teaching that the group ideal prevailed over all, constituted the greater good. Steal a few elections? Exert undue influence? The price of doing business. Can't let Joe Slide Rule and the rest of the GDIs run the place, can we? And as preposterous as it seemed, despite my romantic notion of myself as some campus literary type with intellectual notions about politics and race and class and the way things should be, that primal appeal to my wolf pack instincts still resonated on some level.

That instinct was tenacious and ingrained, and ran much deeper than Theta Chi—it was also the result of growing up white in the South in the 1960s, a place simmering in turmoil and defensiveness, where I was surrounded by people who raged against the way Alabama was depicted by the likes of Martin Luther King Jr. and the Yankee media, by all of Them. "They" were always trying to tell us what to do, what to think, how to live. As I grew up, southerners seemed to talk every day of the critical importance of preserving a way of life under siege. The Civil War still mattered greatly, a century later.

I wasn't immune. As a child I had used the word *nigger* countless times, just like (it seemed) everyone else did, until I came to understand what a vile and hurtful weapon it was. Then I wondered why churchgoing men and women used that word, and why so many Christians had such un-Christian-seeming attitudes toward black people. Children absorbed these expectations early on. In Sunday school we would sing:

> *Jesus loves the little children*
> *All the children of the world*

Red and yellow black and white
They are precious in his sight
Jesus loves the little children of the world

... Except that many kids would pointedly hum through *black,* not willing to concede even that much.

I had my own struggles. Even though by high school I had managed to separate myself from the virulent, overt racism that still pervaded southern life then, I had my mother stitch a patch depicting the Confederate flag on the back pocket of a pair of jeans. I rationalized that it was an ironic and mocking statement against the more transparent rednecks, but I know that I also saw it as a gesture against what I perceived as the savaging of the good name of a benevolent culture. Later explorations into history and my conscience would disabuse me of that attitude, but the more subtle cancer of standing with the world from whence you came was not so easily shaken. And so when the pressure was applied to vote for Fat Joe Williamson, who represented the great white way, over Cleo Thomas, who represented a clear repudiation of the very good-old-boy network that had run the university and the state since its inception, it was something I wrestled with. It was all about guilt: cultural guilt (if I voted for Cleo) vs. personal guilt (if I didn't).

Somehow I marshaled enough gumption to cast my vote for Cleo. (It didn't hurt matters that Fat Joe was arrested in midcampaign for allegedly shoplifting an umbrella from a Tuscaloosa department store on a rainy afternoon, a story merrily trumpeted by the *Crimson White*.) Cleo easily won the endorsement and the election as well—the turnout among independents was unprecedented, plus it was clear from the election results that Cleo had surprising support from some Greeks as well. It was a vicious blow against The Machine, one that presaged its deteriorating grip on power in the coming years. Fat Joe would move to Anniston after graduation, oddly enough, where he was convicted of fraud in connection with some investment schemes and spent time in federal prison. Cleo attended law school at Harvard University and then moved back to Anniston to raise a family. He has never held elective office.

Word got out in Machine circles that I hadn't voted properly, and I caught some mean-spirited grief—even though I had no doubt that Cleo would still have won without the endorsement of the *Crimson White*. But the endorsement was a convenient scapegoat for those unable or unwilling to look at what Cleo's victory portended for the Greek system; thus I was informed by several people that the responsibility for Fat Joe's loss lay squarely with me. I didn't buy that, but I didn't go around the Theta Chi house much after that either. The whole affair reaffirmed that the university, like the state at large, was an incredibly hidebound place, that the rules and the order of things were what they were, and that anyone who dared to rock the boat should be prepared to swim alone.

Not that I cared much. I would return to Anniston soon enough, where things would fall back into the comfortable pace and ritual of the way they always were. I might have changed, but I doubted seriously that Anniston had, or ever would.

My anchor back home was the *Anniston Star*. I had interned there the summer before my senior year at Alabama, and had done well enough to get hired full-time after my days in Tuscaloosa were done. Ordinarily the prospect of getting hired at a 30,000-circulation daily in a relatively small Alabama city might not seem very daunting—especially for a hometown boy who had covered the almighty Bear Bryant—but the *Star* was no ordinary outfit. Here in the middle of nowhere was a newsroom outfitted with graduates from Harvard,

Yale, Columbia, Brown, Duke, Virginia, and a smorgasbord of other prestigious schools, imported to Anniston to kick over tables and rub people the wrong way and gather clips and glory for a couple of years before inevitably moving on to bigger papers.

As a point of *Star* philosophy, townies like me weren't necessarily embraced by owner, editor, and publisher Brandt Ayers, whose grandfather and father had preceded him in the Anniston newspaper business. Brandy had been away to prep school at Wooster in Connecticut and, after graduating from Alabama in 1959, worked as Washington correspondent for an array of southern newspapers amid the glitter of the Kennedy years. He and his formidable wife, Josephine, from a good North Carolina family, admired and broke bread with the leading liberal and progressive minds of the day. But in the mid-1960s his father, the Colonel, fell into ill health; long before he was ready to come home, Brandy Ayers was called back to Anniston to take the reins of the *Star* and get to the business of his predestined life as a small-town newspaper publisher in the Deep South, Camelot be damned.

The Ayers family had always been a contrary bunch. Brandy's grandfather had been an Al Smith man back in his heyday—anathema in the South of those times—while the Colonel was an imperious sort who built a reputation as a progressive southern publisher during one of the most racially perilous eras in American history. (It's a record that doesn't always stand up to close scrutiny. "Dad never got past separate but equal," Brandy has said more than once.) But Brandy—figuring that if he was going to spend his prime years in Anniston, he might as well raise holy hell while he was at it—took the *Star* to an entirely new level. He immediately set about editorializing against the lethal prejudice that permeated state and local politics, and made a mortal enemy of the up-and-coming George Wallace. (For the rest of Wallace's life, any *Star* reporter who crossed his field of vision was due for grief. "It must be hum-blin'," Wallace sarcastically said to me once, "to wuk fo' a man who was immaculately conceived.") Ayers let it be known around Anniston that complaints by advertisers about stories that made them look bad would fall on deaf ears. And he began to recruit aggressive Ivy League grads for his reporting staff, well-educated bird dogs who he well knew would swarm over a town where busi-ness-as-usual was spliced into the genetic code. *Star* paychecks were lousy, but Brandy knew that didn't matter much to the trust-fund types he was bringing south. If they stayed a couple of years, Ayers figured that to be an ample return on his investment. The *Star* had its locally bred infrastructure as well—editors and photographers and some reporters and a columnist or two that made up perhaps half the staff and provided continuity and institutional memory. But it was the imports who provided the edge, the irascibility, the upset-the-applecart mentality that made the paper a very different sort of animal in Alabama journalism. That mentality, combined with Brandy's opinion-page attacks against the status quo, began to make the paper's national reputation. By the time the *Star* became the only newspaper in the state to endorse George McGovern against Nixon in the 1972 presidential election, it had already earned a nickname among many of its readers: "The Red Star." It had also earned a faithful, if restive, local following. "People read every page of it every day," my father was fond of saying. "Don't ever think they don't." And to the rest of Alabama and the South, the *Star* was yet another manifestation of Anniston's out-of-step, eccentric, and obstinately progressive personality.

It was into this milieu that I stepped in early 1977, a few months after returning home from the University of Alabama. I was twenty-three years old and newly married, still dripping with the residue of college life. The *Star* didn't hire me right away, so I went to work at one of my father's grocery stores to pay the bills until they did. When I was offered a job at the *Star,* the store employees and many of its customers seemed mystified that I would abandon a profitable business to work there. Didn't I realize how lucky I was? Didn't I want to take over the business someday? You're going to give this up to go work for . . . *Brandy Ayers*? My father, though, seemed to understand. He could see that my heart wasn't in the grocery business, that writing was in my blood, or at least was something I needed to get out of my system. He gave me his blessing, and I went to work at the *Star* and set to the task of seeing Anniston through an entirely different set of eyes.

Those eyes belonged to my new colleagues, the ones from New York and Connecticut and Boston, who viewed Anniston and its environs as some outrageous, three-dimensional foreign film in which they had been given supporting roles. Anniston, to me, was the perfectly acceptable place in which I had grown up and to which I had returned to continue to live my life, but now for the first time I began to hear it described in stridently negative terms. These reporters would return to the newsroom full of tales about overtly racist language by people in power, about the shocking poverty and downtroddenness of the poor on the West Side and out in the shadowy hills of the surrounding rural counties, about the irreversible rigidity of thinking that seemed to be inherent in virtually everyone, be they white, black, or in between. These Yankees sometimes looked to me, as a native, to interpret the culture. I'm afraid I wasn't much help. I was looking to them for the same purpose. Here, finally, was the dark side revealed, the one inhabited by bus burnings and kidnappings and other simple human black-heartedness, one that all along had existed on a plane parallel to the sunshine-and-goodness side that I knew so well. It was like finding your wife's dusty, dog-eared diary and reading about old forbidden loves: painful to absorb, morbidly fascinating, impossible to put down.

I began my own research. I ventured out into the towns and villages scattered among the pine hills and red clay in the hinterlands of the *Star*'s circulation area, places like Heflin and Wedowee and Fruithurst and Ragland, places where oligarchs in overalls sat on county commissions and thought nothing of spending the public dime to pave roads on private property belonging to their friends and supporters—thought nothing of it, that is, until somebody wrote about it in the paper. I sat through interminable city budget hearings and board of education meetings, watching the subplot of white elected officials battling the dawning certainty that they could no longer ignore the increasing expectation among their black constituents—expectations so easily deflected for so long—that they would be more fully represented in the municipal budgets and payrolls and that their children would be properly schooled. I chased tornadoes when they erupted on a squall line that stretched southwest to the Gulf of Mexico, and marveled at how unfailingly precise and deadly they were at locating and ravaging the poorest and most vulnerable among us—as if God Himself had suddenly taken a powerful dislike to shabby and dilapidated double-wides hidden away in already godforsaken necks of the woods I had never seen in a lifetime of living virtually next door.

Stubborn corruption, racism both covert and not so subtle, outright misery; it was all there on a bountiful platter for my voyeuristic viewing, reaffirming the third-world theories advanced by my colleagues from the North. I drank it all in, just to determine its taste. But that other world, the one that I grew up in and treasured, was on abundant display as well. It was out there in the same places among the overalled oligarchs and the kudzu-clustered trailer parks—you just had to know when to open your eyes and pay attention.

My guide in these matters was Ken Elkins, chief photographer of the *Star,* one of the native Alabamians on the staff and a pure, undistilled, self-taught genius. In physical appearance and artistic temperament, he was the unmistakable love child of Mark Twain and Willie Nelson. He could photograph anything that moved—football players, dogs, politicians, stock-car drivers, firemen, a kid with a hula hoop—or anything that didn't—barns, an old plow, a birdhouse, cemeteries, beauty queens—and render from them a black-and-white piece of gallery-quality art. He wasn't much interested in photographing famous people, unless Hank Williams should suddenly rise from the dead. He was at his best and happiest when he was drifting down the shady side of some obscure dirt road along a rusty barbed-wire fence in an old fishing car, eyes rolling over the landscape, soaking in whatever was there for the seeing. I rode with him many times, the two of us armed with cigarettes, Vienna sausage, crackers, and, most vitally, Cokes in those feisty little high-octane 6½-ounce bottles, one burning sip from which would clear your head like a lightning charge. With Elkins I bore witness to backwoods revivals, domino players, wood-chopping contests, country singings, shade-tree mechanics, any number of rites and oddities; his allegiance to rural endeavor and folk heroism was unswerving.

At dawn one Saturday we loaded up and drove into Georgia to visit what, to Elkins, constituted an A-list celebrity: Chess McCartney, aka "The Goat Man," a living rural legend with a flowing white beard. Over the years he had crisscrossed America countless times on foot accompanied by a large herd of smelly, braying goats. A local artist had tipped Elkins to where the now-retired Goat Man had settled, which turned out to be an old yellow school bus with a decidedly aftermarket wood-burning stove smoking away inside. The man had a face for the ages, like something out of the Bible. We spent the morning there listening to McCartney's Homeric stories of the road, Elkins's motordrive cranking away like mad. The frames he took away from there were stunning. McCartney looked like nothing less than some great ancient hungover Moses. The pictures-and-story package we produced ran not only in the *Star* but in hundreds of papers around the world via the Associated Press. But Elkins had captured more than just the image of this stinking, marvelous curiosity of a man; he had captured his dignity. And I saw then that that same dignity was what Elkins was after in so much of his work—the dignity and worth in his subjects, sometimes buried deep in the creases of a lined and weary face, but there. I began to see that dignity too, or at least look for it, in these people who were so close to who I was and where I was from. I balanced that dignity and worth against the harsher perspectives of my colleagues from New York and Boston, and found that there was much value and truth in both. A great deal of what made up Anniston and its people was worth preserving; a great deal of it was worth trying to change. How to change it?—that was the unanswerable question.

I started covering state politics and, inevitably, George Wallace, who towered over Alabama like a cigar-chewing, Vitalis-slicked monolith, still a political powerhouse despite his paralysis and confinement to a wheelchair since the attempt on his life in Maryland during the 1976 presidential campaign. Wallace had always fascinated me, the way monster movies fascinate a child. The first time I saw him in person was in junior high, when my parents took me with them to Birmingham to the annual convention of the powerful state teachers' association. Wallace was to deliver the keynote address. He was a longtime ally of the teachers' lobby and was greeted like Caesar. I don't remember anything he said, but he had an incredibly menacing air about him and seemed to conjure up a kind of black magic that he cast into the transfixed audience like pixie dust.

He wasn't even in office at the time; in those days Alabama governors were prohibited from serving consecutive terms, so in 1966 Wallace simply ran his acquiescent wife, Lurleen, in his stead—and she won in a landslide. Governor Lurleen Wallace also spoke to the teachers that day in Birmingham, but mainly to introduce her husband. George was the show, and everybody knew it, Lurleen most of all. Wallace's best-laid plans unraveled when Lurleen died from cancer while in office. She was succeeded by the lieutenant governor, Wallace foe Albert Brewer, who quickly cast Wallace and his moneychangers from the temple of state government. Wallace wrested the governorship back from Brewer in 1970 in what is still widely regarded as the bloodiest campaign in state history.

By 1982, when I was assigned by the *Star* to cover the governor's race, Wallace was attempting a political comeback. After serving as governor from 1970 to 1978—the no-succession law had been changed by then to accommodate him—Wallace, unable to run again and in poor health anyway as a result of his wounds, had stepped aside and was replaced by Fob James, a multimillionaire businessman who pledged to run state government like a corporation. That was a laughable notion given the numbing effect of Alabama's antiquated constitution, which essentially had rigged the system to favor in perpetuity the state's moneyed landowners and other powerful interests, but it sounded good and James was elected. After four years of futility James decided not to run again, officially because of a campaign promise to serve only one term, but also because he didn't have the cast-iron hide required to mount a defense against the returning Wallace.

In the early 1980s the Republican Party was still a virtual nonentity in state politics, although Alabama voters had already begun to swing toward the GOP in presidential elections. The Democratic gubernatorial nomination was still tantamount to election. Wallace's chief rival in the 1982 Democratic primary turned out to be George McMillan, a tall, reedy Birmingham attorney who had served as lieutenant governor under Fob James. McMillan was the rarest of Alabama politicians, a progressive intellectual. He was mercurial but brilliant and stood squarely as a New South reform candidate, as a refutation of the "politics of personal destruction" exemplified by Wallace, and as a healer of the various racial and sundry other black eyes Alabama had suffered as a result of Wallace's divisive legacy. Most of the political establishment didn't give McMillan a chance, but a significant minority suspected that perhaps the time had finally arrived for a candidacy such as his. The contrast between Wallace and McMillan was unmistakable. McMillan, not yet forty, was young, incisive, forward-thinking, a tireless bundle of energy on the campaign trail. Wallace, then sixty-three but seeming much older, was shriveled from his injuries, easily fatigued, far removed from the charismatic, fire-and-brimstone bomb-thrower he had once been. I wasn't the only reporter to play up the differences between the two. McMillan began to impress, swelling numbers of voters, and donors began to notice, and before long the polls reflected that McMillan had a legitimate shot, that Wallace had a real fight on his hands. A stream of national media began to troop south, examining this clash of Old vs. New and describing McMillan as the man who might very well write George Wallace's political obituary.

I wasn't convinced. Wallace still held a smothering grip on the hearts and minds of a great many Alabamians. I saw that for myself at Wallace rallies. While McMillan was still forced to seek out voters by canvassing on the street—it was estimated that he personally shook some one hundred thousand hands during the course of the campaign—Wallace, keenly aware of his physical limitations, concentrated on large-scale gatherings at city auditoriums, county fairgrounds, and the like. One night in Decatur I stood among a throng of some ten thousand people at a state park and watched as country superstar Hank Williams Jr. slayed the crowd with a boisterous sing-along rendition of "Family Tradition," and then as Wallace, pathetically crumpled in his wheelchair, manipulated them like a Vegas dealer rifling a deck of cards. He spoke of his worldwide fame, and of how that notoriety would bring "jobs, jobs, jobs to the people of Alabama." He spoke of how he had "stood up for Alabama" and how now he was asking "the people of Alabama to stand up for me." The climax of the event came when country singer Tammy Wynette took the stage and warbled "Stand By Your Man," her arm crooked around Wallace. It was the stuff of redneck genius. "Stand By Your Man," originally composed as a hillbilly article of faith inspired by Wynette's wayward, alcoholic ex-husband, the great country star George Jones, had been converted into an ironic testimonial for a man who, to legions of still-faithful supporters, was no less than a political, even religious, martyr. Wynette's message came through loud and clear: *No matter what they say, he's ours, warts and all.* I looked around and saw tears streaming down the faces of these people in the midst of the rapture, and understood that George McMillan had an immense task in front of him—one that required nothing less than turning around the massive, inexorable battleship of an entire culture.

And yet McMillan persisted. Finally the primary arrived and he ran a strong second to Wallace, forcing a runoff. If McMillan could coagulate the anti-Wallace vote under his aegis and get a big turnout in the urban areas that were overwhelmingly supportive of him, then he had a chance. The polls put him neck-and-neck with Wallace.

Momentum was his, and some experts privately predicted that McMillan would win the runoff in a very close vote. Then some very strange intelligence began to materialize: Wallace, astonishingly, was *targeting the black vote*—specifically, rural, older black voters. He had been making low-profile appearances at churches in the Black Belt, the swath of poor, mostly African-American counties that stretched across the state's midsection, telling congregations that in his period of reflection following the Maryland assassination attempt he had come to regret the effects of his racially charged past deeds, that he had asked God for forgiveness and was asking their forgiveness as well. This never would have played in cities like Birmingham, where memories of church bombings and police dogs were seared onto the black consciousness and where people were simply less gullible, but the word was that out in the hollows the notion of "forgiving George" was actually getting some traction. (The word also was that the Wallace campaign was paying some black ministers under the table to urge their parishioners to vote for Wallace, but no one could ever verify it.) The black vote, of course, was the taken-for-granted linchpin of McMillan's electoral strategy, and in the waning days of the runoff campaign a concerted effort was made to blunt this bold, even galling, maneuver by Wallace, with luminaries like Coretta Scott King trucked into the state to remind people of the lethal impact of Wallace's words and actions and of the related atrocities committed and battles waged in places like Birmingham and Selma and Anniston.

On Election Day, a record number of voters packed the polls. Turnout was especially robust in the larger cities, which boded well for McMillan. Brandy Ayers published a signed, front-page editorial in the *Star* that afternoon that urged readers to vote for McMillan and flatly predicted the end of the Wallace era in Alabama. (Indeed, Anniston and Calhoun County would go to McMillan.) When the polls closed, ABC News immediately projected McMillan as the winner, and an epic celebration began at McMillan headquarters in Birmingham as early returns from the urban areas (where fast-reporting machines were widely employed) sent the lieutenant governor to the lead. Yet there was no sign of concession from the Wallace camp in Montgomery; they would wait for the results from the rural counties, where paper ballots were still in currency and where, ominously, the long-standing Wallace network of sheriffs, probate judges, and county clerks remained in power. Those results began to trickle in, and it became apparent that while McMillan was winning the black precincts, he wasn't winning them by the slam-dunk margins he had anticipated—and sorely needed. His lead began to evaporate. Well after midnight, Wallace inched excruciatingly ahead in the statewide count. And then, at last, the final tally: Wallace had won by less than ten thousand votes out of a million cast. He had done it again. He had seemed mortally wounded; the networks and all his other old enemies had projected him a loser; but he had survived to tell them all to go to hell one more time. Wallace went on to bulldoze his Republican opponent in the general election, Tammy Wynette sang at the inauguration, and all was as it had always been.

George McMillan would run again in four years, and I would quit the *Star* to work for him, so eager was I to reverse what I saw as an egregious defeat of the forces of good. But that campaign never got off the ground, even though Wallace himself decided not to run again and retired permanently from politics. McMillan was depleted, still crushed from his loss in '82. As so often happens with politicians and sports teams who lose the Big One by a whisker, the window had closed. I decided to save my own skin and resigned from the campaign to go to work for the *Birmingham News,* the state's largest and most influential paper, where the pay was good and lots of people were interested in having a good time. But my heart wasn't in it. I had had it with Alabama. I loved the place, but I had decided it was never going to wake up from its self-satisfied slumber, never going to shake loose from the proverbial shackles of its history. The great majority of people seemed primarily concerned about football and religion (and frequently confused the two) at the expense of social and economic progress. I realized that I felt like an outsider. Alabama didn't seem to need me anymore, if it ever had.

Anniston was certainly doing fine without me. It had recently been named an "All-American City" in a national competition. A lot of money had been raised for new industrial development to take advantage of its strategic location equidistant from the booming metropolises of Atlanta and Birmingham on the newly completed interstate. The defense buildup under President Reagan had Fort McClellan and the Anniston Army Depot humming. I had divorced, and I began to dream of big-city newsrooms and of writing books, of becoming an itinerant journalist and roaming free, taking a page from Elkins's book and rolling my eyes over the landscape merely to see what there was to see.

Alabama would never change—the evidence seemed clear on that point. Anniston seemed to be following its usual trajectory, impervious to its environment. People there would continue to do what they had always done and play their assigned roles. I didn't know what my role was. Like so many others before me, the time had finally come for me to leave.

CHAPTER SEVEN

ORGANIZATION MAN

David Baker stayed in New York for nearly twenty-five years. It was everything everyone had said it would be, everything he had hoped it would be. New York was a massive, wide-open, crazy-as-hell place, a civilization unto itself. Almost everything about it was extreme, large-scale: the buildings, the streets, the weather, the people—most of all the people. People were different in New York, particularly black people. Black people in New York were *in your face*. It wasn't that black folks in Anniston didn't stand up for themselves; they did, after a fashion. But as David saw it, a great many black people in Anniston and the South in general were deferential in the way they went about fighting for what was theirs. There wasn't much deferential about New York that David could detect. None of that shuffling-around, head-down, yes-sir-no-sir crap. If you challenged somebody in New York, they would challenge you right back and then some—especially a black man or woman. They would get right up in your grill and see if you were willing or able to back your business up. These people were smart, aggressive, *proud.*

And you had to be all of those things yourself if you were going to hang in there, if you were going to survive, if you were going to be able to hack it. It was a world about as far removed from Anniston, Alabama, as anywhere and anything could be.

But the thing about it was: people are people, wherever they are, wherever they're from, whatever color they are. David had always been able to deal with people. And even though these cats in New York didn't play around, David had never had any problem standing up for himself. Hell, if he could stand up to Coach like he did at County Training that time when he was just a kid, then he figured he could stand up to anybody. But New York . . . it was tough. It took something out of you just to get to work in the morning, just to walk down the sidewalk and hold your ground. After David had been in New York for a while, he had the same realization that many do: he was in over his head, out of his depth, and he could either sink like a stone or start thrashing at the water like all hell and learn to swim like everybody else. At the very least, he figured, he would find out what he was made of, and that would be good information to have.

What David Baker figured out about himself was that he could hack it.

He became a union organizer, maybe as tough a job as there is in God's world. Not right away, of course; it took him a few years to get there, and a little while even to figure out that was what he wanted to do. Plus it wasn't even exactly right to say it had been an ambition of his. Like so many things, it just happened, just sort of worked itself out. One thing led to another, and it seemed like before he knew it he was flying on private jets with Nelson Mandela and Spike Lee and shaking hands with Muhammad Ali. It was just more evidence to back up what somebody had once said: If you want to make God laugh, tell him your plans.

The truth was that David didn't have a plan when he drove into Brooklyn that day from Anniston in the Pinto he had bought off the lot at Sunny King Ford with the windfall that had appeared in his foundry paycheck like a biblical omen. He had family on Flatbush Avenue, and he knew he was welcome to stay with them until he got on his feet. Beyond that, no clue. He would look for work and take it from there. He just knew he wasn't going to work in any damn pipe shop, although he had no idea if they even had pipe shops in New York. (Probably, he decided; New York seemed to have everything else.) He'd starve before he'd do that again. But he needn't have worried. There were plenty of jobs for a man who was willing to work, even if he was black. That was another difference between New York and Anniston. In Anniston, there were two kinds of jobs: white folks' jobs and black folks' jobs. There was very little back-and-forth between the two. In New York, people didn't seem to worry about that distinction very much. If you could talk a good game and seemed willing to work, you could find a job.

He drove a truck delivering soap that was used to make perfume. He worked as a security guard. He even cut hair for a while, learning that trade at an Italian barber shop owned by a man named Salvatore who took a liking to David and thought he had a future. (That was another difference: David had never met anyone in Anniston named Salvatore.) It turned out that Sal had interests in a number of businesses, about which David learned not to ask too many questions. David even chauffeured Sal occasionally as the boss made his many rounds. But David knew this was a dead-end street, or at least a thoroughfare that he had no business getting overly familiar with. He surely knew he didn't want to be a barber for the rest of his life. So eventually he left Sal's employ and went to work as an orderly at Coney Island Hospital, where his destiny began to crystallize.

His coworkers at the hospital gave him a hard time at first. They called him "Country" and "Bama" and every other derogatory nickname they could think of, not letting David forget for a minute that he was just a rough-around-the-edges bumpkin from the sticks. David took it in stride. Hell, he *was* from the sticks. No use pretending it wasn't true. He just gave back as good as he got, told his tormentors that he thanked God every day that he was from a good and wholesome place like Alabama, where the sky was blue and the rabbit hunting was good and people were honest and made cornbread the way it was supposed to be made, and you didn't have to use a hammer and chisel to knock a solid inch of ice off your windshield every morning just to drive to work. He told them he was just up there taking some of that big-city money while it was there for the taking, and soon enough he would be back in Anniston with enough to pay his bills and enjoy the good life the way it was supposed to be lived. When he got back home and was wrapped around a fishing pole in the sunshine and eating lunch at Mama's table every day, he told them, he would be sure to think about them back up there in New York jackhammering that goddamn ice off their windshields. And they would tell David in return that that would be fine, go ahead, and they would be sure to come to his funeral after the Ku Klux Klan hung his wise ass from a tree down there in some plantation cotton field among all the slaves owned by Colonel Sanders. And so it went.

But it was hard not to like David, and he was slowly accepted at the hospital as one of their own. He joined the hospital basketball team and led the way to the industrial league championship—his shot had not deserted him, and he could still play. It was a tough league and there were rough-and-tumble episodes, but this was something that David understood. After a year, he decided to run for the hospital's union council. It was a little extra money for what amounted to a popularity contest, and people had begun to tell David that if he ran he would probably win. He ran and was elected, and found that he enjoyed the work. He liked helping people with their problems, helping them navigate through the minefields that were set by the hospital administration. He took workers' grievances to management, argued their cases, and often prevailed. His natural sense of outrage, the tendency toward umbrage that had prompted fights with Dinky Adams and basketball team strikes, was balanced by his gregarious personality and innate diplomatic skills. He began to establish a reputation as an effective union man. The next year he ran for president of the council and won. In the space of two years David had risen from Country Boy Baker to chief spokesman for the workers at one of the most prominent hospitals in New York. And he found that he loved it—he found that he loved setting things right.

In his position as union council president, David began to deal with other union leaders around New York. Soon he came to the attention of James Butler, head of Local 420 of the AFSCME (American Federation of State, County, and Municipal Employees). Local 420 at that time represented some fifteen thousand hospital workers, which made Butler a man of considerable influence within the AFSCME, which was in turn the largest single union within the AFL-CIO. Butler saw in David a young man who fairly seethed with energy and commitment, two prerequisites for any quality union official, and armed with an arsenal of street smarts that contradicted his down-home background. Butler would take David under his wing and introduce him to the unforgiving world of New York union politics, eventually promoting his protégé higher and higher until David became Butler's full-time right-hand man.

To David, Butler became nothing less than a mentor and father figure. He flourished under Butler's tutelage, and it soon became apparent that he was naturally born to the business of organizing. Local 420 organized a great many hospitals in the late 1970s and early 1980s, and David Baker was the point man on most of those missions. To organize a hospital required a multitude of skills, not the least of which was the ability to persuade a few key employees on the inside to stand firm with him, to take the fight to management, to risk their jobs and serve as the conduit between the union and the workers who would be voting on whether to join the union. To develop that kind of relationship required the creation of a great deal of trust. Through sheer force of personality and a canny appreciation of the way hospitals worked, David more often than not got the job done, wormed his way into the hearts and good graces of opinion leaders in a particular workplace, convinced them to join with him to fight for better working conditions for themselves and their colleagues.

But charisma and knowledge of how to work the system weren't the only assets David brought to the task of organizing. What Butler admired most about the kid is that David truly and utterly believed in what he was doing. David believed that bringing people together to fight for their own betterment was the only way to effect any sort of change that mattered or lasted. Anyone who sat around and waited for people in power to do the right thing was just kidding himself, in David's view. You had to push it, force the issue. Wasn't that the lesson of the civil rights movement? If they hadn't taken to the streets, black folks would still be waiting for equal treatment to be handed down from the mountaintop. They didn't call it the status quo for nothing. The only way to move management off the dime was to resort to the power of numbers, to get people behind you and go to war for what was right and proper. That, or you might find yourself showing up for practice at six in the morning on the day of a county tournament game and hating yourself for it. David believed in the work, and he believed in James Butler. Thus armed, he proceeded to take on New York—and New York accepted the challenge, as it always does.

David organized hospitals. He led picket lines and strikes, and fought the police more than once. He helped organize and lead marches peopled by union members in support of or in opposition to a variety of causes that were deemed critical by Butler or someone above him in the union hierarchy. With unions a big player in New York politics, he participated in many campaigns and worked closely with, among others, Mayor David Dinkins and his staff. When Nelson Mandela was released from prison in South Africa in 1990 and traveled to America to speak to massive gatherings across the country, David found himself on the celebrity-packed private jet that carried Mandela from Miami to New York, where David helped put together an appearance by Mandela at Yankee Stadium. It was heady, humbling, inspirational. David stood on the field at Yankee Stadium in close proximity to Muhammad Ali and Yankee owner George Steinbrenner and marveled at the sight of so many thousands of people gathered to celebrate the deliverance of justice, after nearly thirty years, to Mandela and the fight against oppression he had led in South Africa. He shook hands and spoke briefly with Mandela, who seemed to radiate dignity and inner fortitude. Here is a man, David thought, who conceded nothing in the face of imprisonment and death, a living testament to the power of unyielding commitment to a cause. David pledged silently to do his best to inculcate those same principles in his work within the universe in which he went to battle every day. Compared with Mandela, David figured, his journey was a cakewalk.

But David would be tested, and severely. A civil war broke out within AFSCME, which pitted factions that supported AFSCME president Jerry Wurf against a rebel faction led by a subordinate named Victor Gotbaum. James Butler was loyal to Wurf, who had been instrumental in developing union clout in New York and across the country since the 1960s. According to the AFSCME organizational chart, Butler's Local 420 was technically under the aegis of Gotbaum's District Council 37. But as friction between Wurf and Gotbaum intensified, officials like Butler were forced to declare their allegiance to one side or the other—in deed if not in word. Butler cheerily threw in with Wurf, alongside whom he had fought in many a union contretemps for nearly twenty years. And as Butler went, of course, so did David Baker, who would have followed his mentor into the jaws of hell if such an expedition had been proposed. Wurf used Butler, David, and their crew at Local 420 as his chief operatives in his mission to blunt Gotbaum's insurgency. Gotbaum soon deduced what was happening and attempted to have Butler removed from the leadership of Local 420 on charges of financial mismanagement. Wurf countered by moving Butler's local out from under Gotbaum's DC 37, which not only defused Gotbaum's move against Butler but deprived DC 37 of some $150,000 a month in dues. This in turn eventually forced Gotbaum to cut staff and borrow some $500,000 to meet operating expenses.

Things got very ugly very quickly, with suits and countersuits filed in state court and vicious debates before the AFSCME executive board. David, by now married and with two children, soon found himself involved in a street-level cloak-and-dagger intrigue that consumed great chunks of his time and kept him away from his family. He worked long into the night as Butler and other Wurf loyalists marshaled resources to meet the various legal challenges under way, to protect their membership from incursions by Gotbaum, and to mount their own efforts against the various strongholds within DC 37 in an attempt to erode Gotbaum's power. It soon became apparent to David and certain others within the group that they were being followed, a development they figured was attributable to Gotbaum's desire to keep tabs on who his enemies were consorting with. The situation kept escalating. Repeated late-night anonymous phone calls were made to David's home, telling his wife that her husband was either dead or would be soon. One weekend when the family was away, David's apartment burned in a mysterious arson; he had little doubt about the message that was being sent.

Finally, David's ten-year-old daughter, Twiggy, was struck by a car outside their building in a hit-and-run—a terrifying event, and one that sent David into a rage that lasted for days. Incredibly, Twiggy only sustained minor injuries, for which David was grateful, but he could not be dissuaded from his belief that the incident was no accident, that it was a heinous salvo in the internecine battle between Wurf and Gotbaum. Police investigated and asked lots of questions of lots of people, just as they did with the apartment fire, but the driver was never found and charges were never filed.

For whatever reason, the threats and phone calls and general level of mayhem seemed to diminish after the incident. David figured that either Gotbaum's crew was guilty of the unconscionable act and was unwilling to conjure up more heat, or that they had nothing to do with it but feared being implicated nonetheless. Whatever the case, the episode served notice to David that he was involved in a deadly serious game. But he resolved that he would not be bullied, that he would not back down. He either believed in what he was doing or he didn't—there was nothing vague or gray about the situation. It was yet another lesson about New York: simple lip service wasn't good enough, not in this town. Sooner or later, you were forced to back it up. Any sign of weakness or lack of commitment and you would be set upon by jackals.

David saw this truth demonstrated once again a few years later in an incident that, in retrospect, seemed less like real life than like a scene from some bloody New York cinematic epic directed by Martin Scorsese. His all-consuming professional life had wrecked his marriage, and he and his wife had separated. Money being tight, he moved into a boarding house in Brooklyn populated mostly by immigrants who didn't speak English very well, if at all, and whose lack of communications skills gave rise among them to great suspicions about their landlords and neighbors. David would soon discover that those reservations about the landlords, at least, were well founded. Shortly after moving in, David realized that the landlords—a woman and a handful of her nephews who lived on the first floor—were quintessential slumlords and ran what amounted to a totalitarian regime enforced by terror. Rent control and other housing laws were summarily ignored. If a tenant was late with a rent payment (which might have been suddenly and arbitrarily increased by an illegal whim of the landlords), his water might be shut off, or he might even be forcibly removed from the building—sometimes at gunpoint. Most of the tenants, newly arrived in America, were woefully unaware of their rights and acquiesced to the brutal and illegal tactics employed by the landlords.

David was neither woefully unaware of his rights nor was he acquiescent. After a couple of months in the building he began to organize a tenants' association, to the belligerent dismay of the landlords. When, as often happened, the landlords failed to pay the power bill and the entire building was without power for days, David organized a rent strike. He challenged evictions. He filed peace warrants with the police in connection with the landlords' gun-wielding tactics. He formed alliances among the tenants and set up meetings to educate them about New York housing codes and the rights they were entitled to. The landlords repeatedly tried to evict him and threatened to kill him if he didn't leave. David didn't budge. Compared with what he had been through, this was sport. Besides, he couldn't let these sons of bitches run over these people, could he? It was the principle of the thing.

One evening during the time when the Zodiac serial killer was terrorizing New York (yet another difference between New York and Anniston: no crazy-ass Zodiac killer in Anniston), David was in his room packing for a trip to Indiana, where he had been assigned a union project and would be staying for a few months. His girlfriend was with him, helping him pack. Suddenly the landlady and one of her nephews burst into the room, waving shotguns. The nephew stuck his gun in David's belly, announcing that he was going to kill him. The landlady trained her gun on David's girlfriend, who had fallen to the floor and begun to scream for help. In a fit of anger, the landlady attempted to push a television set over on the screaming woman; David seized the momentary distraction to wrest the shotgun away from the nephew. He swung the weapon around and fired a deafening volley at his attackers, wounding one. The deadly scrum tumbled out into the hallway, where more shots exploded like depth charges. It turned out that a neighbor and ally of David's named Chester had grabbed his own weapon, raced up the stairs, and opened fire on the assailants, killing both of them. In the sudden eerie silence that followed, David fixated on the haphazard splatter of shocking red blood on the corridor walls, incredulous that he was still alive.

The police soon arrived and pieced everything together. The other tenants had been locked in their rooms by the landlords to prevent anyone from witnessing the attack or interfering. Apparently the assailants had planned to kill David and blame his murder on the

Zodiac killer. Because of the warrants David had filed in the past, the police were familiar with the history of disputes in the building, and quickly determined that David and Chester had acted in self-defense. As David sat on the front steps of the building and wearily answered the investigators' questions, a newspaper photographer arrived and snapped his picture. The following day the photo appeared in the *New York Times* with an article that detailed the fatal shootings and the ill will that had preceded them. In the photograph David looked exhausted. In what seemed like a life of close calls, this one had very nearly done him in.

He clipped the story from the *Times* and always kept it in the briefcase that Butler had bequeathed to him, the one battered around the edges from the time Butler had hurled it at a truck that was attempting to bull through a picket line. Whenever David told the story about the time his landlord tried to murder him in New York and two people were killed in self-defense, people either didn't believe him or at least suspected that he was exaggerating. If he detected their doubt, he would invariably forage through the scarred briefcase and present the yellowing article as evidence of the truth. It wasn't a tall tale, he would explain—it was the facts, the nature of New York, one hell of a tough town.

By the early 1990s David was a classic burnout case. It took him a while to realize it, of course, because there was always some union-related shooting war going on somewhere that occupied his frontal lobe, some tar baby of contention that captured his attention and persuaded his subconscious to ignore the mental and physical fatigue that had begun to seep into his system the way water always finds the crack in the reservoir wall. But he couldn't ignore it forever, and it was during a visit home to Anniston that he sat down, took a breath, and began to inventory the situation.

Jerry Wurf was dead. James Butler had retired. The union leadership in New York had gone through a generational change. There was plenty of work to be done, always would be, but David was beginning to realize that what he had come to see as a class struggle between labor and management, between the haves and the have-nots, was one that would be waged long after he was dead, whether he died that night or ten thousand nights into the future. He also knew that whenever he opted out of that struggle, which had swallowed virtually his entire adult life, he would be able to hold his head high because he had done some good work, had defended some worthy causes and even worthier people, and had left every drop of blood he could spare out on the field every single time. He had never shirked a challenge, and he would fight any man who said he had. But he had to admit to himself that he was tired, that he wasn't a young soldier anymore who craved conflict so that he could earn his reputation and his stripes. It wasn't so much about winning anymore as it was about surviving—and David had been around long enough to know that when you started defining the world in those terms, it was time to take a hard look at yourself.

There were other factors to consider as well, personal ones. He had remarried. His old man, Bake, had died. Mama was a widow now and seemed to be growing old before his very eyes—that is, before his very eyes on the rare occasions when he could get away from New York to visit her. The family had scattered, and David began to worry about who would look after her. He was his mother's eldest and only surviving son—he felt that he had certain responsibilities.

David began to make plans to come home.

He went back to New York and persuaded his boss to arrange a transfer to Atlanta, thinking that might provide the solution. Atlanta was about ninety miles from Anniston, a relatively quick drive on the interstate; he could easily make the trip on weekends, even the occasional weekday evening if the need arose. But once in Atlanta, David found that his heart simply wasn't in it. Atlanta and New York contrasted like night and day. He felt like he was starting over, and starting over suddenly felt like something he wasn't willing to do.

He discussed the matter with Betty, his wife. She was from New York but had been willing to move to Atlanta with David; she let him know that wherever he needed to go, she would go with him and make it work. Fortified with that knowledge, David decided the time had come to quit. New York and the union were the city and the profession that had made him a man, and he would miss them both. But it was time to go home. He was needed there. He wasn't sure what he would do for a living, what he would do to occupy his days. But once his mind was made up to return, David didn't worry about that too much. One thing he knew about himself was that he would always be able to find work, would always find something to do.

A vintage postcard of downtown Anniston in 1943, looking south along Noble Street. Always viewed as an unusually progressive small Southern town, Anniston was dubbed "The Model City" by Atlanta newspaperman Henry Grady. *E. C. Kropp & Co.*

Looking south on Noble Street in 2005. Victorian-era facades are still in evidence along the thoroughfare, which after decades of economic difficulty have experienced a renaissance after a refurbishing campaign pushed by Mayor Chip Howell. *Dennis Love*

A century-old statue of Samuel Noble stands at the intersection of Quintard Avenue and Eleventh Street in downtown Anniston. Noble's vision of a ready-made town to support his family's iron works led to the formation of Anniston in the 1880s. *The City of Anniston*

The Freedom Riders' bus was burned by a mob of whites on Highway 202 near Anniston on Mother's Day 1961, an incident that remains notorious to this day. Another bus of the Freedom Riders' was attacked on the same day in Birmingham and many of its passengers were beaten. *The Birmingham News*

The Solutia plant, formerly Monsanto, west of downtown Anniston on Highway 202. The facility was one of only two in the country that manufactured PCBs, the second was another Monsanto plant in Illinois. Monsanto stopped manufacturing PCBs in Anniston in 1971; the U.S. banned production of all PCBs in 1979 due to health and environmental concerns. *Eddie Motes*

An aerial view of the Anniston Army Depot's chemical weapons incinerator, which began operations in 2003 to destroy a huge and lethal cache of GB, VX, and mustard nerve agent stored at the depot—an estimated 7 percent of the world's known chemical weapons stockpile. The facility sits eight miles west of Anniston and began the "burn" after a lengthy and highly political debate about public and environmental safety. *Anniston Army Depot*

A sign on Highway 21, south of Anniston near Interstate 20, shows the official exit route should the "unthinkable" occur—a release of toxic emissions from the Anniston Army Depot's chemical weapons incinerator. Should such an event occur, the Army has warned residents that they may have as few as eight minutes to evacuate. *Dennis Love*

An unidentified Anniston youth tries on a protective hood to be used in the event of an accidental release of deadly toxins from the chemical weapons incinerator at the Anniston Army Depot. The precautionary distribution marked the first time in U.S. history that gas masks were issued by the government to the general public. *Consolidated Publishing/Kevin Qualls,* Anniston Star

The Mars Hill Baptist Church, which launched the first significant major lawsuit against Monsanto in connection with PCB contamination, in West Anniston. The church retained Donald Stewart as its attorney and ultimately settled for $2 million and a van. The church and surrounding property sits near the Solutia (formerly Monsanto) plant and is fenced off from public access. *Eddie Motes*

An unidentified protester makes his feelings known at a Birmingham rally in 2003 against the startup of the chemical weapons incinerator at the Anniston Army Depot. Incineration opponents experienced some successes at burn sites in other states but were stymied in their efforts to halt the process in Anniston. *Dennis Love*

An eroding sign identifies the modest West Anniston headquarters of Community Against Pollution in early 2006. Founded by David Baker, the grassroots organization helped lead the drive to gather plaintiffs for the state and federal suits against Monsanto, conduct PCB testing for the EPA, and lobby for a PCB health clinic as part of the legal settlement with Monsanto and Solutia. *Eddie Motes*

David Baker grew up on Anniston's West Side and would ultimately play a leading role in the town's epic legal struggle against Monsanto. After twenty-five years as a union organizer in New York, Baker returned to his hometown to retire but instead found himself at the forefront of a grassroots movement that would make international headlines. *Eddie Motes*

Montgomery attorney David Byrne of the powerhouse firm Beasley Allen. Byrne was the primary lawyer on the ground in Anniston for the federal lawsuit that pressed the claims of 15,000 plaintiffs against Monsanto. That suit, along with the state case brought by Donald Stewart, led to the historic $700 million settlement with Monsanto and its spinoff Solutia. *Dennis Love*

Anniston attorney Donald Stewart speaks to a gathering of *Abernathy vs. Monsanto* plaintiffs in 2002. A former U.S. senator, Stewart spent eight years on the *Abernathy* suit at great financial risk and won a series of verdicts that ultimately forced a $700 million global settlement that involved superlawyers Johnnie Cochran and Jere Beasley. *Eddie Motes*

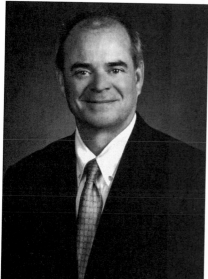

Anniston Mayor Chip Howell, who even as a child was keenly aware of his hometown's military legacy and the burden that came with it. As mayor, Howell helped clear the way for a billion-dollar Army incinerator to begin operations to methodically destroy a vast cache of chemical weapons stored in Anniston since the beginning of the Cold War. *Courtesy of Chip Howell*

Hoyt W. Howell, Sr., a successful real estate entrepreneur in Anniston and influential civic leader until his death in 1988. He groomed his son, Chip, for public service and impressed upon the future mayor the significant and complicated place Anniston held in the Cold War universe. *Courtesy of Chip Howell*

Looking east on Tenth Street toward Noble Street, the "mountain," and beyond. Decidedly more romantic views of the city are available from atop the rolling foothills that surround the city, but here is where the west side begins—and where Anniston finally has confronted the grim environmental legacies left behind by Monsanto and the U.S. Army. Other challenges remain for Anniston, but its residents say the town can now begin to heal and perhaps be stronger for it. *Eddie Motes*

CHAPTER EIGHT

WEST SIDE MYSTERIES

About the time that David Baker was contemplating his return home, Anniston attorney and former U.S. senator Donald Stewart got a phone call at his home on a rainy Sunday afternoon. On the line was Andrew Bowie, a black West Anniston resident and a client for whom Stewart had done legal work in the past. Stewart was a little annoyed about the call—not at Bowie, whom he liked and respected and who certainly had done nothing improper by calling his attorney at home, but at himself for even answering the phone. Stewart was recovering from gallbladder surgery and was struggling a bit with his recovery—he was still using a cane to get around, for one thing, and he had come to value the rest that the weekend afforded him, a respite he had never needed in the past. Stewart had been lazing about the house after church, an unaccustomed pleasure for a workaholic who usually found some reason to go into the office on Sunday afternoons to prepare for one case or another. He had been enjoying himself, and the damn phone had rung. And he answered it because . . . well, because you never knew what the day was going to throw at you, and you might as well get a handle on the situation and take it from there.

Bowie's purpose in calling intrigued Stewart right away. He told the attorney that the Mars Hill Baptist Church, a small, predominantly black church on the West Side where Bowie served as a deacon, had been approached by an attorney for the Monsanto Corporation. For decades Monsanto had operated a large plant right across the highway from the church, not far from where State Highway 202 branched west from downtown Anniston. Now, to the immense surprise of the church, Monsanto wanted to buy the church property. The offer on the table was one hundred twenty thousand dollars. The Mars Hill deacons were at that very moment meeting at the church to discuss the offer and decide what to do next. Would Stewart be willing to drive out to the church and participate in the conversation, perhaps provide some guidance? Stewart told Bowie he would be there in about fifteen minutes.

The distance from Stewart's East Side home to the church was only about four miles, but the cultural and economic separation between the two was in many ways immeasurable. Stewart lived in a restored, vivid-yellow Victorian-era beauty of a house on Tyler Hill, one of the oldest neighborhoods in the city and so named for city cofounder General Daniel Tyler. Tyler Hill and its surrounding neighborhoods had during the last few decades been encroached upon from the north by the expanding hospital complex of the Northeast Alabama Regional Medical Center, but the area still boasted some of the most historic and treasured homes in the city and was located but a few blocks from the Anniston Country Club, the nexus of local society.

The Mars Hill Baptist Church, by contrast, was very near the geographic center of what was probably the most impoverished area of the city. Originally a grouping of neighborhoods for the blue-collar legions that had worked at the nearby pipe shops, the portion of West Anniston that bordered Mars Hill had long ago succumbed to the forces of disintegration. Some middle-class families had hung tough and could be found here and there, but mostly the area was populated by poor blacks and whites who were struggling greatly to get by and who lived in dilapidated trailers and houses that had long since frayed around the edges and were now deteriorating from the inside out. Even Shirley McCord, who had run her supermarket down on Clydesdale Avenue for as long as anyone could remember, had moved to a house in Golden Springs. The Monsanto plant, belching steam and noise, loomed over this tableau like some giant, unapproachable cauldron on the hill.

It had been a while since Stewart had driven through this part of town, and as he sloshed through the rain he was surprised by what he saw. Many of the houses that once bordered the Mars Hill church had disappeared, as if into thin air. They had been replaced by vacant lots that appeared to have been scraped bare by bulldozers and then fenced off. It was very odd, and something about the scene made Stewart uneasy. It wasn't just the absent houses either; it was something intangible, unsettling. His lawyer's radar had picked something up. His experience as an attorney over the years had taught him that his gut was sometimes more perceptive than his brain. His gut was telling him something now, and it had nothing to do with the gallbladder surgery, of that he was sure.

Stewart reached the church and was greeted by Bowie and the others. Someone said a prayer before the meeting continued, asking for God's guidance in this and all matters concerning the church. Once the discussion resumed, it quickly became clear that three factions had developed: one that favored recommending to the Mars Hill congregation that Monsanto's offer be immediately accepted; another, more cautious group that believed the situation deserved more investigation; and a third that wanted to stay put no matter what. Bowie belonged to the cautious faction, and had been the one to lobby for legal advice.

Stewart asked some questions and began to get some interesting answers. Monsanto wanted to buy the property because, even though the company hadn't come right out and said as much, there was some problem with contamination in the area—a problem about something called PCBs. It was the first time Stewart had ever heard the term. It was rumored that the issue had something to do with the massive Monsanto landfill that had operated across Highway 202 for decades and from which drainage water cascaded downhill onto the land around Mars Hill. Anyway, the deacons mused, *something* must be up for Monsanto to offer enough money to buy a piece of property on the other side of town if they wanted to.

There was more. Monsanto had been quietly buying up other properties in the area, as evidenced by the vacant lots Stewart had noticed on his way there. The company had even gone so far as to set up a trailer on plant property where Monsanto representatives had entertained offers from property owners in the area. Stewart had heard nothing about this. He didn't believe anything had been in the paper about it. Now his lawyer's radar was sounding off like a firehouse bell. Something definitely was afoot here, something significant. Any fool could see that.

After much discussion the deacons decided to hire Stewart as their counsel and authorized him to contact Monsanto and ascertain the situation as best he could, then report back to the church. When the meeting broke up, Stewart visited individually with Bowie and some of the others and then hobbled outside toward his car. The rain had paused, and the lawyer scanned the lay of the land and could see for himself how the runoff from the elevated landfill drained across the highway and collected in streams and puddles on the acreage that surrounded the church. Propped on his cane, Stewart stood by his car, watched the water run, and wondered to himself just what in the hell was going on in West Anniston.

David Baker, back in town, was beginning to wonder the same thing. Something was wrong, he knew that much. You didn't have to be Lieutenant Columbo to dope that out. And somehow, he had landed right in the middle of it. He had come back to Anniston to retire—not from work, necessarily, for he figured he would work as long as he was able. But he had come back to Anniston to relax, to take life a little easier, to enjoy his family and the people he grew up with. Sometimes David felt like a soldier who had returned from a faraway war. He was lucky to be alive and he had stories to tell of battles won and lost, and he figured he would happily spend the remainder of his days resting on his laurels and trading insults with friends he had known since he was barely old enough to walk around. But now, this.

Upon his return to Anniston David had lounged around for a few weeks, getting his bearings. Then he had gone to work part-time for two of his old friends, Sylvester Harris and Tombstone Williams, both undertakers who serviced Anniston's black community. Historically the African-American population in Anniston had been concentrated in two general locations: on the West Side, and south of the downtown, starting below Tyler Hill (where Donald Stewart lived) and spreading more or less southward toward Oxford and Hobson City. Working with Harris and Williams had provided the first clues, although David didn't really figure it out at the time: the incidence of people who died from various (and sometimes freakish) cancers on the West Side seemed dramatically higher than that to the south. A lot of people seemed to die awfully young. It was extraordinary, actually, and something that people had remarked upon for years, but nothing that anyone had ever studied in any empirical way. It was just the way it was, and it was interesting.

Some while later David got a lead on a job opportunity from somebody who worked at the unemployment office. Monsanto was looking to hire a group of "environmental technicians" to perform a series of cleanup duties on and around the plant site. The company had contracted with a North Carolina–based environmental staffing company to hire the workers, which in turn had contacted the unemployment office and other agencies in the Anniston area. David wanted the job, but there was a hitch—to get the required testing and licensing would cost about nine hundred dollars. David didn't think he could spare it, even for a good job, but Tombstone offered to loan him the money. David accepted the loan, took about a week of training, and even helped recruit other employees. In the end, however, only about three or four local men were hired to work on the Monsanto site. The rest were shipped in from places like Detroit, New Orleans, all over. David thought that development was strange; why pay to put people up in hotels when you could hire perfectly qualified local folks who went home to their own beds at night? But no matter, David thought. Let them do things as they wished. It seemed like a good job and he was glad to have it.

It soon became apparent to David that "environmental technician" was Monsanto-speak for "dirt mover." All the job seemed to involve was moving dirt and worrying about dirt. The crew, dressed in protective hoods, suits, and gloves, would be dispatched from the plant with a truck or two to some nearby property, where they would spend the day digging up dirt, moving dirt onto the trucks, moving fence lines around, taking the dirt to the landfill across the highway, dumping it, then returning to the plant, where they would spend lengthy amounts of time spraying down the trucks in what amounted to an elaborate sterilization process. Clearly they were dealing with soil that was believed to be contaminated in some way, but David wasn't terribly concerned about it at first. He figured the exacting decontamination process was probably a classic exercise in overkill, something he was highly familiar with from his years of working in and around hospitals. Anyway, it seemed like these days it didn't take much to get people all freaked out about worker safety; David knew something about that subject too, having wrestled with safety issues time and again back in New York. It was all very different, and a tremendous pain in the ass, but all in all David didn't see much to be concerned about.

One afternoon, David's crew was working on a property along the highway that sat across from a row of houses. They decided to take a break and were sitting around with their masks off, shooting the breeze. An older white man emerged from one of the houses and made a beeline to the fence where the men were relaxing. "Why y'all wearing all that stuff?" he asked. "You fellows look like you're expecting trouble."

"Why? Because this site is contaminated with PCBs," replied one of David's coworkers, a man from Detroit. "That's why. The stuff's everywhere around here: soil, water, air, everywhere." This was not only news to the old man who had asked but to David as well. PCBs? What kind of crazy thing was that? They tossed the subject around for a while longer. Detroit wasn't exactly an expert, but he had been with the staffing company for a while and had heard some talk. Soon enough it was time to go back to work, and the old man drifted back to his house.

The next morning a supervisor from Birmingham appeared at the morning meeting and chewed the room and spit it out. From now on, she said tersely, if anyone asks anything about your work, you immediately direct them to the plant office and *say nothing else.*

Clearly, David surmised, the old man had made an inquiry of some kind and had put the place in an uproar. People didn't get this upset over some minor situation. Something was up. These folks were *alarmed*.

From then on David made sure to keep his mouth shut on the job, but it wasn't his nature to be the strong, silent type around the clock. He began to talk to his friends and neighbors on the West Side, wondering if they had heard anything about the situation around Monsanto. A few had heard that some people around the plant had sold their property to Monsanto, cheap, and left. There was some murmuring about something going on at Mars Hill Baptist Church. Suddenly there seemed to be a lot of fragments of information floating around, but nothing David could ever hang on to and nail down. He would go hunting with Sylvester Harris, his undertaker buddy, and they would talk about it. David told Sylvester that he was beginning to get the feeling something was very wrong. He didn't know what it was exactly, but there was some sort of contamination issue on the West Side, and he felt certain Monsanto was squarely in the middle of it.

David bided his time, and events developed further.

Monsanto moved a trailer near its front gate, and word began to circulate that the company was soliciting offers to purchase property that surrounded the plant. Details about Mars Hill bobbed to the surface in the *Anniston Star*. The church had apparently retained Donald Stewart as its attorney, and Stewart had negotiated a two-million-dollar settlement with Monsanto, with the company acknowledging—for the first time that David was aware of—that the Mars Hill property was contaminated with PCBs that the plant had discharged into the environment for a thirty-year period that ended around 1970. But there was no mention of contamination anywhere else.

David started asking around again, and it became clear to him that Monsanto was focusing almost exclusively on buying properties in what were known as the Cobbtown and Sweet Valley neighborhoods, predominantly poor, black areas east of the landfill, on what amounted to a flood plain that led away from the landfill site. No mention was being made of contamination, but David had no doubt about what Monsanto was doing. The company, it seemed clear, was buying up property along the landfill waterway before property owners wised up and began to sue. It was just a theory, but it made sense. And it gave rise to other questions, mainly: What if Detroit had been right about his claim that PCBs were spread not only through the water but through the air? If that was true, didn't it stand to reason that property had been affected on a much larger scale than merely within the confines of Sweet Valley and Cobbtown?

David talked to Betty about his concerns, at first sporadically and then incessantly. She asked good questions, helped him to think things through. Her main argument was that David needed to educate himself about PCBs, what they were, how they spread, their effects, whatever he could find out. Learn what he could, and then decide what, if anything, to do about it.

And so, gradually, David gathered materials that spelled out the history of PCBs and the continuing scientific debate about their impact on the environment and on human health. PCBs, he found, were everywhere, a naturally occurring element in the environment, but increasingly widespread due to their inclusion in countless manmade products from paint to newsprint. He read about Monsanto's leading role in the manufacture of PCBs beginning in the 1930s and how its Anniston plant had been the major North American point of origin for the compounds. He read about how scientists had discovered skyrocketing levels of PCBs in the environment in the 1950s and 1960s and about how Monsanto had quietly stopped making PCB-related products a few years before the U.S. government banned them outright in 1979.

And, inevitably, he read about medical studies that pointed to a host of maladies found among people who had experienced prolonged exposure to PCBs: bizarre cancers, hardening of the arteries, enlarged organs, learning disabilities—the list seemed to go on forever. He thought of the cancer-corroded corpses that had filled the West Side mortuaries of Sylvester Harris and Tombstone Williams for all those years, so many of them people who had died before their time. And he thought of his little brother Terry and the childhood he spent in the dusty looming shadow of the Monsanto plant, of Terry's gruesome death, which had stymied the doctors, a death that had seemed to have no explanation other than a God who worked in terrible and mysterious ways.

David thought of Terry, whose picture was tucked away in his wallet at that very moment, and he began to get very angry.

David trained like a prizefighter for what was to come next.

For as long as he could remember, he had been able to bring people together, to unite them behind a common cause. Not on the scale of a Nelson Mandela, of course, or even a James Butler. But in his own way, on his own scale, he had succeeded in becoming a leader. It is one form of accomplishment to stand up for one's self; people defend their own lives and property and honor every day, in ways big and small. David himself had nearly fifty years' worth of scars and sea stories about holding his own against a hostile world, from Dinky Adams to shotgun-wielding landlords. But to rally people to a mutual purpose—standing up to an abusive coach, forming a tenants' association, organizing a hospital, whatever—required singular ability. People who knew David were often hard-pressed to isolate a particular characteristic of his that might explain his talent for moving the herd in a positive direction. He wasn't especially smooth. He certainly was not an exceptional public speaker. What people usually pointed to in analyzing David was a personality that filled the room and a tenacity befitting a bloodhound. Once David committed to a mission, then he simply would not quit until the job was done. Some might think it stubbornness. David preferred to think of it as conviction.

David's conviction in Anniston in 1998 was that the people of the West Side were not receiving justice. He couldn't prove it; it was difficult to explain his case to people, largely because there was so much about the situation he didn't understand himself. The learning curve seemed endless. But there was something out there on the edge of town that had scared those Monsanto folks half to death. He had seen it for himself, in the eyes of the female supervisor who had read them the riot act at that morning meeting. He knew fear when he saw it, and he had seen it that day.

It was all about the PCBs. People needed to know about the dangers they posed. People needed to band together to demand information. People needed to come together, demonstrate unity, and then move forward from a position of strength. David might not have known a PCB from a black-eyed pea, but he knew how to form a coalition of hearts and minds. You started with one person, and then another, and another and another. It was like evangelism, in a sense. *And where two or more are gathered . . .*

David began to hold meetings about the Monsanto situation. The first one of any size was held at Tombstone Williams's funeral home. About fifty people showed up. David shared his still-meager findings about PCBs, his suspicions about his brother, spoke about the need for education, perhaps even legal help. He encouraged those in attendance to share their own concerns and recollections. A few rose to speak and wondered aloud about loved ones who had passed away from ravaging cancers. They resolved to meet again, and to bring others with them.

It was a start.

It wasn't long before David was suddenly pulled away from the decontamination work for Monsanto and sent to North Carolina for a few weeks to clean up an oil spill. When he returned to Anniston, he was told that there was no longer work for him at Monsanto. Which was odd; when he checked with the men on the cleanup crews, he was told that there was more work than ever, that they could use every able-bodied man sent their way. It finally got back to David that word was out about the meetings, and that his activities had begun to concern people.

Well now, David thought to himself, *we must be getting somewhere.*

By the mid-1990s I was living on the westernmost edge of Los Angeles in Santa Monica, renting a ninety-five-year-old house about a mile from the beach. My block of Euclid Street was, and is, a good wide avenue with a mostly undistinguished mix of single-family homes and apartment complexes, bordered on the south by Pico Boulevard, one of those massive, teeming thoroughfares that run from the ocean to downtown L.A. To the north, a half-block from our house, Euclid gave way to the steep, ivy-covered slope of the Santa Monica Freeway; it seemed as if, like so many Angelenos, we were pinned down on all sides by the perpetual fury of L.A. traffic. Sometimes, in the pink haze of dawn, I would walk to the cul-de-sac's edge, stand at the guardrail, and peer down at the eastbound commute below, already humming like a power main toward the heart of the city. And I would think: *All these ambitious, driven, desperate, yearning people.* I didn't pity them; I pitied myself for not being one of them—anonymous, focused, locked in, part of the California multitude, consumed by the same things that had consumed them the day before and the day before that. I was forty years old then, a long way from home, and lost.

The previous summer I had quit a good-paying job as a staff writer for Arizona's largest daily newspaper to move to California and finally write the novel I had been boring my friends about for years. My then wife had taken a job as an editor at the *Los Angeles Daily News,* and the house on Euclid featured a small, isolated upstairs office with a wide-angle view of the Santa Monica Mountains, a perfect writer's perch. We moved in just in time for the violent adrenaline surge of the Northridge earthquake, both terrifying and exhilarating, which left our house and the city in a shambles. By then I was beginning to realize that my marriage, laced with a variety of fault lines of its own, wasn't going to hold together much longer either. But I repressed that knowledge, just as I had repressed the awareness that I had spent the last several years running from something—and that I had just run out of room. I was at the precipice of the continent; I could go no farther, save swimming. Los Angeles seemed about as far away from Anniston, Alabama, as one could get, and that was fine with me. I sprouted a goatee, grew my hair to my shoulders, walked along the crashing beach at sunrise among the preening tai chi practitioners and past the oblivious homeless having sex beneath dirty blankets, and I began to entertain the notion that I was a Californian.

There were sporadic reminders of home. My parents would visit each summer, trooping into town in their forty-foot RV with a minivan in tow, for leisurely visits of a week or two. They would pitch camp on a towering bluff in Malibu overlooking the Pacific Coast

Highway and the immense sea. In the afternoons, once the marine layer had melted away, I would take them for long, mostly aimless drives around the L.A. basin, pointing out the sights, rattling on about the city and the weather, while they swallowed the dense enormity of the place. "All these people!" my father would invariably observe. They would in turn update me on old friends and enemies, family members, local politicians, who was prospering, who had died. And they would inquire, gingerly, about when I was coming home. I never knew what to tell them. Home, for me, had become a shifting, mutating, malleable entity, subject to wild interpretation. "We miss you," they would tell me, then load up the forty-footer and, with an exhalation of air brakes and regret, head east in the slow lane on the Santa Monica Freeway toward home, a place that to them was clearly defined, sensible, solid, reliable.

One Saturday afternoon my phone rang, and I was surprised to hear the voice of Cody Hall, longtime executive editor of the *Anniston Star*. He was in town visiting his daughter in Venice, and offered to buy me a drink. I was thrilled. Though we had fallen out of touch, I had always revered Cody, and he had carried the flag for me on many occasions at the *Star* and elsewhere. He was all the things you would expect an old-school southern newspaper editor to be: homespun, crusty, pugnacious, droll, ever mindful of history and its twisted ironies, cruel, funny as hell, occasionally bellicose, and given to nonfiltered Camels and Irish whiskey neat. My most effective reference, he never failed to secure me a job offer when a prospective employer gave him a call. He had also long battled a series of health problems; some affliction or another had prompted a forearm to swell to Popeye proportions, and he had been covered with liver spots for as long as I could remember. Even so, I was shocked by his appearance when he swung open the door to greet me that afternoon in Venice. His pallor was dingy and forbidding and he looked tired and old, even though he was not yet sixty-five. "Let's walk to the joint on the corner," he said, and with much effort and heavy breathing we made it to Casablanca, a Moroccan restaurant furbished in 1940s style with white tablecloths and white-jacketed waiters, reminiscent of Rick's in the iconic Bogart movie.

It was late afternoon, the weakening sunlight floating through the west windows. We had the place to ourselves. Cody ordered whiskey for me—"the good stuff," he instructed the cufflinked waiter—and a glass of white wine for himself. "Doctor's orders," he explained, looking mournfully at his wine as it arrived. "Doesn't mean *you* have to suffer. Drink up." I did, and we began to catch up on small talk, how things were going in Anniston and at the *Star.* But it was perfunctory stuff, and I could tell he had something else on his mind. Finally he got to it. "I'm not well at all," he said. "I'm barely working anymore. If I'm here a year from now I'll be damned lucky." I started to offer some awkward condolences, but he waved them off. "I tell you that to tell you something else," he said. "There are three people in this business that have been very special to me." He ticked them off. First was the late Steve Traylor, who had served as managing editor at the *Star* in the mid-seventies and had hired me for an internship when I was a junior at the University of Alabama. Traylor was a gruff, capable newsman with an eye for talent who battled alcoholism and died prematurely at the age of fifty after moving on to help manage a newsroom in Tennessee. I had never realized he and Cody were close. "Steve was like a son to me," Cody said. "Then there's Bragg"—Rick Bragg, the gifted, lightning-rod reporter who spent his formative years at the *Star,* made it to the *New York Times,* and was on his way to winning a Pulitzer for feature writing. "And you." I was amazed. "That means a lot, Cody," I said. "You've been very special to me too. A champion." It seemed a lame response, but what can you say? He reached over with his glass and clinked mine, then looked away. The cranky old bastard had tears in his eyes, and so did I. It was a wonderful, maudlin, terrible moment, and I wish it could have lasted forever.

Then he swung back around on me. "Listen," he said, and I could see him taking me in with a long hard look. "Don't lose track of who you are. Don't distance yourself from the people and places that make you distinctive." He drained his glass and looked at me again. "Don't get too far from home. This place out here, these people . . ."

"Never," I lied. He let it go.

And that was that. Cody threw some bills on the table and struggled to his feet. We negotiated the half-block back to his daughter's home, where he gave me a palsied handshake and clapped me on the shoulder. "Good luck, boy," he said, and disappeared inside, leaving me out on the sidewalk with the palms swaying in the cool rush of evening air. He died soon afterward. I didn't make it back for the funeral.

A coin-operated laundry stood at the intersection of Euclid and Pico, between a liquor store run by an irritable Pakistani and a dry-cleaning establishment owned by a very sociable Chinese family. I always figured the Chinese, who nearly always fell all over themselves in their zeal to greet me, were purposefully trying to balance out the local strip-mall karma against the black-cloud Pakistani. Or maybe they were just euphoric that I had finally rematerialized to claim the boxcar load of laundry I invariably stuck them with for God knows how long.

One evening I hauled the week's wash into the Laundromat and stumbled onto an unlikely conversation. Sitting on the folding table near the back was a large, scraggly young white man in his late twenties, wearing a Kentucky Wildcats bill cap. He was in a deep discussion with a slight and elderly black woman, outfitted in a cotton print dress and white canvas sneakers, who sat nearby on one of a row of indescribably uncomfortable chairs. It seemed clear that they had been talking for a while, having one of those serendipitous conversations that sometimes seem to evolve into being on planes, in bars, at the Department of Motor Vehicles, wherever strangers find themselves spending time together. I began eavesdropping immediately, as is my despicable habit in public places, and it took only a couple of exchanges between them to determine that they were speaking nostalgically of home, which for both of them was indisputably the South.

I could tell the conversation was winding down. I could tell they had already covered the chapters of their respective stories that told from where, exactly, they hailed, be it Pikeville or Meridian or Lake Charles or Greenville, and how they wound up here, so far away from those fondly remembered places. Now, as the last quarters were dropped into the slot for the last dryer load, they were getting philosophical. They speculated about what would have happened had they stayed put, had they resisted the confluence of events that led to their various uprootings, had they remained home with Mama and them instead of striking out for this distant land of sun-baked streets that sometimes shifted beneath your very feet.

"I'm sure I'll go back," the young man said.

The woman wagged a friendly finger at him. "You better be careful," she said. "You'll be like me, turn around thirty years later and wonder what happened. I still tell myself that I'll go back one day, and I guess I still believe it. But I have all my children here, and their children now. . . . I couldn't have imagined it."

The Kentucky fan, too young, really, to know a damned thing, good-naturedly pretended that he understood. "I'll be careful," he said, smiling.

Then he said: "The South will always be there."

I stared at him wordlessly from across the room, amid the scraping of the dryers and the smell of powdered Cheer, and wondered if that could possibly be true.

CHAPTER NINE

THE ANNISTON THEATER
OF OPERATIONS

As the new millennium began, "The Model City"—created from the drawing-board vision of Samuel Noble and nurtured for more than a century by a series of elected leaders and unofficial but widely acknowledged town patriarchs and matriarchs—showed distinct signs of splintering apart.

The 2000 census would confirm what many already suspected from a wealth of anecdotal evidence: the City of Anniston was losing residents at a breathtaking rate. The census revealed that Anniston's population at the turn of the century was some 24,000 and change—a figure that represented an eardrum-popping plummet of 20 percent since the 1990 count. The shuttering of Fort McClellan explained part of the hemorrhage, but only part. People seemed to be leaving virtually en masse.

The reasons for this precipitous blood-loss were readily apparent for anyone who cared to investigate. Atop the list was the Anniston city school system. The increase in black students that had slowly begun in the late 1960s and early 1970s had turned into a juggernaut. Cobb High School, once the pride of the West Side, had been converted to a middle school and then shut down altogether. African-American kids were funneled into Anniston High School at an exponential rate. Even Tenth Street and Golden Springs elementary schools, once the standard-bearing, unassailable outposts of white Anniston, became predominantly black. By the time Chip Howell entered the mayor's office in 2000, more than nine of every ten students at Anniston High were black. White families with school-age children began to vote with their feet: they were gone. Families that could afford it—and some that couldn't—sent their children to the Donoho private school at a cost of thousands per year, or exercised less expensive (but nonetheless costly) options such as the Faith Christian Academy in Golden Springs. But a much greater number of people decided to desert the city completely, dispersing to the outlying towns and communities where public schools still had white majorities and where money that in Anniston would have been used for private school tuition payments could be converted into house payments.

The chief beneficiary of this quintessential case study in white flight was the City of Oxford, which bordered Anniston to the south. Anniston had always maintained an attitude of condescension toward Oxford, viewing it essentially as a village of hayseeds who stood around scratching themselves. Anniston, on the other hand, from its very inception had been populated by people of status and culture, titans of industry and the arts—or so its self-impression went at least (never mind its inescapable blue-collar legacy). Over the years, a not-so-friendly competition developed between the two towns. The annual game between Anniston and Oxford high schools traditionally kicked off the Calhoun County football season, routinely drew as many as ten thousand spectators, and was widely viewed as one of the most hotly contested rivalries in the state. Oxford, proudly carrying its chip on its shoulder, more often than not prevailed in football. But Anniston was the undisputed economic king of the county—that is, until the schools-related exodus was launched in earnest in the 1980s and began to erode Anniston's vitality.

The outpouring of middle-class whites from Anniston filled new subdivisions in Oxford and gave rise to new retail and other commercial opportunities there. That dynamic played a critical role in Oxford's attempt to shake off its weak-sister status, but the primary factor was nothing less than a heaven-sent stroke of luck in the form of Interstate 20, the superhighway that stretched from east of Atlanta deep into Texas. For decades, the primary artery between Atlanta and Birmingham was U.S. 78, a narrow, treacherous, slow-moving route with all-too-infrequent passing lanes, notorious for spectacular, road-jamming accidents as well as unconscionable speed traps laid by corpulent rural sheriffs. Once upon a time, U.S. 78 had unfurled directly through downtown Anniston, prompting congestion and eternal complaints about how the traffic was bringing the fair city down. Shortly after World War II, however, a federal highway project rerouted 78 away from Anniston and through Oxford instead. The chief sentiment in Anniston was good riddance. But while Noble Street and its environs continued to thrive for many years afterward, the downtown Anniston merchants would live to rue the day they complained about the constant stream of cars and trucks that lined not only their streets but their pockets. When the U.S. interstate system was launched during the Eisenhower administration, planners drew the proposed route for Interstate 20 through Oxford alongside the existing U.S. 78, and fate was cast.

When Bill Love opened his IGA supermarket in 1967 at the corner of Quintard Avenue and Snow Street in Oxford, about a mile north of U.S. 78, the store stood virtually alone in an expansive field of broom sage, with but a couple of disconsolate gas stations interrupting his line of vision. A few years later, northeast Alabama's first indoor shopping mall—complete with a Sears and J. C. Penny's—opened on a plot of land directly across the highway from Love's IGA. Other businesses sprouted. Finally in 1978 the interstate came through, complete with an exit that funneled traffic directly onto South Quintard Avenue in the heart of Oxford—and the boom was on. Restaurant and hotel chains appeared. New shopping centers materialized. Almost overnight, it seemed, Oxford had a multiplying tax base and was rapidly becoming a regional economic power. Overseeing this new dynamo was Oxford mayor Leon Smith, a crafty, heavy-lidded good old boy with a gravelly drawl for the ages and an extraordinary gift for local politics. Smith's background was as an Anniston package srore owner who sold the occasional cold six-pack to underage customers; in heavily churched Calhoun County, still he was elected time and again to public office.

It's one thing to be dealt a good poker hand; it's another to know how to play it. Smith played Oxford's cards well, building infrastructure, throwing the city's doors open to business, and gobbling up more land in annexation deals. In one of his most admirable coups, Smith annexed land farther east along I-20, including a site that became yet another exit for Golden Springs, which in turn became another boom area—and one Anniston would love to have annexed itself. Finally, Smith's crowning achievement: the announcement that a Wal-Mart Supercenter would be constructed in a giant plaza just south of the interstate. In the Deep South, at least, nothing says you've arrived quite like a Wal-Mart.

Meanwhile, Noble Street and the rest of downtown Anniston went into a steep decline. The Ritz and the Calhoun, the two movie theaters that had anchored Noble Street since the war years, closed down, as did the Sears store farther north on Noble. The only sign of life, it seemed, was the phalanx of automobile dealerships that lined Quintard Avenue just north of the viaduct that separated Anniston from Oxford (the "motor mile"). These and other clues to Anniston's deterioration began to appear in the late 1970s and 1980s; by the 1990s, with even the staunchest white supporters of the public schools pulling their kids out of the Anniston system, it sometimes seemed as if the place was in free fall. Baby boomers who had been raised in Anniston to believe that it was better to swallow poison than to live in Oxford found themselves moving there—and sending their children to Oxford High School to boot.

Chip Howell saw it all as a disturbing state of affairs, although he had valiantly attempted to put a positive face on matters during the mayoral campaign. But the truth was that there was a lot to be done, and the problems didn't all have to do with the schools or economic jousting with Oxford, as concerning as those matters were. There wasn't a lot Chip and the city council could do about the schools anyway—the city board of education made the calls there, and school funding came from the state. He planned to use his influence to see that the most able and qualified people possible were elected to the school board and hired as administrators, but the reality was that in many ways the mayor and council were out of the loop on school issues. As for reviving downtown, Chip had some strong ideas about refurbishing Noble Street, taking advantage of its still-salvageable Victorian-era architecture, and encouraging a transition to an appealing corridor of restaurants, boutiques, and lofts where people could live, work, and play. That formula had worked in other towns, large and small, and Chip was reasonably optimistic that it could work in Anniston. Downtown Anniston might have lost the battle for the big-box stores and fast-food outlets that seemed to be proliferating in Oxford like a contagion, but Noble Street had a territorial claim on charm that Oxford could never match.

All that could be dealt with, in Chip's view. But there was the larger, more intangible issue of Anniston's image—its self-image, even—and how it related to the city's future. For a variety of reasons, some dating back to the city's inception and Samuel Noble's gift for promotion, Anniston had enjoyed a reputation as an outstanding place to live and work deep into the twentieth century. An energetic economy, relatively good race relations (the occasional bus burning notwithstanding), a progressive newspaper—these characteristics and more had long contributed to Anniston's generally accepted status as a forward-thinking New South city. But Chip well knew that good reputations, while originally deserved, often outlived reality. The reverse was also true; once a reputation turned negative, it could be a very difficult thing to turn around. For proof one only had to look as far as Birmingham, Anniston's neighbor to the west. Modern-day Birmingham was a prosperous white-collar town with medicine and banking as its most notable economic engines and, for a Deep South metropolis, almost seamless race relations. But because of its history with the likes of Bull Connor and U.S. Steel, many people still viewed Birmingham as a smoky mill town with racist cops and snarling police dogs roaming the streets. It wasn't fair; Birmingham had changed dramatically. But perception often dwarfed reality, and Chip worried that Anniston had arrived at its own critical juncture in terms of its reputation, status, and prestige.

Like the downtown development strategy, there were some things over which Chip had some control; like the school situation, there were some things he could do little or nothing about. A troubling situation that fell into the latter category was the massive lawsuit with hundreds of plaintiffs that had been launched by Donald Stewart against Monsanto and had begun to attract national attention. The suit claimed that a wide swath of residents in West Anniston had sustained damage to their property and health due to the decades of PCB-dumping by Monsanto. Stewart could be fractious and was disliked by many in town as a result of various disputes and entanglements. But no one ever shortchanged his intellect or doubted his ability as an attorney. If any country lawyer could bring the monolithic Monsanto down, it was Stewart. Anniston was being depicted as a cancer-ridden environmental disaster zone. It was a germinating public relations disaster. And while Chip had no role in the proceedings, he was acutely aware of the worst-case scenario: a spectacular verdict against Monsanto would undoubtedly provoke the kind of fallout that the town might never overcome. He was all for people receiving justice if that justice was deserved, but as mayor he couldn't help but fret over the ramifications. There were even rumors that David Baker, a West Side activist who seemed to have materialized out of nowhere, was attempting to interest famed superattorney Johnnie Cochran in coming to Anniston to take on even more clients and press a separate case against Monsanto. Chip couldn't imagine that actually happening, but the mere prospect of the renowned Cochran riding into town was enough to prompt discomfort in anyone entrusted with protecting Anniston's image.

There were other matters. Prominent on the agenda was the massive redevelopment of the Fort McClellan property, which soon would be turned over by the Army to the city and presided over by a joint powers authority featuring a mix of city and county officials.

The disposition of the Fort was an undertaking that would impact Anniston for decades to come, and Chip—who as mayor held a seat on the joint powers authority—would have a say. Helping to chart a positive and prudent course for McClellan would be a giant step toward ensuring that Anniston would flourish in the years ahead, and Chip expected that a significant chunk of his time as mayor would be devoted to that.

And then, finally, there was the Anniston Army Depot. After much debate and gnashing of teeth, the Army had begun construction on a one-billion-dollar incinerator to destroy the sprawling cache of chemical weapons that lingered on in West Anniston like some quiet cancer that might metastasize at any time. To Chip, the wisdom of disposing of the weapons once and for all seemed indisputable. There really wasn't much wriggle room—by the tenets of an international treaty, the United States was obligated to eliminate its chemical weapons stockpile by 2007 (though no one realistically expected that deadline to be met). To burn some of the most feared weapons of mass destruction in the world in your own backyard carried undeniable risk, but to even contemplate moving the increasingly unstable agents seemed like unalloyed folly. The fact was that the weapons were in Anniston, and the Army intended to destroy them in Anniston. And as far as Chip was concerned, the sooner the burning began, the sooner the community would be rid of the last remaining threat of the Cold War—the war that Hoyt had told him about over the dinner table all those years ago.

But it wouldn't be easy. The situation had already grown immensely complicated. A small but vocal group of opponents had made its local presence known, abetted by a Kentucky-based environmental group led by a pugilistic Vietnam veteran, Craig Williams, who was to the U.S. chemical weapons incineration program what

Zorro was to Spanish authority in old California. Legal challenges were being mounted. The Calhoun County Commission, initially accused of not advocating aggressively for state-of-the-art safety precautions and other considerations from the Army, was beginning to throw up roadblocks. And there was the matter of general public opinion, always a fluid and enigmatic quantity. Somewhere down the road, Chip knew, the people of Anniston and Calhoun County would have to be sold on the viability of the weapons burning concept—and more than likely he, as mayor, would have to do some of the selling.

One only needed to look west for a glimpse of what the future might hold for Anniston's incinerator, although that glimpse would be far from conclusive. There were two primary track records to be considered: the Rocky Mountain Arsenal in Denver, Colorado, and the Tooele Army Depot in Tooele, Utah. Neither facility was perfectly analogous to Anniston—especially the Rocky Mountain Arsenal, whose pioneering incineration program had been shuttered for a quarter of a century—but the evidence was nonetheless there for the taking. Whether that evidence provided hope or despair, of course, depended greatly upon who was conducting the examination.

In May 1942, less than a year after the Japanese bombed Pearl Harbor and the United States entered World War II, the U.S. War Board announced that it would convert 19,883 acres of farmland eight miles outside of Denver, Colorado, into the site of a large-scale chemical weapons manufacturing facility. A number of factors were considered by the Army in choosing the site. It needed a stretch of land far removed from the coastline to protect against enemy attacks, but also required an area with established transportation routes. Combining an airport and a web of highways and railroads with its relative isolation, the Denver area seemed ideal. By selecting property outside the city, the Army reasoned that the facility would be adequately buffered from the downtown area, although even then thousands of people lived in outlying cities like Commerce and Aurora.

Construction on the Rocky Mountain Arsenal began in June 1942. The complex was quickly completed at a cost of about fifty million dollars. In the beginning, the arsenal manufactured three primary "war" chemicals: mustard gas, white phosphorus, and napalm. By the end of the 1940s it had produced more than a hundred thousand tons of chemical incendiary weapons. In the 1950s, the Army began manufacturing another type of chemical: GB nerve agent, or sarin. GB, which was loaded into munitions, would be manufactured at the Rocky Mountain Arsenal well into the 1960s. During this period, the Army also leased areas of the arsenal to Shell Oil for the manufacture of herbicides and pesticides. But by the late 1950s, damage to nearby crops indicated widespread contamination from a mélange of chemicals resulting from the operations of the Army and Shell Oil. Groundwater contamination was also documented, and a public outcry, albeit rather muted, began.

By the early 1970s, against a backdrop of growing public awareness, the Army began searching for a disposal method for the 3,071 tons of mustard gas and GB nerve agent stored at the arsenal. (Tens of thousands of tons of the agent and munitions had already been shipped to storage sites around the country, including the Anniston Army Depot.) The disposal program was dubbed Project Eagle and consisted of incinerating and neutralizing the chemical agents and their explosive components. The incinerator used at the Rocky Mountain Arsenal in the 1970s would be considered extremely primitive by contemporary standards, particularly in regard to the task of neutralizing GB nerve agent contained in rockets and other weapons, such as M-34 cluster bombs and Honest John warheads. According to a 1987 chemical stockpile disposal program report issued by the Army, levels of GB agent were detected in the dried salt that was a by-product of the neutralization process. Incineration, however, was used to destroy the explosive components of the weapons.

"The designs of the incinerators used today are much more advanced," Charles Baronian, a former program manager for the Army's chemical demilitarization program, told the *Anniston Star* in 1997. "We didn't have the afterburners or the pollution-abatement systems that are on incinerators today. I assure you, the 1997 model is much better than the 1970 model."

The disposal process at the Rocky Mountain Arsenal ended in 1976. Eleven years later, the arsenal was designated a Superfund cleanup site; two years after that the Army, Shell Oil, the EPA, and various other interested parties developed a plan to clean up the site. That cleanup continues still, but in 1992 the arsenal was designated a National Wildlife Refuge and today hosts some forty thousand visitors each year who turn out to observe bald eagles, mule deer, prairie dogs, and other wildlife. A 1996 study prepared by the U.S. Department of Health and Human Services concluded that no significant adverse health effects resulted from the operations at Rocky Mountain Arsenal—including a finding that there were no discernable increases in the number of cancers that could be linked to the types of chemicals manufactured at the site.

The Rocky Mountain Arsenal and its incinerator were planned, built, operated, and then mothballed during an era when environmental restrictions and public awareness were mere blips on the screen compared with the exhaustive scrutiny prevalent today. While proponents of incineration could in large part take heart from the relatively unblemished track record of the chemical weapons burn in Colorado, even the staunchest advocates had to concede that the Rocky Mountain Arsenal had existed in what amounted to a time capsule that no longer had much relevance to the new, more extensive round of burning envisioned by the Army at eight other sites around the United States.

The 1990s brought a brand-new ball game with a new rule book, exemplified by the saga surrounding the first new mainland incinerator since Rocky Mountain, which began operations in Tooele, Utah, in 1996. (An incinerator on Johnston Atoll, a 637-acre island eight hundred miles southwest of Hawaii, began burning in 1993.) In one respect, Tooele (pronounced too-WILL-ah) was the ultimate manifestation of the federal government's strategy of locating weapons depots in remote, sparsely populated areas where what little population existed could be counted on to be supportive of the Army. From the Vietnam War era on, the Tooele Army Depot was by far the largest repository of chemical weapons in the United States. When burning began in 1996 it was estimated that fully 43 percent of the chemical munitions in the *free world* were stored there, more than thirteen thousand tons' worth, or 1.1 million items. At the peak of the Vietnam War, the depot employed five thousand people in a county of eighteen thousand people. "Everybody worked at TAD," Tooele mayor Charlie Roberts recalled in late 2003, "and if you didn't your neighbor did." The Depot's influence on Tooele County was so pervasive that plans by private industry to set up shop there—after all, Tooele was a convenient thirty-mile drive from Salt Lake City—never got off the ground because too few workers were willing to leave the good pay and benefits of the Depot. The exceptions: two commercial incinerators that burned hazardous waste shipped in from across the country. But given the Depot and an Army bombing range that encompassed two-thirds of the county's land area, Tooele was probably in as close to lockstep with the U.S. military's priorities as a community could possibly be.

That allegiance seemed to reaffirm itself in the runup to the incinerator's start-burn date. A public hearing about the plant—the type of meeting that typically drew hundreds of worried citizens in other parts of the country—attracted four people. The Sierra Club, which along with Craig Williams's Kentucky-based Chemical Weapons Working Group and the Vietnam Veterans of America Foundation served as the point organization in filing a lawsuit to attempt to block the burning, could only claim fifteen members in the entire county. And the plant's most strident critic, former safety chief Steve Jones, was fired in 1994 by contractor EG&G Defense Materials after he cited a variety of problems at the incinerator site. By 1996 he was selling kitchen appliances to make a living while he conducted a legal battle in an effort to get his job back.

Even in with-the-program Tooele, however, Jones's firing made waves and presaged what would be a series of shutdowns, whistle-blower controversies, and other troubling episodes once the incinerator started burning in 1996. As word of Jones's firing spread, the House Committee on Armed Services announced it would conduct an inquiry, and the Army itself said it would investigate. The *New York Times* published a story that quoted plant officials who described Jones as "overzealous" and said he was fired not because he pointed out safety flaws but because of "differences in management style and methods and philosophy." But the *Times* also noted that Jones was a well-respected administrator who had presided over safety and security operations at several Navy facilities; the *Times* also excavated a radiation safety expert at UCLA who had toured the Tooele facility at Jones's request and said that he too had noticed several "design problems with the potential for injuries," specifically in the system for unloading chemical arms. Jones himself told the *Times,* "The real problem is this facility can't support the technology. The temperatures are too hot. The pressures are too great. The plant infrastructure cannot support what this plant is intended to do. There are going to be parts failures." In a subsequent interview with *USA Today,* Jones was more succinct: "It'll be like Three Mile Island."

None of this sudden turmoil sat very well with local residents, who mostly professed to be at peace with the incinerator and blamed the growing controversy about the facility on outside agitators from Salt Lake City and Colorado. ("The Army has a good track record around here," Mayor Roberts explained. "When they explained what they wanted to do with the incinerator, there was buy-in from the get-go.") But the confluence of events—Jones's firing, the Sierra Club lawsuit, national media attention—served to underscore the contrast in arguments by both sides about the propriety of incinerating chemical weapons.

The arguments essentially split as follows: Opponents like the Sierra Club and Craig Williams claimed that no matter how assiduously the exhaust from the burn was "scrubbed," tiny amounts of highly toxic gases would inevitably be released into the air over a long period of time—with no one really aware of the effects of such exposure on humans and crops. Instead, the argument continued, the Army should have investigated alternative methods that didn't involve smokestack emissions—methods such as neutralization, which uses chemicals to break down poison gases. For its part, the Army countered that its new breed of incinerators burned lethal chemical agents so effectively that the smokestack emissions would actually be cleaner than the air into which they were released. As for neutralization, the Army contended that the technology would take a decade or more to develop—too long. The weapons, leaking and unstable, were time bombs in the literal sense. A rocket could always self-ignite, the Army warned, possibly setting off a chain reaction—as could some unforeseen disaster like an earthquake or a plane crash.

The ultrasensitive issues of cost and deadline overruns were also given an airing. The *Times* noted that the Army's initial cost estimate for its entire chemical demilitarization program was $1.2 billion, with the elimination of the weapons to be completed by 1994. A dramatically revised estimate put the cost at $10 billion and the completion date at 2004. (Indeed, at the Tooele facility alone the original cost was estimated at $450 million; the final price tag was some $1.7 billion.) Even at that, the General Accounting Office later predicted that the costs would most likely approach $20 billion in the end.

Money was also the issue as the Tooele County Commission haggled with the Army over "economic considerations" for the impending burn. County officials wanted the Army to pay up to thirty-five million dollars a year to offset the economic hit expected to occur from businesses steering clear of the area while the incinerator was in operation. The commission and the Army ultimately agreed on thirteen million dollars to be paid over eight years—$970 for every ton of chemical agent destroyed, with payments made incrementally as the burn proceeded. According to Roberts, the commissioners played hardball to get the funding agreement. A green first-term city councilman in 1995, Roberts was present at the Pentagon when a contingent of Tooele officials met with the undersecretary of the Army. A powerful county commissioner, Gary Griffith, let it be known to the undersecretary that he would block the state-issued burn permit if the Army didn't "bring its checkbook." Roberts recalled that the undersecretary was incensed: "You can't do that— that's bribery!" Griffith responded, "Bottom line: no check, no permit." After the agreement was reached, Griffith told the Associated Press that he didn't think the thirteen million "was enough, but we believe that's what we could get without going into litigation. We're pleased, if not happy with [the agreement]." The haggling over payments from the Army was closely monitored in Anniston and the other sites where incinerators were planned, and would impact those negotiations as well.

Finally, on August 21, 1996, with the initial wave of lawsuits rejected by the courts and the necessary (and thanks to Griffith, expensive) permit issued by the Utah Solid and Hazardous Waste Control Board, the Army began to move thousands of M-55 rockets filled with GB from their protective igloos to prepare for the first round of incineration. The next morning, as about a dozen protesters gathered outside the incinerator gates—one University of Utah student carried a sign that read STOP BURNING AWAY OUR FUTURE—the first rocket was reduced to molten aluminum and ash. According to plan, burning then stopped as the remains of the rocket were removed and analyzed. The Army then moved ahead on a twelve-hours-per-day, seven-days-per-week "trial burn" schedule until some nine thousand rockets were destroyed. The plan then called for a halt in the burning for a governmental review, which would be followed by a ramped-up, twenty-four-hours-per-day burning schedule.

Then a parade of problems began, all duly reported in the national press. Two days after the first burn, operations were shut down when a trace of GB was found inside a sealed vestibule bank protecting the facility's air filtration system. The incinerator resumed burning six days later and destroyed eight thousand pounds of agent until September 18, when a hairline crack was discovered in the concrete floor of the facility's decontamination room, where workers cleaned their clothing. Plant officials reported that no chemical agent had leaked through the crack but said that a small amount of decontamination solution, containing mostly sodium hydroxide, had dripped from the contamination room into the electrical room below.

The facility resumed operations about two weeks later but would be plagued with three more shutdowns before the end of the year, including a day-long stoppage during Christmas week when a rocket jammed in the feed gate of the plant's explosives containment room. But the on-again, off-again burn schedule quickly became second-tier news when reports surfaced that a team of EG&G and Army investigators had appeared at the facility in late November to look into allegations from a former plant employee that the incinerator was unsafe. The Army and EG&G refused to name the whistle-blower, but the *Deseret News* later identified him as Gary Millar, a twenty-two-year EG&G veteran who had replaced the fired Steve Jones as chief safety officer at the facility—and who himself was fired, albeit quietly, in late 1995. The *News* also published portions of a leaked twelve-page letter from Millar to Utah officials that claimed the incinerator posed a "significant risk" to employees and surrounding residents. The letter compared the potential for accident in Tooele to the Three Mile Island nuclear reactor incident and the explosion of the space shuttle *Challenger*. Millar wrote that he attempted to develop a long-term plan to resolve what he described as "several thousand safety, quality and operational deficiencies," including three hundred "serious" problems that he did not specify, but said his efforts were resisted by other EG&G managers and retired Army employees who worked at the plant. He said a series of short-sighted, temporary "fixes" at the facility "will eventually line up to trigger a high-risk event." Millar also claimed that he was "forced to retain" some managers who in his view did not follow proper safety precautions.

EG&G officials quickly attempted to discredit Millar's charges, with a company spokesman, Martin Reynolds, contending that Millar did not make the allegations until he was fired. "The plant is running. It is safe, and it will continue to operate," Reynolds told the Associated Press. "Safety is the most important consideration at this facility." But concern about Millar's allegations was immediately registered by various monitoring agencies and organizations. The director of the state agency that issued the Tooele burn permit was quoted as saying he would "expect the Army to do a long-term fix" if the allegations proved to be substantive; a senior member of the National Research Council, an independent group of scientists charged with watchdogging the U.S. weapons incineration program, said its stockpile committee would "be actively monitoring how this particular situation is resolved." Apparently stung by questions about just how exacting its internal investigation could be expected to be, EG&G announced that it had hired an independent consultant to examine Millar's complaints. But Craig Williams of the Chemical Weapons Working Group—whose fingerprints were all over the Millar memo and its leak to the *Deseret News*—denounced the various investigations as a "joke," pointing out that the "independent consultant" retained by EG&G, Amoretta Hober, was "the Army's main booster" for incineration in the 1980s. Williams also derided the Army's chief investigator, Brigadier General Thomas J. Konitzer, who had headed the military's inquiry into the charges made by Millar's predecessor, Steve Jones, which had exonerated EG&G.

Within a matter of weeks, Hober and Konitzer would indeed

issue reports that, despite Millar's allegations, concluded the Tooele facility was safe. More damaging to the efforts of incineration opponents like Williams, the Utah Solid and Hazardous Waste Control Board voted unanimously to allow the incinerator to keep operating after a hearing that featured anticlimactic testimony from Millar. Under a withering cross-examination by an EG&G attorney, Millar conceded that he could not name five serious safety problems at the plant, although his widely publicized memo had said he had noted three hundred such issues. "I don't believe there will be a catastrophic number of deaths because of the plant, short of an earthquake," Millar conceded to the board. "The risk is much more to workers and employees of the plant."

Despite Millar's disappointing performance, Williams and other activists continued to press their opposition to the Tooele incinerator. At a Salt Lake City symposium in January 1997 sponsored by the Chemical Weapons Working Group, a procession of speakers urged Utah residents to be dubious of Army claims that minuscule levels of agent emitted from the facility's smokestacks posed no danger. "This is the same Army that has been slow to accept any connection between illnesses suffered by Gulf War veterans and their children," said Jim Tuite, a former Senate investigator and founder of the National Gulf War Research Foundation. "The Army tells us, 'Trust us, it's safe.' They have to expect that people are going to question what they say based on their history." Williams pressed the case for alternative technologies like neutralization, and claimed that his group had confirmed no less than a dozen releases of live agent into the atmosphere at test facilities on Johnston Atoll and at a pilot test facility two miles from the Tooele incinerator. Moreover, he said, two more such releases had been documented at the new Tooele facility—a claim the Army quickly disputed to the Associated Press. Less than three weeks later, however, the state ordered the incinerator to halt operations for several days while it investigated an internal sarin leak into an observation corridor from a sealed area where a container of the agent was being drained. Investigators ultimately blamed the incident on a control-room-operator error that apparently caused an imbalance in the plant's ventilation system.

The legal battles and whistle-blower claims would continue. In January 1997, at Williams's direction, the Chemical Weapons Working Group filed yet another motion in U.S. District Court in Salt Lake City for a preliminary injunction to stop the burn at Tooele. At about the same time, another ex-EG&G employee at the facility filed a complaint with the U.S. Department of Labor claiming that he was harassed and fired from his job as an "entry-level" engineer-technician for pointing out safety problems at the plant. A weary-sounding EG&G spokesman, Skip Hayes, told the AP that whistle-blower allegations were "getting to be the general theme for anybody who falls out of favor with EG&G." Hayes said that although the former employee, John R. Hall, was indeed "a problem child," he was fired because he wasn't prepared to go back to work as required after a disability leave. In his complaint, Hall said he took the leave because of severe depression and stress over his treatment by fellow employees and supervisors after he discovered sealant cracks in the floor and evidence of battery acid leaks in the plant's toxic maintenance area. A subsequent in-depth inspection of the plant's emergency power system found battery leakage throughout the facility, Hall claimed. According to the complaint, Hall's supervisor became "irate" when the findings were reported, and then Hall was reassigned. Hall said he subsequently was harassed by his coworkers because of his actions and at one point found feces-filled underwear in his locker. He also claimed that he was harassed because he filed a notice with the Occupational Health and Safety Administration, which alleged that sulfuric acid from life support system transformers was leaking onto hydrogen bottles that were used for sampling nerve agent—a problem he said he had previously brought to the attention of his EG&G supervisors to no avail. Hayes, the EG&G spokesman, denied that Hall was harassed as he claimed: "EG&G is not accustomed to attacking entry-level workers," he told the AP. (More than one cynic suggested that that was probably true, that EG&G was clearly more practiced at discrediting higher-ranking employees—such as its safety managers.)

When yet a fourth whistle-blower surfaced in June 1997, it seemed as though everyone—the ousted former employee, EG&E, the state regulatory agencies, incineration opponents, and the press—simply went through the motions of a familiar drill, to little effect. Trina Allen, the former chief of hazardous waste operations at the plant, claimed that she was coerced into signing off on the plant's safety and was then forced to quit when she protested. In making her allegations at a news conference at the Salt Lake City offices of the Sierra Club, Allen characterized EG&G management at Tooele as "typical of the senior management at Three Mile Island before their nuclear accident or at NASA before the *Challenger* accident"— analogies used previously by Steve Jones and Gary Millar. EG&G spokesman Hayes said that Allen was fired because she altered transportation records at the facility, a charge that Allen denied. Dennis Downs, the director of the Utah Division of Solid and Hazardous Waste, said Allen's allegations were "old news" and that "she's obviously got some employee-employer relationship issues." Allen's complaint essentially went nowhere.

Then a sea change seemed to occur. In Salt Lake City, U.S. District Judge Tena Campbell, after reviewing arguments presented by attorneys for the Chemical Weapons Working Group, refused to issue an injunction to halt burning at Tooele. The Army expressed considerable relief at the decision and, having weathered the difficult first several months, began a public relations counteroffensive.

Shortly after Judge Campbell's decision, an op-ed piece by Tim Thomas, site project manager at the Tooele incinerator, appeared in the *Anniston Star*. Describing the aging chemical weapons stored at Anniston and elsewhere as "a threat to the very same people they were designed to protect," Thomas wrote that research by the Army had "concluded that the risk of indefinite storage is 45 times greater on a daily basis than the chosen disposal method of incineration." He further asserted that a "Quantitative Risk Assessment" showed that "the risks associated with the entire incineration program at Tooele . . . is equaled by the risk of only 11 days of storage." The article made no mention of the six shutdowns the Tooele plant had experienced thus far, but noted instead that the facility had "operated for more than 618,000 hours without a lost-time accident." Thomas concluded, "Experts agree that continued storage poses more risk than incineration. Incineration will dispose of our stockpile in a safe, efficient manner. Most importantly, once the disposal process ends, the risk is reduced to zero."

Similar-themed, Army-generated opinion pieces appeared in other publications around the country. A few months later, an unadulterated coup was presented to the Army and other incineration advocates, compliments of the U.S. Centers for Disease Control. Concerned about the charges made at the Chemical Weapons Working Group symposium in Salt Lake City that low-level nerve gas emissions could cause Gulf War syndrome, a retired National Guard colonel and leading member of a prominent incineration oversight commission asked the CDC to evaluate smokestack safety at the incinerator. The retired colonel, John L. Mathews, said he requested the study from the CDC because he believed that agency to be credible and because it had no ties to the Army. The incinerator passed the CDC's evaluation with flying colors. Dr. Henry Falk, director of the CDC's Division of Environmental Hazardous and Health Effects, reported that the incinerator had never released even one-fifth the allowable amounts of nerve agent through its smokestacks—a finding that Falk noted was even more impressive given that the allowable limit itself was set very conservatively to ensure public safety. "To date," Falk wrote, "our review of this information has led us to conclude that the stack emissions of the Tooele incineration system will not pose a threat to Tooele employees or people living near the facility."

The Army and EG&G followed up with a public relations tool that would prove so effective that it would become its public outreach bread and butter: relentless updates on the progress of the burn. Any milestone would do. In April 1997, the Army announced that the Tooele plant had destroyed three million pounds of agent; even though that figure represented less than 5 percent of the stockpile at the plant, the news was enthusiastically reported across the national wires and picked up by dozens of newspapers, including the *Star*. Three months later, another announcement: the destruction of the last of 4,463 750-pound MC-1 bombs filled with GB agent. The report didn't mean that GB, regarded as the most lethal agent in the stockpile, had been eliminated at Tooele—far from it. It merely meant that the destruction of one type of weapon that *contained* GB was complete. Nonetheless, the AP's story carried a dramatic tick-tock account:

The last of the MC-1 bombs at Tooele was punched and drained at 1:47 P.M. on Sunday, said depot spokesman Joel Pettebone. It was the first chemical agent of any single type to be eliminated from the depot's chemical weapons stockpile, he said.

"Over the years, the MC-1 bomb has been one of the most difficult to maintain in storage," Army Col. Joseph Huber, commander of the depot, said in a news release. "Completion of this campaign represents a significant decrease in risk to our Rush Valley neighbors."

The story was flawed in that no chemical agent had been "eliminated"—one had only to read further down in the article to learn that an additional eight hundred thousand GB-loaded projectiles in the arsenal had yet to be destroyed. No matter. The incessant drumbeat about the incremental burn milestones, big or small, met several aims, including the simple reality that the more the public read or heard about the activities at the incinerator, the more ordinary (and risk-free) they seemed. The stories also provided perfect opportunities for the Army to hammer away at the notion that incineration was "good" while any other option was "bad"—as exemplified by Huber's comment in the AP story about the difficulty of storing the MC-1s.

Given this onslaught of progress reports, which usually received wide play by news outlets anxious for any news about the controversial incinerator, it was difficult for Craig Williams and the other incineration opponents to keep pace—but they did their best. A high-water mark occurred in the fall of 1997, when an administrative law judge recommended that Steve Jones, the Tooele safety chief fired by EG&G in 1994, be given his job back and awarded back pay and damages totaling some seven hundred thousand dollars. Jones said he was "overjoyed," that EG&G had "made me unemployable, and I feel that this decision is a vindication." Jones's attorney said that her client "lost his job for telling the truth and trying to protect the public." Williams claimed that the ruling demonstrated that the Tooele facility and others like it on the drawing board "are threats to human health and the environment and must be stopped."

Yet, mostly, once the burn started in Tooele and the legal challenges played out, the impact of the anti-incineration efforts by Williams and other opponents seemed to resemble that of rocks and bottles hurled against advancing tanks. Williams, especially, had pulled out all the stops: lawsuits, whistle-blowers, disturbing scientific research, political pressure, virtually any tactic he could think of. But as 1996 blurred into 1997, and 1997 into 1998, it became increasingly clear that barring some horrendous catastrophe—and Williams certainly wasn't rooting for that—the battle against the Tooele incinerator was essentially lost.

Time to move on to the next theater of operations. The efforts of the Chemical Weapons Working Group actually had scored significant progress—and in some cases outright victories—in Oregon, Indiana, Maryland, and Williams's home base in Kentucky, all depot sites where the Army's plans for incineration had either been stymied or slowed dramatically. But the two remaining sites—Pine Bluff, Arkansas, and Anniston—were different, obstinate creatures. Pine Bluff was especially hard-core in its inhospitality to incineration opponents. Williams had been threatened with bodily harm there on several occasions, and he considered it the only regular stop in his travels where he literally was forced to keep looking over his shoulder. Anniston harbored a sampling of that same menace, but there was also a small but committed group of enlightened peo-

ple on the ground there who were helping—asking questions, causing problems, making their presence felt. Williams didn't know if
the resistance there would be enough to make the difference, but he
knew that it was enough to try. There was a chance, and all you
could ask for, really, was a chance.

So it was on to Anniston, to try.

CHAPTER TEN

PROSELYTIZING

Donald Stewart was fond of describing himself as "just a fair country lawyer," but he was no tin-pot rube with a shingle. He might have been born in the tiny Talladega County burg of Munford, and his father might have been an unassuming farmer and cotton-gin operator, but Stewart demonstrated early and often that he had the wits, ambition, and ice in his veins required to become a considerable force in politics and the law. One doesn't become a U.S. senator at age thirty-eight by blind-stumbling into a lucky alley. Yes, his term only lasted two years—a complicated story, but Stewart always was a complicated man. And while it was fortuitous that Stewart was the attorney whom the Mars Hill deacons elected to ring up that Sunday afternoon in 1995—a three-hundred-million-dollar phone call, in the end—the call from Andrew Bowie could also very well have meant Stewart's ruin, and on several occasions threatened to be. It could have gone either way. Stewart was sometimes reminded of the aphorism attributed to Groucho Marx: *You have to be in the right place at the right time, but when it comes, you better have something on the ball.* Stewart had something on the ball, all right: a smoking fastball, wicked curve, slider, knuckleball, insatiable desire to win, all the tools. He had something else, too: a mean streak a mile long. Everybody knew it. Crowd the plate against Donald Stewart, and he wouldn't just brush you back; he would adjust his cap, spit in his glove, rear back, and aim a beanball with a comet trail right at your temple . . . and then smile, just to let you know it wasn't an accident.

Stewart's family moved to Anniston when he was eight. They were devout Methodists, and Stewart's father was careful to ensure that his twin sons, Donald and Ronald, rejected the regional attitudes about race and class prevalent at the time. He taught them that everyone, even if black or poor or both, deserved to be judged on their own merits, to be heard. This was, to be sure, a minority view in Anniston and throughout the South in the 1940s and 1950s when Stewart was growing up; it was a direct contradiction of the status quo, a position with which he would become very comfortable in the years to come. He attended public schools in Anniston and went on to the University of Alabama, where he was student body president and editor of the yearbook before going on to the university's law school. Stewart returned to Anniston, got married, started a family, established a law practice, and prepared for a career in politics. In 1970 at age thirty he was elected to the Alabama House of Representatives, where he immediately became known as a tough, abrasive liberal who seemed to go out of his way to confront establishment interests, sponsoring a raft of consumer protection bills along with air and water pollution control legislation. In 1974 he moved up to the state Senate, where he led a movement to institute some of the first reforms in the state budget system since 1935 and was named Outstanding Freshman Senator by his peers. In 1976 the Alabama Power Company requested a then-staggering

$106 million rate increase from the Public Service Commission; at his own expense, Stewart intervened in the case and so cogently attacked the powerful utility's rationale for the rate hike that the commission reduced the increase by $83 million. When the power company filed for a $205 million increase later that same year, Stewart intervened again and persuaded the commission to reduce the hike by more than half. He later pushed through legislation that beefed up the Public Service Commission staff to more effectively monitor the state's utilities. Stewart was establishing a reputation as a maverick Democrat who was building an unusual populist coalition of lower-income white voters, labor, and blacks.

As the 1978 elections approached, Stewart strongly considered a run for the U.S. Senate seat long held by Democrat John Sparkman, who had announced his intention to retire. Just the contemplation of such a bid was audacious—Stewart had never run statewide and had no congressional experience to boot—but the competition was stiff and Stewart wisely held back. Then a wholly unexpected event: the fatal heart attack of Alabama's other fixture in Washington, U.S. Senator James Allen. The senator's widow, Maryon Allen, was given a temporary appointment to the seat while a special election was arranged, with the winner to serve out the remaining two years of Jim Allen's term. Allen announced her candidacy for the Democratic primary portion of the special election, as did Stewart and a host of others. Allen was considered the front-runner, but Stewart launched a maniacally paced campaign and presented himself as a youthful, up-and-coming contrast to the pleasant but staid Allen. Stewart ran a respectable second to Allen in the Democratic primary and then won by a landslide in the runoff. He easily defeated his Republican opponent in November, and suddenly, eight years after entering politics and not yet forty, he found himself a member of the exclusive U.S. Senate.

Stewart took on the office and Washington with his customary rush and seemed to be entrenching as the 1980 election for a full six-year term approached. A complimentary profile in *Alabama Magazine* declared that "barring a stunning reversal of his fortunes— a reversal which grows more improbable by the day—he is likely to be a very big man on the Alabama political scene for years to come." But 1980 presented a number of problems for Stewart. Ronald Reagan was presenting a shoot-up-the-saloon challenge to President Jimmy Carter, and an anti-incumbent fervor seemed to be sweeping the country. The economy was leaking jobs and causing panic within the labor voting bloc. Questions about financial contributions to Stewart's 1978 campaign continued to receive media attention. Still, Stewart appeared to have the whip hand in the 1980 Democratic primary; his chief opponent, Jim Folsom Jr., son of a much-beloved former governor, was having trouble raising enough money for an effective race. Polls showed Stewart in fine shape. In a shock, however, Stewart on primary day fell just short of winning outright and so was forced into a dangerous runoff with Folsom. The Stewart camp blamed the fiasco on the presence on the primary ballot of perennial also-ran Mrs. Frank Stewart, no relation to Donald, who finished far back but fared just well enough to make observers wonder if her last name had confused some of the senator's would-be supporters. But one Stewart insider had a simpler explanation: victory had been taken for granted. "It was not a breakdown," the unnamed insider told *Star* political editor Mike Sherman. "Just overconfidence." Awarded new life, Folsom went on to upset Stewart in the runoff— only to himself lose to GOP nominee and war hero Jeremiah Denton in November in what turned out to be a very Republican year.

Thus was Donald Stewart sent unceremoniously home. It was a humbling transition. He formed a law firm in Birmingham but fell out with his partners, the result being a $500,000 law suit filed against Stewart by his associates and a $250,000 counterclaim by Stewart. The suits were ultimately settled in "amiable fashion," Stewart said at the time, but by 1985 he was back in Anniston, a sole practitioner, having come full circle back to where he had begun. He was forty-five years old and essentially starting over. More than a little quiet satisfaction was expressed around town at how things had played out. Donald had gotten ahead of himself, it was whispered, had gotten too big for his britches. Now he's back, the thinking went, and we probably won't hear very much from him anymore.

But Stewart reoriented and worked his way back in. There were some other financial struggles; a business deal went sour and landed him in hot water with creditors. But he began to win some cases and settle some others favorably, one for four-million-dollars against a local wholesale firm. By the time the Mars Hill Baptist Church called in 1995, Stewart had been up, down, and finally leveled out in stable financial condition. He had been doing some good lawyering, in his view, taking some cases no one else wanted to touch because "they might upset somebody." Stewart didn't worry much about upsetting anyone. "They" were usually upset with him anyway, always had been. Stewart didn't mind representing somebody on the West Side against their East Side employer, if the case was sound. He took black business when a lot of white lawyers tried to avoid it, and this was known and appreciated west of the tracks. Donald Stewart had been a good politician for black folks, and a good lawyer for them, and Andrew Bowie was mindful of these realities when he suggested that the deacons ask Stewart's advice on the matter of the Monsanto purchase offer.

It didn't take Stewart long to understand that the Mars Hill case was worth a great deal more than one hundred twenty thousand dollars.

He filed suit against Monsanto on behalf of the church; the company promptly retained the services of the elite Birmingham defense firm of Lightfoot, Franklin & White, which maintained a long roster of distinguished and high-profile corporate clients. Warren Lightfoot was that firm's most prominent partner, had been a law school classmate of Stewart's, and assured Stewart in an initial conversation that he was wasting everyone's time with this Monsanto business. But Stewart started digging and working the phones and asking around, and learned that the Environmental Protection Agency and the Alabama Department of Environmental Management had been notified two years earlier by the Alabama Power Company that a plot of land it had acquired from Monsanto in a property swap had serious PCB contamination issues. A quiet resolution had been worked out among all the parties, with an interesting stipulation: any release of information would come from Monsanto. Stewart could find no evidence that information regarding possible health hazards resulting from that incident was ever released to the community. Stewart saw to it that word began to get out, encouraging some publicity in the *Star* about the Mars Hill case, and soon Monsanto's settlement offer rose to one million dollars.

This development caused a division within the church, as a faction materialized that pushed for acceptance of the one-million-dollar offer. Stewart, confident that Monsanto would go higher, advised against it. The church voted to reject the offer after a contentious debate. (According to Stewart, a leader of one faction of the church was erroneously convinced—and then convinced other members—that the settlement would be divided among individual church members rather than going to the general mission of the church.) Stewart would later learn that a lawyer at Lightfoot was talking to a member of the congregation who wasn't a client of Stewart's. Stewart would ultimately get the church $2.5 million and a van, but the church would break up in the end over what to do with the money.

While the Mars Hill case was in play, Bowie placed another call to Stewart. Would the attorney address the church as a whole? Many of the church members had been approached by representatives of Monsanto about selling their homes, and were concerned about acting hastily, since the purchase agreements stipulated that the sellers would voluntarily forgo their rights to sue Monsanto. Stewart showed up at the church a few nights later and spoke to a full house. He outlined the various options open to residents— among them his offer to represent a group of them to make sure that they received the monetary damages they deserved.

Word of the meeting ricocheted about the West Side. For the next several days, Mars Hill church members and other West Side residents clawed into Stewart's office and clamored to sign up for "the lawsuit." On a number of occasions, Stewart and his staff would look around and realize that more than a hundred people were crammed into his modestly sized office. The would-be plaintiffs jostled and elbowed and muscled their way in, a stream of humanity that never seemed to quit, all of them anxious to tell Stewart or anyone who would listen about how they always knew something was going on "over there," about parents and siblings and friends besieged by cancer, about how happy they were that someone was finally doing something about it, about how it was About Time.

Stewart listened and counseled and signed people up. (His initial suit would list some four hundred plaintiffs; he would eventually amend it to include more than thirty-five hundred, and no doubt could have signed up three times that number.) He had never seen anything like it, had never witnessed such a sustained outpouring of emotion and need. Nothing had been proved, no one had admitted liability for anything, and it would take some hellacious doing to

ever get that far, he knew. But it seemed to Stewart that the Mars
Hill case and now this suit had driven a lance into some dark beast
of suspicion and fear that had lurked on the western fringe of
Anniston for more than half a century. Something had been awakened. It was as if people just wanted to hear, after so many years,
that they weren't crazy after all, that something had been *wrong all
along.*

And the damn thing of it was—they would tell Stewart these
things and then they would say, "You know, we don't really expect
any money out of this. We just want someone to make it right."

And whenever anyone said that, Stewart would give them the
same reply: "Hell *yeah,* we're gonna get you some money."

Circuit judge Joel Laird came through the door of his office in the
Calhoun County Courthouse on that morning in 1996 and understood immediately that his secretary was peeved. You work with
someone long enough, you start to pick up on such things. He arched
his eyebrows in a silent question—What?—and she responded with
a jerk of her head toward the new file sitting on the printer. Laird
picked up the folder and thumbed through it. Well, well. *Abernathy
et al v. Monsanto et al.* A toxic tort case, filed by Donald Stewart, four
hundred-plus clients. The file had apparently landed in Judge Sam
Monk's office—cases are randomly assigned by a clerk in the order
they arrive—and Monk, with no explanation, had passed the file over
to Laird's office, all of which explained Missy's bad humor. It was a
case that had all the appearances of being a pain in the butt, a lot of
paperwork, complicated, plus the added feature of dealing with the
stickling Stewart—trying enough on the simplest of matters. As it
happened, Laird had already presided over two PCB-related lawsuits
Stewart had brought against Monsanto: the Mars Hill church case,

and another one on behalf of a black minister, the Reverend Thomas Long, seeking individual damages. Those cases had been contentious and required a lot of attention, but of course that was nothing new where Donald was concerned. And now this. Laird assumed Monk had transferred the file over because Laird had handled the earlier cases.

"So you want me to get rid of it?" Missy asked. Translation: *I'll ship it back to Judge Monk, or foist it off on somebody else.*

"No," Laird said. "I'll just keep it." Missy rolled her eyes, shrugged, and went back to work. Laird walked into his chambers and got started on his day. He wasn't concerned about the new case. He had learned a long time ago that things happened for a reason. Trying to micromanage everything just made life more difficult. Yeah, he would keep it. No big deal.

David Baker felt like he was back in business at last.

It had been a very tough year, perhaps the toughest of his life. It just went to show you how the world can lay you low, just absolutely shear your head off your body, right when you think you got it all going on. And David *did* have it going on. He and Betty had come back to Anniston. She was feeling comfortable and happy—he had been a little worried about how she would settle in, but she was doing fine with it. And he was finding his footing with this Monsanto business—he was feeling the old New York juices again. He had started to realize that maybe this situation with the PCBs was what New York had been all about—that New York had been God's way of preparing him for Anniston. Wouldn't that be something? Everybody thinks that *New York* is what it's all about, an end unto itself—and that's certainly how David felt when was there in the middle of it, that he had left Anniston to fight in some foreign war with the world in the balance. But his generation of soldiers had moved on, and so had he. He had thought he was coming home to be with Mama and Betty and kick back and just enjoy being back in the old town again. And then one thing had led to another, and damn if he wasn't organizing his ass off all over again. David had to admit it felt good to be in the mix again, raising Cain.

And Betty had been behind him 100 percent—in fact, it was Betty who made him promise he would see it through. She was the one who saw the purpose in it all, the big picture. He would talk on the phone to Butler about it too, keep him updated about Monsanto and all the happenings. Butler would offer advice, ask the right questions, but mostly he would just chuckle and say, *Go, son*. But it was Betty who convinced him that he could take it to the next level, form an organization, get a staff together, start delegating. That was how CAP got started—Community Against Pollution. That was the beginning, anyway. Every worthy endeavor has to begin somewhere, and so it was with CAP.

But when Betty died—man, it was a hard thing to take.

It was a bad car wreck at a bad intersection while she was on her way to the hospital in the rain to visit somebody who had just been in an auto accident himself—the craziest and most terrible sequence of events you could imagine. And he lost her, just when he least expected it, as if you could ever truly expect it to happen. They had found each other and made it to Anniston and found their purpose, and then one gray, wet afternoon it was over, with no good-byes.

After he buried her David fell into a deep depression. He had never minded a drink once and again, but now he was drinking every day and rarely leaving the house. He knew that Betty would have been disappointed in how he was handling things, but it seemed like he had fallen into a deep hole and couldn't see his way out. And he knew it wasn't just the loss of Betty in and of itself, as tragic and incomprehensible as that had been, as much as she had meant to him. It also had to do with the reality that David had never done very well without a woman in his life. It was as if he needed someone to provide for, someone to bear witness to his battles in life, someone to *strive* for. It was like that comic strip *Hagar the Horrible*, about the Viking who was always setting off with his men to raid castles in England, risking life and limb, having all these splendid adventures out in the world. But he always came home— bruised and battered, arrows jutting from his tough hide—to his wife, Helga, who gave him a hard time but was always *there*. From childhood, David had always kept a lot of people around him and he took sustenance from that, but he needed that home base to keep it solid. Didn't everybody? Otherwise it was just emptiness. The truth was that since Betty had died, CAP and the work he was doing in the community about Monsanto—he had let it languish. He was just going through the motions. And slowly he had started to think about going back to New York. It would break Mama's heart—she had been so happy when he had come back for good. Others were counting on him. But it had been nearly six months since Betty died, he wasn't doing any better, and it didn't look like Anniston was going to work out after all.

One rare Friday night out, as he was sifting through these thoughts, David found himself at the Elks Club. There was a pretty good crowd in there, and his mood had lightened a bit. After a while a young woman approached him, a woman he knew well, a friend of his niece's. She sat down and gave him a big smile.

"My mother wants to talk to you."

"Your *mother*?" David had to laugh at that. He knew he was getting some age on him, but now the young ladies wanted to fix him up with their mothers? Another sign of the times. "Where's your mother at?"

"Right over there."

David peered through the smoky nightclub haze and spotted her—and stopped laughing.

"*That's* your mother?"

"Yeah."

"Well," David said, getting up, "I better buy her a drink, just to be polite."

Her name was Shirley Williams, and she sipped Sprite while David had a couple of drinks. Shirley had grown up around Anniston but had moved to Chicago to live with her father and attend high school. She had spent some years up there, had gotten her nursing degree and moved back south. Now she was working in Fort Payne and was in town to visit her daughter. She was pretty; that was what had drawn David to her table from across the room. But he quickly realized that she was smart, deep, and spirited—was she *ever* spirited. Maybe *feisty* was the better word . . . and they had a lot to talk about. Both had been away to the big city, seen some of the world, and come back home to family and friends. They talked for two hours, and when she left, David asked for her phone number.

So began their courtship. And Shirley began to attend some meetings with David, to get her own handle on what he talked about all the time, the Cause. And she got *in* to it. It was the type of work, she discovered, that appealed to her nature. These people needed help. They needed medical information. They needed a place to come with their problems associated with the Monsanto mess, somebody to tell them where to go to a doctor, find legal assistance, whatever. They needed someone to advocate for them, to take their concerns to the city, Environmental Protection Agency, Alabama Department of Environmental Management, and other government agencies. And she could see that David needed help too. He was a big-picture operator who tended to let the details slide. He was a passionate motivator, a wonderful strategist, and seemed to know every family in town; but he wasn't going to pore over the specs for an EPA grant application, or get letters out to potential contributors, or mind the thousand-and-one details that come with running a grassroots organization.

After a few months with Shirley, it occurred to David that he had not thought about New York for quite some time. He still mourned Betty and always would, but he also knew he had fallen in love with Shirley and wanted her in his life. Shirley agreed to move to Anniston and help him run CAP. Shortly thereafter she agreed to marry him. Everyone said it was a textbook match. If anyone could channel David Baker's energy and outrage and headstrong determination to change his corner of the world, it was the loyal, vocal, steely, wily, committed Shirley. In Shirley, David had found his purpose again. His stride and swagger were back, and David Baker resumed his raids on the English castles, arrows be damned.

David had been a major player in the recruitment on the West Side of plaintiffs for the *Abernathy v. Monsanto* lawsuit. Via CAP meetings, other gatherings, and just working the streets, he helped put out the word that Donald Stewart was signing people up. He advised Stewart about prospective clients who had lived near the Monsanto plant for many years, still owned property there, or had exhibited significant health problems. David himself was an *Abernathy* plaintiff. (Tests would show that he had PCB levels in his fatty tissue of 341 parts per billion; anything above 20 parts per billion is considered extraordinary. Over the years he had also had several operations to remove a series of small lesions that had cropped up on his face and arms.) As Stewart had explained the legal process to David, and as David had in turn explained it to many others, the trial would be divided into several phases: The first, centering on a sampling of test cases, was intended to show that PCBs had contaminated property, rendering homes and businesses less valuable or in some cases worthless. If those damages were proved, then Stewart would attempt to show that Monsanto was responsible for that contamination and, as a result, liable for damages. Then the case would move ahead to consider health claims. It would all take years. The best result, of course, would be some sort of settlement, in which Monsanto conceded its liability and paid some money to the plaintiffs. But the word from Stewart was that Monsanto did not appear to be in any mood to settle for anything substantive, and in any case Stewart himself could be a difficult man to settle with, whether the issue was a toxic tort case or who was paying for lunch.

Yet what David found himself explaining over and over again to people was why Donald Stewart wasn't signing up more plaintiffs for the *Abernathy* suit. Stewart had stopped when he reached about thirty-five hundred clients. As David understood it, Stewart believed he had listed the most deserving clients with the best cases; the other element was that Stewart, as a small-town lawyer with a relatively modest operation, could only manage so many plaintiffs and only so large a case. David had heard that Stewart was actively seeking financial backing and other assistance from larger law firms to help him handle the crushing load that the *Abernathy* suit portended. But still David was approached by people who wanted to be involved in the case, many of them, it seemed to him, who had claims with as much merit as many of the Stewart plaintiffs. Finally, David began telling people that he would attempt to find another lawyer or lawyers to take their cases. Well, people would reply, we don't want just *anyone*. We want a lawyer as good as Donald Stewart.

One afternoon David was discussing the matter with James Hall, a retired teacher and activist concerned about West Anniston. Hall mentioned that he had a distant relative, Eddie Harris, who was an associate in Johnnie Cochran's law firm in Los Angeles. Cochran wasn't a plaintiff's attorney, of course; he was a defense attorney, as anyone who walked the planet well knew. But Hall offered to place a call to determine if someone with the Cochran firm might be interested in taking on clients, or at the very least, if he might recommend another attorney somewhere. Sure, David said, chuckling at the audacity of the idea, let's call up Johnnie Cochran. It can't hurt. What the hell, let's call up Perry Mason too, and see if *he's* interested. Why not aim high?

A few days later, Hall called David with news that bordered on the astonishing. Hall had reached Harris in Los Angeles. Harris had expressed interest and promised to get back to him after looking into the matter. And not only did he call back, he did so with the news that Cochran was scheduled to appear soon in nearby Talladega to deliver the commencement address at a predominantly black college there—and that Cochran would allot ten minutes of his time that day to meet with Hall and Baker at the college. No promises, no guarantees. Just the commitment that Johnnie would see them and hear them out—for ten minutes, anyway.

David couldn't have been more excited if President Clinton himself had agreed to meet with them. *Johnnie Cochran.* In the African-American community, at least, Cochran came as close as one could come to living, breathing sainthood. His inspired, swashbuckling defense of O. J. Simpson had mesmerized that Los Angeles jury as well as TV viewers everywhere. For David and countless others, the Simpson trial, as it neared its conclusion, was not a question of whether OJ was guilty of murdering his wife. No, the question was: *Can Johnnie Cochran prevail?* No one could say for certain whether Simpson did it, although David had his strong suspicions. The way David viewed it, if OJ was guilty, then Almighty God would exact his retribution no matter what any jury of common men and women said. If OJ was guilty, then he was already living in a hell of his own making and would continue a life of torment whether he spent that life in prison or on a golf course. If OJ did it he deserved to go to jail; but God worked in mysterious ways that mere mortals could barely fathom. For some reason, events had transpired to put Johnnie Cochran in that place and time before that judge and jury. Cochran was chosen to hold the prosecution to account, to make the state prove its case, and it became readily apparent to anyone who watched with any interest at all that Cochran was in total control of the proceedings. He was smarter than everyone else, more articulate, craftier, and more cunning. How often in real life did black America see one of its own beat the establishment—the legal establishment, at that—at its own game? The guilt or innocence of O. J. Simpson became almost secondary. David had heard all the theories about how the Simpson trial was "payback" for all the black men wrongfully convicted at the hands of a prejudiced legal system. Maybe that was so, he couldn't say. To David, it had been all about Johnnie. The trial became Johnnie Cochran's world; everybody else just lived in it. David's mother was typical in her reaction to the entire affair. Say what you will about O. J. Simpson, but she *loved* her some Johnnie Cochran.

David was surprised to learn that Cochran wasn't exclusively practicing criminal law any longer. He was now concentrating on cases that threw the spotlight on civil rights and other social justice issues. He had handled a few environmental cases. The more David thought about it, the more he came to believe that there might be a fighting chance that Cochran would get interested in Anniston. The presentation to Cochran would be the key. David knew exactly how to handle it. All he had to do was tell the truth. He just needed to explain how so many folks in West Anniston, most of them black and poor, had been sick and dying beyond all reason for many years, how the impact of PCBs was becoming known, how property in the area had become unmarketable because of it, how Monsanto was refusing to accept responsibility, to do right by people. All he had to do was tell Johnnie Cochran about his little brother, dead at seventeen, and how there were so many more just like him that they could never bring back. But *something* could be done, some level of justice attained. The people in Donald Stewart's suit had a chance to get theirs. But there were many, many more who deserved the same chance, the same justice. Just put it to him straight, David figured. What was there to lose?

But David knew better. To attach Johnnie Cochran's name to the proceedings against Monsanto could rework the entire equation. If Cochran didn't bite, then surely some other superbly qualified attorney would. But no one could bring the instant credibility and outright clout that Cochran represented. It could mean everything. And David would have his shot—all ten minutes of it.

David, James Hall, and Barbara Boyd, a legislator whose district includes parts of Anniston, made the twenty-mile drive to Talladega on a sunny, warm day that promised better weather to come. They arrived on the Talladega College campus and were ushered into a conference room where they waited for a lifetime, give or take a few years. Then suddenly, in a rush, the room seemed to fill with people, and then Cochran entered, looking every bit the man of the hour. Introductions were made, everyone settled in, and David found himself eye-to-eye with the most famous lawyer in the world.

"So, Mr. Baker," Johnnie Cochran said, "tell me what's going on in Anniston, Alabama."

A few weeks later, David borrowed the newest, shiniest, plushest hearse that his undertaker buddy Sylvester Harris owned and headed to the Atlanta airport, where he picked up Johnnie Cochran and Eddie Harris. If Cochran saw any irony in David's choice of vehicle to transport him to Anniston—where, if the reports were to be believed, cancer and all the rest were causing people to virtually drop in their tracks—he didn't mention it. Everyone simply started working, with Cochran and Harris peppering David with questions about Monsanto and the situation in West Anniston as the group sped westward on I-20 into Alabama.

Upon arrival in Anniston, David provided Cochran and Harris with a brief tour of the impacted areas around Monsanto, with particular attention to some of the properties marked by "Contaminated" notices posted in front yards, the hearse drifting through West Anniston like an omen. Then, as they made their way toward the Cobb Community Center, David's cell phone rang. It was Shirley. "David," she said, "you have *thousands* of people over here."

David thought she must be exaggerating. CAP had put the word out about the meeting arranged to bring attorneys from the Cochran firm together with people who had been left out of Donald Stewart's suit. The notice had included the nugget that Cochran himself was scheduled to appear, and David had been optimistic that several hundred people would attend, maybe even upward of a thousand. But it was a Tuesday night, after all, and people had to work the next day, so it wasn't as if the whole town was going to show up. But as the hearse approached the meeting center, it became apparent that Shirley was right, and that even David had underestimated the drawing power of Johnnie Cochran. Cars and people clogged the streets and yards around the center, making the area impassable except on foot. The hearse would have to go over the curb and cut across a field just to dodge the mob and get anywhere near the back door. Even though hundreds of people had been through the CAP office in the last few months, David had not fully grasped the level of interest among the rank and file in suing Monsanto—especially if *Johnnie freaking Cochran* was going to lead the charge. Besides, how many times did Johnnie Cochran come to town? What were people going to do, stay at home and watch *JAG*? Of *course* there was a crowd for the record books.

The hearse made its way to the back door, and David, Cochran, and the rest began to make their way inside. People seemed to be clinging to every square inch of space in the building, a great frothing mass of folks. David was told that a huge overflow crowd was milling in front of the meeting center as well, unable to get in. All told, an estimated five thousand people had shown up, a staggering number, fully one-fifth of the population of the city. As people spotted Cochran a great roar of applause began to build and the crowd began to recede before him, as if Moses were parting the Red Sea. David gently took Cochran's arm and steered him toward the front row of seats where members of David's family sat, including his mother, dressed as if it were Easter Sunday. David quickly introduced Cochran to the group, and the attorney made a special point of speaking to Mama Baker, who looked as if she might grin until she burst. Her reaction mirrored that of the rest of the packed hall: *It's really him, and he's really here.*

Finally the Cochran retinue settled at the table behind the podium while David made a few welcoming remarks, thanking everyone for attending, and reminiscing about how CAP had started with just a tiny handful of people meeting at the Seventeenth Street Baptist Church. "To see all these people here tonight is a powerful thing," he said. A few others spoke as well, including Jock Smith, an African-American attorney and Cochran partner well known throughout Alabama's Black Belt. Smith had made millions as a plaintiffs' lawyer and maintained his office in a grand, renovated mansion off the Tuskegee town square. He had previously made a fact-finding foray into Anniston at Cochran's behest, and had strongly recommended that the Cochran firm take on the case. "Anniston reminds me of a war zone," Smith told the audience. "There are an awful lot of red signs around here that need to come tumbling down."

Eddie Harris introduced Cochran ("Heeeeeeeeeeeere's Johnnie!"), who took the podium to a revival-meeting ovation. Poised, in command, looking splendid in a perfectly cut gray suit and with cufflinks glittering in the pale fluorescent light, Cochran did not disappoint. He told the crowd that he was in Anniston because David Baker and a group of others had recently met with him in Talladega and asked him to "take a look" at what was going on in their community. "Baker and [James] Hall told me that there were people here who were unrepresented, people who were ready to fight for themselves, people with courage," Cochran said. "They told me there were people here who cared about what's happening with Monsanto, and what's happening to their city. . . ." He invoked Rosa Parks and her historic role in the Montgomery bus boycott, and how her "act of courage" sparked the civil rights movement in the South "against Jim Crow. Jim Crow is dead now, but we have his son, Jim Crow Junior, and you have to be careful." He invoked the biblical story of David and Goliath, in which against all odds David slew the giant. "I look out into this audience," Cochran said, "and I see a whole bunch of Davids. I don't think you know how much power you *have*. . . .

"We have our basic rights in this country, and one of those is that every citizen should live free of pollution, live free of PCBs, live free of mercury, of lead, anything that is deleterious to our health. We've not been told about the dangers here . . . there's always some study and they'll study it to death and then thirty years later you find out it's bad for you. I'm here to tell you tonight we know it's bad for us right now!"

The crowd was with him, urging him on. "If we embark on this journey together, it's a major battle," Cochran continued. "You're gonna get tired. You're gonna wanna quit. You can't do that . . . you have to have the courage of your convictions. And if you have that, you can change this community." He told the audience that they wouldn't be fighting just for themselves, but for generations yet to come. He called the name of a young boy he had met a few minutes earlier—"Devon Shields, where are you? Come up here"—and a stunned-looking youth in a bright blue shirt joined Cochran at the podium. Cochran put his arm around the boy. "This young man was talking to me, telling me he's doing well in school. I asked him what he wanted to do and I was hoping he might say he wanted to be a lawyer, but he said a doctor. But one day I will pass from the scene and others will pass, and Devon and these other young people will take our place. We have to leave a better place for these young people. . . . With the numbers and the strength and the resolve you've shown here tonight, you can do that. . . . If you take that and put God first and at the center of your life, blessings will flow. Things you never dreamed possible will happen! If you go before the board of education, they'll listen. If you go before the city council, they'll listen . . . even the courts will pay attention!"

The hall erupted in applause and a chorus of *Amens* and *Hallelujahs*. Cochran waited for quiet, preparing his summation. "Injustice anywhere is injustice everywhere," he finally said. "If you don't get justice here, that affects me where *I* am. . . . I want to come back to this community in five years and see this young man here grown up and feel a lot of pride about what has happened here. When these kids are grown up this place can look a lot different. You are empowered! Not to dominate others but to be the best that you can be. . . ." The rest was lost in the whooping and the cheers and the adulation. The line to sign up to be represented by Cochran had already begun to form, and ultimately would slither out the front door into the street and would stay there for hours. David Baker had brought Johnnie Cochran to town, and everyone agreed he had put on one heck of a show.

Cochran's suit in federal court would come to be known as *Tolbert v. Monsanto* and would be filed on behalf of more than fifteen thousand plaintiffs.

CHAPTER ELEVEN

THE RUN-UP

Donald Stewart had needed help with his litigation against Monsanto, and he had found it.

Through a Mississippi lawyer acquaintance named Dan Barrett, who had handled a number of toxic tort cases, Stewart was introduced to the principals of the New York firm of Kasowitz, Benson, Torres & Friedman. On the surface, the chances for an alliance between Stewart and Kasowitz, Benson seemed remote. The New York firm was known for its toxic tort defense work, not as a plaintiffs' shop. But Kasowitz, Benson shared with Stewart a maverick streak. The firm's founder and managing partner, Mark Kasowitz, had defected in 1993 from the prominent Manhattan firm of Mayer, Brown & Platt. From his old firm Kasowitz imported eighteen lawyers and two main clients: the chemical company Celanese Corporation (now Celanese AG), and a large real estate company. Almost immediately after the formation of the new firm, Kasowitz, Benson was plunged into thousands of lawsuits alleging that a Celanese compound widely used in fitting plastic pipes was faulty and responsible for damage to homes caused by leaking. But it was in 1996—the same year Kasowitz and number two partner Dan Benson were introduced to Stewart—that the firm created shock waves that reverberated across the legal industry by engineering the startling withdrawal of client Liggett Group Inc. from a joint defense of the cigarette industry. Kasowitz, Benson formulated a strategy to turn over secret business documents as part of a settlement with plaintiffs' lawyers and state attorneys general and saved Liggett millions of dollars in the process. According to *American Lawyer* magazine, the headline-grabbing defection by Liggett "gave Kasowitz, Benson a reputation for fierce loyalty to its clients. But it also fostered a view among fellow defense lawyers that Kasowitz, Benson attorneys were untrustworthy, a sentiment that remains."

Dan Barrett had been one of the plaintiffs' attorneys in the tobacco and toxic tort litigation and an adversary of Kasowitz, Benson. When Stewart let it be known that he was looking for cocounsel, Barrett thought that Kasowitz, Benson might be interested. Stewart at that time was representing the Mars Hill church and was contemplating the *Abernathy* action. Stewart met with Kasowitz and Benson in New York. The two partners liked the case and were impressed by Stewart. The firm signed on with the Mars Hill case and then stuck with Stewart when he made the considerable leap into *Abernathy*.

In the beginning, Stewart was looking for someone to foot the bills and manage paperwork; that suited Kasowitz and Benson, who anticipated that their financial outlay might be in the one-million-dollar range. But Stewart and, especially, Benson, who would become the firm's point man in Alabama, developed an intimate working relationship, and soon Benson and some fifteen other Kasowitz, Benson attorneys were involved in discovery, briefs, pretrial motions, and trial argument. It was an arrangement that would last seven and a half years and involve an investment by Kasowitz, Benson of some fifteen million dollars, with expenses during one period running at five hundred thousand dollars a month.

Per their understanding, Stewart not only would be the public face in the case against Monsanto but would have the last word on all tactical decisions in the courtroom. "They never faltered," Stewart would say much later. "And we didn't have a damn thing in writing between us. Here I was, a sole practitioner in Anniston, Alabama, and they took this on with me. . . . I told them from the beginning, 'I have my people [plaintiffs] to worry about—don't ever put me in a position where I have to consider going against their best interests.' Mark looked me dead in the eye and said, 'You have my word.' He backed it up all the way." Thus a team was assembled that included Stewart, Benson, and Bennett, with the occasional assist from Kasowitz.

Two incidents in the early going demonstrated to Stewart that his new partnership with the New Yorkers could be counted on. During an early encounter with Monsanto lawyers from the Lightfoot, Franklin firm, Warren Lightfoot was talking expansively to Kasowitz, Benson, and Stewart about the difficulties the plaintiffs had ahead of them, how the defense had no inclination to settle, how they were in it for the long haul. The message was clear: *This case will break you; you're in over your head.* Kasowitz fixed Lightfoot with an even stare and said quietly: "You think you're going to bankrupt me with *this* case?" It had been an understated, almost offhand reply, but it carried the unmistakable undercurrent of cold-blooded commitment. Stewart prided himself on being able to gauge people, be they members of juries or other lawyers or the guy behind the counter at the grocery store. In that exchange between Kasowitz and Lightfoot, Stewart read that Kasowitz was a winner who was ready to knock heads for all four quarters and then overtime if that's what it took—and he took huge comfort in that knowledge.

The final evidence came some two years into the proceedings. A trial date still seemed far away. Stewart had steadily built his case, and the defense had upped its settlement offer to thirty million dollars. It was an offer that had to be considered, if for no other reason than because by that juncture it had become clear that the *Abernathy* case was going to be no mere one-million-dollar investment by Kasowitz, Benson. Things were getting tense; the Mississippi lawyer Dan Barrett, for one, was pushing to accept the offer. Stewart was opposed. The offer, in his view, didn't serve his clients well, in the first place. Beyond that, he was feeling good about the case. The evidence seemed to be coalescing in their favor. Stewart felt confident that the defense was growing more concerned, that it was likely that much larger settlement offers were ahead if they could just ride it out. And if that didn't happen, Stewart liked his chances in the courtroom. As Stewart was prone to remind everybody, including the defense team, he had "whipped Warren Lightfoot's ass" every time they had squared off on a case. He saw no reason why he should lose the upper hand now. But Stewart also knew that the case had probably reached a pivotal stage for Kasowitz and Benson. Thirty million dollars wasn't all the money in the world in a case like *Abernathy,* but it was certainly a decent sum. It was enough to put a good face on things and get away clean. It was enough money, in other words, to put the lie to tough talk of "going the distance," if the lie was there.

One Monday morning, with the thirty million dollars newly on the table, Stewart placed a call to Barrett in Mississippi. Barrett's secretary reported that Barrett was out of town, "meeting with Mark and Dan in New York." *Oh shit,* Stewart muttered to himself. Barrett had said nothing about going to New York, nothing about a meeting with Kasowitz and Benson. What was happening was easy to see: Barrett was making an end run. He was pushing settlement, and by all appearances Kasowitz and Benson were listening to what he had to say. And why wouldn't they? *They know Dan Barrett one hell of a lot better than they know me.*

Stewart's intercom buzzed shortly. "Mark and Dan on the phone from New York," his secretary said. *Here we go,* he thought.

"Dan Barrett came up here," Kasowitz said. "He didn't have your permission to do that, did he?"

"No, he didn't," Stewart said.

"Well, Dan's out," Kasowitz said. "He's not involved anymore. All you've ever done is exactly what you said you would do. We see no reason why that won't continue."

End of conversation. It would be the last time Stewart ever had even a glimmer of doubt about the New York firm's commitment to the *Abernathy* case, or to him. He would take that commitment and ride it toward the kind of battlefield glory that most lawyers only dream about.

It was like picking up the faintest of radio waves from across space and time, faint yet intelligible signals emitted from some now-extinct source buried within a swirl of stars in some distant galaxy, evidence of . . . well, evidence of something that couldn't be fathomed, even guessed at, unless the signals were tracked all the way back to the source.

Stewart kept picking up radio waves about the documents. The waves were just a murmur, an ebbing, a soft disturbance in the atmosphere. He wasn't even conscious of receiving them at first. But they were there, pulsating ever so delicately, waiting to be noticed. It was like monitoring those big SETI receivers, the gargantuan satellite dishes the government maintained out in the desert somewhere, attuned to any extraterrestrial message beamed our way. Probably a useless exercise; but you keep the listening post up and running all the same because who knows when the sign may come that provides the key to everything?

The one saving grace about litigation is that those who engage in it aren't necessarily required to reinvent the wheel every time out. Every case is unique in its way, but every case is also like countless cases that have played out during the vast history of jurisprudence. Part of the game of law is dredging from the past, to apply to the present, long-ago court rulings that may help today's judge see it your way, legal arguments from some mothballed proceeding that just might open a fruitful line of questioning. Evidence—especially evidence. One clear advantage of the plaintiffs in the *Abernathy* case was that Monsanto had been sued many times before. Witnesses in other cases had been deposed, experts queried, documents subpoenaed. In a case like *Abernathy*, it was crucial that the plaintiffs avail themselves of what had transpired before. Which is how a Kasowitz, Benson attorney named Ellen Mallow found herself in Texas, sifting through the documents from a previous case against Monsanto. She ran across some documents—some internal Monsanto memos—that indicated that the company's knowledge and concern about PCBs and their impact on the environment went back substantially further than the company had admitted. There were only a couple of them, but they were about as titillating as a set of corporate documents could be. "Donald, you won't believe this stuff," she told Stewart over the phone.

Stewart was intrigued and told her to keep digging. He had believed all along that over the years, somewhere in the labyrinthine bowels of Monsanto's corporate headquarters in St. Louis, there were those who had known about the deadly effects of PCBs long before they became general scientific news in the 1970s and 1980s. Moreover, he was confident that some Monsanto officials were aware of the pervasiveness of PCB contamination in Anniston and had managed to keep it quiet. But intuiting something and proving it in a court of law are different matters. The documents unearthed by Mallow alone wouldn't do the job, but it stood to reason that more documents existed where those came from. Human nature dictated as much. In his experience as a lawyer and politician, it seemed to Stewart that people had a compulsion to document the most damaging evidence imaginable against themselves, the Nixon White House being a monumental example. Monsanto was a huge, carefully controlled corporation populated by scientists and others who liked to do things by the book. It was reasonable to imagine that somewhere in the annals of time, uncomfortable information had been committed to paper in the name of proper information flow. The question was whether those papers still existed. If so, it was also very likely that somebody at Monsanto knew where they were. As many times as Monsanto had faced litigation, Stewart figured that any smoking-gun documents had been secreted away by now. It was a long shot, but what the hell.

The truth was that at this phase of the case, some three years in, Stewart believed things were going quite well for the plaintiffs. The case was inching toward trial in fits and starts. The first order of business was to establish that damage had been inflicted on the community and specifically on the plaintiffs whose cases would be heard first in a series of test cases when the trial began. Then the task would be to prove that Monsanto bore liability for that damage. Evidence that PCBs had saturated the community was mounting. Soil tests commissioned by Stewart showed conclusively that PCB levels in residential and commercial soils in and about West Anniston posed a public health hazard. Blood sampling data from three thousand West Anniston residents coordinated by David Baker's CAP organization and financed by an EPA grant showed that about half the people tested had detectable levels (greater than 3 parts per billion) in their blood; about 15 percent showed blood PCB levels that indicated "elevated environmental exposure" (greater than 20 parts per billion). Depositions of Monsanto officials and the geographic evidence made it clear to Stewart that he would be able to prove that it was Monsanto that had launched the PCBs into the environment, sometimes recklessly, and therefore should be held responsible for the subsequent damage.

It was easy to anticipate what the counterargument from the defense would be: No one has ever definitively proved that PCBs harm human health. Monsanto would argue that PCBs are everywhere, present in the bodies of every person on earth, and yet the human race has not come to an end. It is simply a part of life. Monsanto did not fully understand how PCBs affected the environment when they were discharged. Some forty million dollars has been spent in a good-faith remediation effort. The suit is just a blatant money grab by opportunistic plaintiffs under the influence of a greedy trial lawyer. Stewart could hear it all now. But Stewart felt that the evidence was too vivid to ignore, and would not be easily shrugged off by any fair-minded jury. He believed that he could convince that jury of his version of what had happened, especially against any lawyer that Lightfoot, Franklin could prop up there.

The historical record concerning the monitoring of Monsanto's PCB releases by regulatory agencies had also come into focus. As far back as 1985, the Alabama attorney general had notified the EPA that PCBs existed in Snow Creek, the waterway that ran past the Monsanto plant and into the Choccolocco Creek watershed area that furnished Anniston with its water supply. The EPA deferred the matter to the Alabama Department of Environmental Management, or ADEM. The low-profile process essentially resulted in Monsanto being allowed over the next several years to police itself and develop its own programs for groundwater monitoring and sediment removal from Snow Creek. But in 1993, an official from the U.S. Soil Conservation Service snagged a fish from Snow Creek that was horribly deformed; he submitted the fish for testing, which determined that the fish contained PCB levels in its fatty tissue that were off the charts.

This development would prove to be the beginning of a new and certainly more public phase of the PCB saga in Anniston. ADEM officials became more aggressively involved and later that same year issued a "no consumption" advisory for fish caught in Choccolocco Creek between Snow Creek and Lake Logan Martin. The advisory sparked a round of media attention, although the warning and subsequent news accounts were widely ignored by residents who had fished from the creek for generations. ADEM in 1994 also launched an assessment of Monsanto's unlined dump, which sat across Highway 202 from the plant and the Mars Hill Church. That resulted in a consent order negotiated between ADEM and Monsanto—again, all handled very quietly—that led to Monsanto initiating the buyout and relocation program in which the company ultimately purchased some one hundred residential, commercial, and vacant properties near the plant site, not to mention two churches—including the Mars Hill Baptist Church, which was where Donald Stewart had entered the picture. It was that under-the-radar buyout program that had led to the ghost-town tableau Stewart witnessed on that fateful afternoon when he drove to the Mars Hill church for his first meeting with the deacons.

It was a sorry accounting of things, in Stewart's mind. It seemed to him that every regulatory official charged with protecting the public had managed to drop the ball at virtually every step along the way, dating back nearly fifteen years. When the time came, he intended to make sure the jury understood that apparent neglect of duty—and he intended to argue that it was the jury's responsibility to right those historical wrongs. As for what Monsanto knew about PCBs and what it didn't—that could very possibly be the deciding factor in the case. The documents Mallow had uncovered would help, but they needed more.

Another significant event occurred during the pretrial portion of the case. In 1997, one year after Stewart filed the *Abernathy* case, the Monsanto Corporation announced that it was spinning off its chemical operations into a new, independent, self-contained entity. The new company would, like Monsanto, be headquartered in St. Louis. Its new name would be Solutia ("Applied Chemistry. Creative Solutions."), and under its corporate charter it would assume the defense and liabilities involved with the litigation against Monsanto's Anniston plant. *Creative solutions, indeed,* Stewart thought. Although Monsanto officials denied it, the spin-off was widely seen as a transparent attempt by Monsanto to indemnify itself against the growing litigation and to insulate itself against the inevitable public relations trauma the litigation promised to create, win or lose. ("I think they just changed the name," U.S. Senator Richard Shelby would say later.)

As if by magic, Monsanto was now technically out of the chemicals business, its primary meal ticket since its inception in 1901. Now it would concentrate on its burgeoning biotech operations, including its foray into genetically engineered crops, and attempt to distance itself from the Anniston mess. Meanwhile, Solutia officials were now free to claim that their shiny new company had had nothing to do with Monsanto's increasingly blemished past. "We never produced PCBs," Solutia CEO John Hunter became fond of saying. Stewart often wished he could see the billing statements for the marketing and PR operatives who dreamed up this galling new organizational constellation. But he managed to win a number of rulings in the months and years to come that would force Monsanto to stand behind Solutia and make good on any damages and cleanup costs that Solutia was deemed unable to pay.

Other machinations had to be dealt with. One involved an inevitable change of venue. As the *Abernathy* case had progressed and media interest had grown, it became clear that the trial would have to be conducted outside of Anniston. Publicity surrounding the case wasn't the only issue. With thirty-five hundred plaintiffs, approximately one of every nine Anniston residents was part of the lawsuit. Finding jurors who were not related to or acquainted with at least one plaintiff would be a nearly impossible task. So the trial would be moved—but where? Stewart argued for Etowah County, which sat adjacent to Calhoun County to the northwest. Its county seat was Gadsden, a city of about sixty thousand that, much like Anniston, had an economy traditionally anchored by heavy industry. (A Goodyear tire factory had long been the city's primary employer.) Etowah County also had similar demographics to Calhoun County—that is, a substantial black population. Stewart argued before Judge Joel Laird that it was essential that the trial draw from a jury pool that reflected the socioeconomic and ethnic characteristics of the plaintiffs themselves. The defense team argued for relocation of the trial to Blount, DeKalb, or Marshall counties, smaller, more distant, and more rural counties that were virtually all white. In a terse decision, Laird ruled that the trial would be held in Gadsden in Etowah County and wrote that he "certainly hopes that Defendants aren't attempting to inject issues of race into this case." Defense attorney Adam Peck took exception to Laird's comment: "This is the first time race has come up, and it wasn't by us, it was by the court," he told the *Anniston Star*. Stewart, having won the argument, could afford to be gracious. "He's the judge, so we'll do what he says," he told the *Star*.

The reality was that Judge Laird and the defense weren't getting along. Stewart obviously viewed this development as yet another arrow in his quiver. Not that he and Laird were close friends by any means—he knew Laird, but everybody knew everybody in Anniston. Stewart also knew Laird's father, Richard Laird, a long-time legislator from nearby Randolph County, and had served with him, but they weren't close. Joel Laird was one of the less experienced judges on the Calhoun-Cleburne County circuit, and Stewart had butted heads with Laird in the past. But the judge had always impressed him as evenhanded and thorough, which was all you could ask from a judge, and so Stewart had been generally satisfied when he learned that Laird would be presiding over *Abernathy*.

But Laird and the defense team seemed to have clashed out of the gate. The case had barely started when the defense, led by Franklin, Lightfoot partner Jere White, attempted to go over Laird's head on a jury selection matter and filed a petition with the Alabama Supreme Court to direct Laird to rule a certain way. To petition for a writ of mandamus is a drastic step, and one that the Monsanto lawyers employed on four different occasions during the course of *Abernathy*—including one very late going attempt to have Laird removed from the case. Stewart wasn't the only one who saw the petitions to the supreme court as attempts to intimidate Laird and to delay the start of the trial, nor was he alone in believing that White and the other defense lawyers were following a terrible strategy. (There was also speculation around the courthouse that the defense was laying the groundwork for an appeal in the event that they lost the case.) Stewart didn't know Laird well, but he knew him well enough to understand that the judge was a prideful man who took his service on the bench very seriously—and would fight like hell before he allowed a group of hardball-playing Birmingham lawyers to take over his courtroom.

One such petition filed by the defense tied up the case for nearly two years. It was time that Stewart and his allies used wisely. Had they been forced to go to trial in 1999 or 2000, which had been their original expectation, Stewart believed that he could have mounted a good case but probably not his strongest one. Such was business as usual for a trial lawyer—rarely was there enough preparation time. Usually there were other cases to worry about, other deadlines and demands, and you simply tried to hang on and do an adequate job. Even though Stewart was devoting all his time and attention to *Abernathy,* the work load was enormous. The material was voluminous and extremely complicated. The extra two years were a godsend. By the time a concrete trial date of January 2002 was set, Stewart felt that he had mastered every aspect of the case, felt in total command, like an athlete at the peak of his training. He had memorized every deposition, knew the contents of every file, had probably become one of the world's leading authorities on PCBs, their manufacture, and their consequences. For the first time in his some thirty-five years as an attorney, he believed he was as prepared for a case as he could be.

Which was a good thing, because everything was on the line. The plaintiffs had been dragged around for years now. The Kasowitz, Benson firm was in so deep financially that Stewart could hardly bear to consider it. Stewart's own financial situation had become perilous again as well. He was sixty-two years old now and had essentially worked on nothing but *Abernathy* for six years. All his eggs were in one basket, and if they lost this case Stewart feared he would have to declare bankruptcy. It would be damned hard to start over again at his age. He would have no idea how to begin. His wife, Lulu, had read *A Civil Action,* the bestseller about a Massachusetts lawyer who spent himself into oblivion pressing a similar case against the W. R. Grace Company, and it had shaken her more than any Stephen King novel. Stewart swore to himself he would never read it.

So yes, the additional two years had been welcome. But the extra time had served another purpose as well: it allowed Stewart to tune in to those radio waves, to remember what he had been trying to remember about the documents.

It finally reoccurred to Stewart, amid the crush of preparing for trial, that years back, Monsanto's in-house attorney had casually mentioned in a deposition in St. Louis that a cache of documents had been stored in a library in the North Carolina law offices of a Monsanto defense attorney. For some reason the issue had gone unremarked upon, although Stewart had made a mental note of it. Now, as the memory finally floated back to him through the ether, he wondered if that had been Monsanto's method of disclosing the existence of important documents during the discovery phase without drawing attention to them. At his first opportunity during a subsequent hearing, Stewart quizzed the in-house attorney on the subject, who reiterated that the documents existed but said that most of them were protected from discovery because they had been classified as attorney work product. How many pages of documents? Stewart wanted to know. About five hundred thousand, came the reply. Half a million pages of attorney work product? Bullshit, Stewart said.

He dispatched a representative to North Carolina to examine the documents at the law firm, where a vicious argument developed. The Monsanto lawyers insisted that Stewart could only properly examine documents selected as relevant by the Monsanto team. The hell you say, Stewart said, and appeared before Laird to request that he be allowed to depose the in-house counsel yet again on the matter. The defense raised objections to the heavens, but Laird agreed with Stewart. Stewart spent a month preparing for the deposition. He went to St. Louis and, as one witness would describe it later, "pinned his butt to the wall." He successfully established that the index of the documents prepared by the attorneys could well have been attorney work product, but the documents themselves were not. Stewart returned to Anniston and argued before Laird that he was entitled to the documents. The defense filed a motion which revealed that other plaintiffs in other cases had attempted to obtain the same documents, but each time, a judge had ruled that the documents were protected.

Laird ruled again for Stewart, a decision that plainly staggered the defense. *This stuff must be dynamite,* Stewart thought, and immediately put a Kasowitz attorney on a plane to North Carolina to start picking documents that the law firm there was now obliged to copy at the plaintiffs' expense. It soon became apparent that a wealth of damning information lay hidden in the rows and rows of files in North Carolina. Documents were found that seemed to clearly establish that Monsanto had known for decades that PCBs were harmful to the environment and to humans, and had taken steps to keep that information under wraps and maintain its very profitable market position vis-à-vis PCB products. Documents were found showing that as early as the 1960s, Monsanto officials had convinced at least one Alabama state health official to suppress the critical information that the waterways in and around Anniston were contaminated with PCBs and that fish in those areas were saturated with them. It was revelation after revelation, and finally Stewart called Dan Benson in New York and recommended that they have all the documents copied, every page, and have them shipped to Anniston. It would cost a small fortune, but these documents could very well be worth one, Stewart told him.

Benson sighed deeply. "Do it," he said.

Eventually the documents arrived, and Stewart and anyone he could recruit pored over them until their eyes bled. There were to be no shortcuts. Stewart demanded that every last page of every last document in every last file in every last box be examined. It was tedious labor but was an approach that paid dividend after dividend. It soon became apparent that the order of the documents had in some instances been significantly altered. There would be a file of invoices, for example, containing invoice after invoice after invoice—and then, abruptly, an internal memo marked CONFIDENTIAL that might discuss the results of fish tests in Snow Creek. Then the invoices would pick up again, in order. A score like that could keep someone going for hours. Stewart and the other paper chasers kept at their search until every page had been eyeballed—and in the end they had quite a haul.

Absorbed in their entirety, the documents told the story of a dispassionate corporation that clearly understood the implications of its actions and consistently rejected its moral obligation to inform the public in Anniston and elsewhere of the dangers of the PCBs it had produced for forty years. There was simply no other way to interpret them. Stewart and Benson shared their conclusions with the defense team and suggested they find a way to settle the case. Surely, Stewart figured, the defendants would do anything other than try to explain the documents in court.

The defense team came back with their response to Stewart's entreaty for a settlement: an offer *lower* than the figure already on the table. The defense was basically suggesting that Stewart take the documents and shove them.

Stewart was flabbergasted. He had truly believed that the documents would force Solutia to the negotiating table. He certainly believed that if *he* were in the defense's shoes, he would have pushed his clients like hell for settlement—he would have *made* them listen to the facts of life—the documents were that powerful. Stewart just couldn't understand why the defense conducted business the way they did, angering the judge, big-timing the opposing lawyers, not dealing realistically with devastating evidence.

Well then, Stewart thought, so be it. He would take the documents and flog the defendants with them like some recalcitrant mule back on his daddy's farm in Munford. With the Monsanto memos, Stewart could very well start to fantasize about the two most popular words in the vocabulary of every plaintiff lawyer on earth: *outrage verdict*.

David Byrne was getting to know Anniston very well. Sometimes that familiarity could be a grim business.

Byrne was the main attorney on the ground in Anniston for the Montgomery firm of Beasley, Allen, Crow, Methvin, Portis & Miles, probably the most feared plaintiffs' firm in the South. The firm's founding partner, Jere Beasley, was a plugged-in former lieutenant governor of Alabama who had run unsuccessfully for governor in 1978. Done with politics, he created a firm that espoused the same populist values he had adhered to as an elected leader, with a sharp focus on consumer safety issues. Beasley, Allen won huge verdicts against the automobile industry in connection with faulty air bags, and had developed a reputation as a firm that was adept at mastering highly technical cases. So it had been no surprise when Johnnie Cochran, shortly after his visit to Anniston and his decision to take on the Solutia case, called Beasley to ask if he wanted in. If Beasley would handle client contact and the science, Cochran offered, he would handle the courtroom. Beasley said yes, which is how the fortyish Byrne, efficient, studious-looking, and low-key, found himself arranging for Manuel Washington's autopsy.

Washington was a forty-year-old African-American who was one of the approximately fifteen thousand plaintiffs represented by the Cochran and Beasley firms in *Tolbert et al v. Monsanto et al*, and who was slated to be one of the test cases in the early phase of the trial in U.S. District Court in Birmingham before Judge U. W. Clemon. Washington had grown up near the Monsanto plant and worked as a grocery clerk at McCord's Supermarket in West Anniston for several years until he became ill. He was diagnosed with liver disease and diabetes, and became so incapacitated that he was forced to move into a residential nursing facility in Oxford. According to Washington's medical history, he ate fish from local streams several days a week for most of his life until he became ill;

he also had consumed homegrown poultry, pork, and vegetables several times a week. Moreover, about once each week he ate dirt from around his West Anniston home, a common practice among some poor southerners. A medical examination of Washington before he died, conducted by a plaintiff's expert, concluded that Washington's liver disease was linked to his very high exposure to PCBs while he lived near the Monsanto plant.

Washington had been doing poorly, and Byrne had been concerned about him, but his abrupt death was something of a shock. Not only was there the tragedy of his passing to consider, but Washington's death also had to be dealt with in the context of the *Tolbert* case. The results from Washington's autopsy might prove to be valuable evidence in the courtroom. So Byrne received permission from the grieving family to proceed, and soon he was keeping a vigil at the Ervin Funeral Chapel in West Anniston while he waited for a doctor who was being flown in from South Carolina to perform the autopsy.

When dealing with thousands of clients, it was easy to think of them as so many names, addresses, and compilations of medical data. Byrne prided himself on remaining mindful of the people behind the numbers, but in big cases like *Tolbert* the temptation always existed to become numb to it all, to look at people in the abstract. Even as he resisted it, Byrne saw that numbness as a survival skill, a natural psychological defense against the illness, suffering, and death that these cases often involved. But Anniston . . . Anniston had been different from day one. It was virtually impossible to compartmentalize what he saw there. And it wasn't just the Manuel Washingtons. Of the fifteen thousand plaintiffs, some forty-five hundred were children. Of those, nearly a hundred had cerebral palsy. Where else could you find a cluster of CP like that? It was amazing, and humbling. A very real need was being addressed there. As Byrne sat patiently in the funeral home waiting for his somber mission to play out, Manuel Washington's diseased body resting on a large table in the next room, it occurred to him that if it was possible to do God's work as a lawyer, then Anniston, Alabama, was about as close to it as you could get.

CHAPTER TWELVE

WHAT-IFS

Vietnam changed Craig Williams, but not in the corrosive and some-times deadly way he saw it change so many of the men he fought with, or in the way he saw the experience of Vietnam haunt and gnaw away at those men once they returned home. He certainly had his own issues as far as that went, but Williams had survived Vietnam essentially intact—or as intact as someone can remain after witnessing the ass-backward cluster-fuck for the ages that Vietnam had been. Sure, he had been scarred by his tour of duty over there; everyone had, no matter what they said. For Williams, leaving that dripping, lethal jungle and coming home to Long Island in 1969 had been like stepping gingerly through some hallucinatory time warp. It wasn't anything he couldn't handle—it just took a while, is all.

What he discovered about himself when he came back is that, against very sizable odds, he had become a more altruistic and less hedonistic person—and even though *altruistic* and *hedonistic* were the sort of precious words used at one's peril growing up around New York, they fit. Williams had seen too much physical and emotional carnage, too much of life, to come back and resume his previous self-absorbed existence. He had come to realize that the world was a bigger place than the one chiefly concerned with whether he could afford a new car or how the Yankees were doing. And so, even though he came from a fairly conservative family where activism, while not a vile term, was certainly a foreign concept, he began to get involved. Before long he became president of the Long Island chapter of Vietnam Veterans Against the War (a grassroots organization that ultimately would become the influential Vietnam Veterans of America) and threw himself headlong into that cause, marching in Washington, smoking dope with John Kerry, the whole schmear. He not only pressed the antiwar case but also became immersed in the issues confronting returning veterans, beseeching the Army and the rest of the federal government to help the many soldiers who had fought in Southeast Asia and who had returned to pain, turmoil, and despair. He saw it as duty, and patriotic duty at that—even though Williams learned early on that to speak critically of the U.S. military establishment was to be painted with a very different brush. He learned a great many things, including the dispiriting, if unsurprising, knowledge that the Army as an institution did not like to be challenged or even questioned, and that when it was questioned or challenged about its treatment of its veterans or the conduct of its wars or you name it—whatever—it very often could not be believed. A reality soon became apparent to Craig Williams: that in most instances the Army would rather climb a tree and lie rather than stand still and tell the truth. Which was good to know, as Williams increasingly devoted his life to challenging and questioning that same Army on a variety of matters.

Soon enough, however, the 1980s appeared, and Williams found himself attempting to live a normal life in Berea, Kentucky, in the rolling horse country near Lexington and the Bluegrass Army Depot.

In 1984 the Army announced that it would undertake a massive program to rid the United States of the chemical weapons stored around the country in depots like Bluegrass, and began to hold public hearings in Lexington and at the other depot sites to discuss the disposal options on the table. Williams, ever curious about the Army and its pursuits, attended a hearing with his wife. It seemed clear to him that despite the Army's rhetoric about investigating the various methods of destroying the weapons and giving them all equitable consideration, incineration was already the anointed choice. It also seemed apparent to him, merely on the face of it, that to set fire to some of the most dangerous weapons on the planet in a populated area like Lexington, Kentucky, was about the most stupid fucking idea he had ever heard. Of *course* it would be preferable to be rid of the weapons—there was no disputing that. It was common sense. But what actually was involved in that? What were the risk factors? Just how seriously had alternative methods like neutralization been studied? Was it truly more dangerous to let the weapons atrophy than to undertake to essentially blow them up in a "controlled" setting? Just because the Army said it was so, was it necessarily true? Williams didn't know the answers to any of those questions save the last one. He stood up that first night at the hearing and didn't get satisfactory answers. He and his wife had kids. Did they really want them to be sucking down the exhaust from a chemical weapons incinerator? He was concerned, and so was his wife. On the drive home, she said, "Somebody's got to do something." He said he would.

Williams kept attending hearings, meeting people, educating himself. It soon became plain to him that incineration was a concept steeped in risk. Worthy-seeming alternatives, namely neutralization, existed, alternatives worth a serious look. But the Army was fixated on incineration and, to Williams, appeared intransigent in its resistance to other technologies. Why? He couldn't exactly say, other than to recollect his own lengthy experience with the macho, gung-ho stubbornness of the Army, whose management style resembled not so much a bull in a china shop as a thousand bulls in a china warehouse. Defense contractors who stood to make billions off a national incineration program were no doubt being heard in the glossy corridors of the Pentagon. Whatever the thinking, reason, or motive, in 1985 the Army announced that its decision was made. Incineration was its preferred method of disposal for America's chemical weapons stockpile, and that was how the Army intended to proceed.

During the last half of the 1980s, Williams managed to hot-wire a coalition of Kentucky interests to provide a public monitor for the "chem-demil" (short for chemical demilitarization) process. Having been unable to blunt the Army's incinerator initiative at the local level, he began to consider the merits of bringing together the various fledgling public-interest groups like Kentucky's that existed—sometimes barely—at the other chem-demil sites around the country, as well as representatives from the South Pacific, where Johnston Atoll was at issue, and even Russia, which had the world's largest chemical stockpile (forty thousand tons). After much outreach and networking, an unwieldy but committed group of a few dozen people gathered in Kentucky in 1990 in an attempt to arrive at some sort of working arrangement to combine forces at the national and international level. Their goal was to affect policy in Washington and other world capitals and to augment each individual battle on the ground—in Blue Grass, Kentucky; Tooele; Anniston; Umatilla, Oregon; Pine Bluff, Arkansas; Aberdeen, Maryland; Newport, Indiana; and Pueblo, Colorado. It was difficult because different groups had differing views and objectives. Someone from Pueblo might get up and suggest that the approach to coalesce behind was to ship all weapons west of the Mississippi to Tooele and deal with them there—this with the highly unimpressed

Tooele delegation in the room. But they kept at it, and from that beginning grew the Chemical Weapons Working Group, which would go on to lead anti-incineration efforts at chem-demil sites across the United States and abroad and to establish a significant presence on Capitol Hill. (Oddly enough, Williams would forge a collegial working relationship with Kentucky's conservative Republican U.S. senator Mitch McConnell, and even filmed a campaign spot for McConnell at the senator's request. The spot never aired, which Williams figured probably saved them both considerable grief from their respective constituencies. But if U2 lead singer Bono can cozy up with Jesse Helms about forgiving third world debt, then perhaps Williams and McConnell bedfellowing up on chem-demil isn't so astonishing.)

The tiny Anniston delegation consisted of Pete Conroy, a museum official and head of the Alabama Conservancy; Alan Lindell, a Christian minister and his wife, Brenda; and another couple, Jim and Donna Harmon. Conroy would eventually bow out of the anti-incineration movement and focus his environmentalist energies on other projects. Donna Harmon would die of cancer. But it was a foothold, a beginning.

Others would ultimately join in and play varying roles, most notably Jacksonville State University professor Rufus Kinney and Anniston architect David Christian. They would in turn draw in others; as in most "movements," people would come and go and make (or not make) contributions large and small. But it would be Brenda Lindell, David Christian, and Rufus Kinney who ultimately proved to be Anniston's most prominent local anti-incineration voices. The bearded and tweedy Kinney was the most vocal of the three; supremely well informed, a born lecturer, he constantly argued for neutralization and was frequently quoted in newspapers around the country, the classic "go-to guy" when an out-of-town reporter appeared. Christian, another highly capable intellectual but more subdued than Kinney, pressed his own offensive, making erudite arguments to the press and proving valuable in helping shape the legal battle against the Army's plans. But it was Brenda Lindell who would prove to be the most dogged of them all, attending every meeting, filing comments at every hearing, traveling to speak at environmental rallies and other events no matter how tenuous their connection to the incinerator issue, indefatigable and relentless even when her husband melted away and conceded to her the role of family activist. In any movement of any aim or stripe that gains any traction at all, there is always one person, one tenacious soldier, standing at the end; in Anniston, that soldier was Brenda Lindell. Craig Williams, who knew what that brand of soldiering was about, tried to prepare her for what was to come.

The subject matter was complicated, for starters, sometimes incomprehensible. Anyone who meant to be an effective voice in this mind-bendingly technical arena would be forced to become an expert, for example, on the specifications and characteristics of dozens of arcane weapons, to be able to read Army documents and understand, say, that the project manager at the Tooele incinerator chose specific M-55 rockets that, because the chemical agent stored inside them for decades had gelled, would be most likely to pass the Deactivation Furnace System GB agent trial burn, and to be able to further understand enough about M-55 rockets and trial burn procedures to be able to lobby effectively for more stringent trial burn requirements in Anniston. There were reams of Quantitative Risk Assessments and GAO reports and the like that contained ample ammunition but had to be read and understood and applied. A basic understanding of the convoluted way the Army does business was required. One had to be willing to beseech and debate and lobby and kiss the garment hem of the many politicians involved: the mayor, the county commissioners, the congressional delegation, the governor, the state legislators . . . not to mention the players in the regulatory agencies, state and federal . . . the newspapers, radio, TV . . . the chamber of commerce types. . . . Basically, a working relationship was required with everyone who was anyone. Raise money or be prepared to spend your own. And by the way: *You can never be wrong about anything,* because the Army and the press and everybody else will holler bloody hell and never let you forget it. The Army can be wrong every other day. You, on the other hand, must be perfect, because that is the cross that the opposition must bear. It was a lot to expect of anyone, and Williams knew it. "It's a hell of a burden, just enormous," he would reflect much later on. "You're up against the world, and you're a housewife."

All that was difficult enough to explain and absorb. Yet there was a more pervasive obstacle, one that Williams had wrestled with but whose brick-wall ramifications he had only begun to grasp: the closed-ranks psychology of a Depot town. The Army, back so long ago, had indeed chosen its sites well. An insulated community that has perceived the Army and its local Depot as an economic patriarch for half a century or more is not prone to critical reevaluations of how that Army or that Depot conducts its business. To question the modus operandi of the Army was to assault the town itself.

He had seen it in Tooele, where that mind-set was enhanced by an inbred Mormon reluctance to question authority. He had seen it in Pine Bluff, where there might as well have been billboards that proclaimed ENVIRONMENTALIST, DON'T LET THE SUN SET ON YOUR ASS. And he had seen it in Anniston, where the Army had been the largest employer for generations, and where agitation against incineration was lumped into the same category as agitating against the Depot—the same sort of reasoning by which people who oppose war are assumed to oppose the troops dispatched to fight that war. Just because someone disagrees with the premise for war doesn't mean he doesn't pray for the safety and success of the men and women in harm's way; someone who fears that the Army may be following an ill-advised chem-demil policy isn't necessarily anti-Army and/or anti-Depot. But that is a difficult distinction to draw in a setting where emotions are exacerbated by long-held perceptions about economics and history, not to mention a deep fear of change.

Moreover, Williams knew you only had to do some very broad demographic math to get a sense of what opposition voices like Brenda Lindell's were up against. The Anniston Army Depot in the 1980s and 1990s employed about five thousand people. Factor in the immediate families of those employees, and you could most likely triple that number. Throw in extended family and close friends and others who operated in the swirl of the Depot—those who knew full well when "Bynum payday" rolled around, because much of their own prosperity depended on it—and you could probably triple that figure yet again. And you began to look at a number approaching fifty thousand people in a county of about a hundred thousand. Not all of those people marched in lockstep, of course, but it was a daunting thing to consider.

That sort of saturation made it extremely difficult not only for activists to gain traction but for elected officials to consider the concept of incineration on its merits and demerits. It meant very tough going for politicians such as Calhoun County Commissioner Eli Henderson, a gregarious bantam rooster (or in southern speak, "banty rooster") of a man whose district encompassed West Anniston and his beloved alma mater Wellborn High School. After serving in the Marines, Henderson worked at the Depot for twenty-four years; many of his sixteen siblings were also on the Depot payroll at one time or another. Henderson—whose pet project was a memorial to Confederate war veterans in the rural village of Ohatchee—was a classic, impossible-not-to-like country politician who still drank beer with his buddies at the Eagles Lodge on Friday nights and seemed to know every human being who had ever drawn breath in Calhoun County, who their daddies were, and the names of their daddies' dogs. As much as anyone, he appreciated the chromosomal nature of the Depot's influence on the life and times of his district; the Anniston Army Depot essentially was his political base, and he knew to tread carefully whenever the facility was at issue.

For Henderson, in the early going at least, the question of incineration was a no-brainer. He had handled the chemical weapons stored there himself, had lived in and around those igloos for years, in one legendary incident had had GB pelt his protective suit like a sudden summer rain. He was for incineration 100 percent, primarily because his experience taught him that to move the weapons elsewhere was doomsday behavior. Plus he trusted the Army—he had served in the military himself, had made working at the Depot his career before he was summoned by politics. Ultimately he would change his mind about that trust, and would become a case study in just how much gumption and tolerance for frustration it took to contend with the Army on what amounted to its home turf. But if challenging the Army was difficult for Eli Henderson, who surely qualified for the blue-collar hall of fame in Calhoun County, then for the likes of Craig Williams and Brenda Lindell it looked to be damn near impossible.

Then there was the *Anniston Star*. A Vegas line on the liberal, contrarian *Star* editorial page allying itself with the pro-incineration groupthink would probably have been a number containing several digits-to-one. But support incineration the *Star* did, with a fervor that amazed the paper's longtime observers and with a sarcastic rancor toward incineration opponents that was equally striking. In a fairly typical editorial, the *Star* in 1995 weighed in on a pledge by the Legal Environmental Assistance Foundation, or LEAF, to

> protect our community from toxic pollution by the Army's proposed incinerator. That's nice. Would the lawyers like to suit up in the hot and heavy protective gear and do the real work of protecting us from chemical weapons leaks already here?
>
> ... LEAF would block disposal of nerve agent in rockets and other munitions stored in considerable quantities at Anniston Army Depot. The rockets are notoriously leak-prone and cause legitimate fear of spontaneous ignition because of their age and uncertain decay rate.
>
> The M-55 rocket designed for mass casualty rates does not respond well to legal writ, does not obey a court injunction. So perhaps this latest legal "dream team" and homegrown critics of weapons disposal alike would wear the sweaty rubber outfits required for clean-up and disaster response. The danger from unstable weapons, after all, will only get worse as opposition delays timely disposal.
>
> A distinct lack of realism marks many opponents to incineration.... Incineration might not have been everyone's idea of a perfect solution but remains the soonest acceptable way our community can climb out of the box of nerve agent that leaks from canisters like venom dripping from a viper's fangs. That image is real.
>
> Not so true is the opposition's intellectually dishonest harping on "alternative technology" that is not developed, tested and applicable to large scale projects like Anniston's on a responsible timetable.
>
> ... A disinformation campaign party orchestrated by activists

who do not even live here has persuaded some well-meaning residents that our community is better off to delay destroying the toxic threat that rattles and slithers here in the box we live in. . . . Realism calls for getting rid of what threatens us. Who would sit and stare at a coiled rattlesnake until it decided to bite? The creature won't listen to legal debate. The romance of protest movement won't stop the strike from coming.

The time is here to dispatch this snake and quit imagining there is some painless way to remove the fangs while we're in this box.

Some months later, when Judge Campbell in Salt Lake City denied the request by the Chemical Weapons Working Group to issue an injunction against starting the burn in Tooele, the *Star* was quick to assail Anniston opponents with the news.

It is safer to burn than to keep storing chemical weapons in arsenals like Anniston Army Depot. The truth keeps coming back like an eternal flame.

Now a federal judge has told environmental groups that she won't block incineration at another Army depot in Utah. The disposal furnace could ignite this week.

The law will not override what science and common sense keep telling Anniston: We're better off to light a match to our nerve and blister agent and their explosive containers under extremely controlled circumstance than to keep storing the leaky and volatile threat in our own midst.

The opposition looks petulant, stubborn, counterproductive. The essence of good environmentalism is a poison-free Earth for human habitation, and incineration opponents are on the wrong side of public safety.

... It's time for opponents to quit heckling the progress of our community's torch of freedom from threat of chemical weapons.

A week later, three events occurred on one very busy day: the Tooele burn began, an explosion occurred at a military ammo dump in Texas, and two public hearings on incineration were convened in Anniston. The *Star* took note, arguing that

Scary coincidence drives home the point: Incineration opponents tempt the tragedy of our lives.

While a U.S. Army disposal plant yesterday began burning Utah weapons identical to missiles stored in Anniston, an ammo magazine at a third military depot burned uncontrollably.

What if? What if the accident that blew the door off that Texarkana storage bunker had ignited chemical weapons similar to our own stockpile instead of threatening conventional artillery rounds?

... We and the military run together in a race to dispose of the leaky and volatile nerve agent munitions stored in our midst. But while civilian and Defense Department engineers at Tooele lit up the fire that pioneers weapons destruction here, activists were agitating against incineration at two public meetings in Anniston last night.

They have the right. They also have no sense of the moral import of their opposition to incineration. How devastating for them personally and ethically if an actual accident locally and not merely the Texarkana portent of one here proves exactly how wrong they are. What a terrible consequence to live with.

... Incineration opponents have it wrong. How hard it must be for them to admit.

Let the news of the week do it for them: The facts show a conventional weapons storage blaze took place at one Army depot, raising the dread "what if?" question. An exquisitely engineered burn at the same time began safely eliminating the chemical weapons threat in Utah. Fail-safes work.

And the Anniston Army Depot stockpile still sits mute at the center of the incineration debate, waiting to see whether we win the race for disposal or lose our lives in tragic consequence.

The anti crowd considered the editorials an outrage. *What if?* What if a malfunction prompted a deadly leak? What if an explosion occurred within the incinerator and sparked a billowing toxic fire? Whose hands would be slathered in blood then? The weapons had existed in a virtual vacuum for more than forty years. No one was arguing that the arms be left there indefinitely (in any case, the United States was obligated by treaty to destroy them). But where was the harm in spending more time to fully contemplate the potential of neutralization? Neutralization was being seriously considered in Aberdeen, Newport, Pueblo, and Lexington. Were the players at those sites all idiots? Was there not even room for reasonable discussion?

To be fair, the *Star* was no rubber stamp for the Army and its machinations, despite its pro-incineration vehemence. One of the foundations of the paper's support for incineration was assurances that the facility would never be used to eliminate any weapons other than those stored at the Anniston Army Depot. This issue had flared in 1995, when Colorado senators Hank Brown and Ben Nighthorse Campbell tried to require the Army to revive the concept of transporting chemical weapons by rail from depot storage centers to "regional" incinerators—namely, Tooele and Anniston. That notion, as it turned out, had been the Army's concept of choice according to a 1993 environmental report by the Army's Chemical Materiel Destruction Agency. The Army estimated that some fifty-five rail shipments would be required nationally to move the chemical stockpile to the two sites. The report noted that the Army had safely moved chemical weapons since World War II without incident and as recently as 1990, when 435 tons of nerve agent were moved by truck, rail, and boat halfway around the world from Germany to Johnston Atoll. The Colorado senators depicted their move to reopen the weapons-transfer debate as rooted in concern over the spiraling costs of the demil program, but it was also viewed as simply a maneuver to get the weapons out of their backyard and let someone else assume the risk of disposal.

Brown and Campbell went so far as to write a weapons-transfer study into the fiscal 1996 defense budget bill, but Alabama Democratic congressman Glen Browder, Bill Nichols's successor and a member of the influential National Security Committee, managed to quash the provision. The fear was that Anniston could become a national dumping ground for chemical weapons, "another Emelle"—a south Alabama toxic waste dump that notoriously accepted shipments from around the country for many years and was reported to have shadowy financial connections to George Wallace via his unsavory businessman brother Gerald.

So when the Army began to lobby in the late 1990s to leave open an option to bring outside weapons into the Anniston Army Depot, the *Star* waded in:

> The Army reached all the way back to Julius Caesar for its divide-and-conquer tactics against us, living in the shadow of its chemical weapons.
>
> Didn't work.
>
> The consensus emerging group by group, leader by leader is

that we don't want any more nerve agent or other military chemicals shipped into Calhoun County. We have plenty already.

That's why we made a social compact to accept incineration as the fastest, safest way to reduce the existing stockpile to zero.

Our understanding was clear: The Army wouldn't ship any more weapons here, wouldn't extend the life of the incinerator for other purposes and wouldn't try to make us the assembly area for its problem of disposable munitions.

Endless Pentagon assurances won our agreement, if not exactly our trust—for good reason.

. . . If the Army wants to operate its permit peacefully, the Pentagon better stick by its bargain.

We've done our share, struck our devilish bargain, and don't like the nervy way the Army has been shopping around. . . . Army finagling has succeeded in uniting us against a common enemy, its attempt to circumvent consensus. It takes a lot to make Calhoun County of one mind, but military deviousness did it.

But that stance was a rare exception to the *Star*'s policy of giving no quarter to Army and incineration critics. Most of the *Star*'s editorials on the subject were written by then–editorial page editor Chris Waddle, a veteran news executive who had come to Anniston from the *Kansas City Times* in the mid-1980s. Waddle was usually the smartest person in the room, and knew it; that self-awareness often caused grinding conflict with those he worked with, especially when he first came to the paper as managing editor. But his was a formidable, influential presence, and during his tenure as editorial page czar he brought to his opinion writing the same slashing, no-room-for-argument style that his worst critics said he employed as a newsroom manager. Waddle enthusiastically quarterbacked the *Star*'s hard line on the incinerator, which he explained as nothing more than a position grounded in good horse sense and supplemented by science and history. If that disappointed the sansculottes among the readership, tough shit. As for his cutting treatment of incineration opponents, he offered no apologies.

Williams, Lindell, and others of the loyal opposition were left to bat around theories about why the *Star* took such an uncompromising stance in favor of incineration; it mystified them that a newspaper with such a well-earned reputation for pounding away at the establishment as if it were a railroad spike would, in this once-in-a-lifetime, high-stakes, history-altering instance, take the path of least resistance. Some believed that Brandy Ayers, distracted by extensive traveling and by consorting with Washington-axis types, was exerting less of his influence on the paper, a void that Waddle had happily filled. (A focused Brandy never would have bought this bill of goods, the argument went.) Others wondered if the *Star* was simply being stubborn, having staked out a position and then burrowing ahead, blinders on, unwilling to admit that its position might be too closed-minded. Still another, much less gracious theory held that the *Star* had simply paid heed to the fear-mongering promulgated by the Army about the insanity of pursuing any option other than incineration, and used that as an excuse to accede to its own economic self-interest. Wasn't the *Star* just as interested as anyone in keeping the Depot and its payroll up and running? The gargantuan investment the incinerator represented obviously presented a very convenient means to that end. It was one thing to endorse George McGovern for president, or to catapult boulders at George Wallace and his ilk from beyond the parapets. But to engage in messy hand-to-hand combat over something that history might judge very harshly—well, that took real guts. Maybe when it came down to it, the *Star* didn't have the prerequisite sap.

But that was all speculation. The bottom line was that Waddle and the *Star* were launching great searing balls of flame at the opponents of incineration, and it made the going that much tougher. But as Williams liked to say: Deal with it. You want easy, start a book club.

As it happened, 1997 was a pivotal year—perhaps *the* pivotal year—in the extended wrestling match that was the debate over what to do with chemical weapons in Anniston.

Much was happening. The U.S. Senate ratified the Convention on the Prohibition of the Development, Production, Stockpiling and Use of Chemical Weapons and on Their Destruction—commonly known as the Chemical Weapons Convention. This was essentially a preordained event; eleven years earlier, Congress had directed the Department of Defense to destroy the nation's chemical stockpile "in a safe manner," and the DOD in turn directed the Army to set up and operate the chemical demilitarization program. These events were parallel to a series of global conferences among a consortium of nations that harbored chemical weapons, during which it was agreed that the use of chemical weapons would be prohibited and a deadline of April 2007 established to destroy the existing stockpiles. There were some notable absences from these discussions—Iraq being one—but the United States, Russia, and more than 150 other nations signed on to the historic treaty that aimed to rid the world of a manmade scourge that had been a cruel and dastardly last resort of war for centuries.

But 1997 was also the year when significant fissures, both operational and political, began to show in the Army's incineration initiative in the United States. Technological headaches, permit snafus, administrative confusion from the Pentagon down to the disposal sites—all contributed to what had become (and would continue to be) a perpetual pushback of the program's projected completion date and ever-escalating cost estimates. In a series of reports, the GAO recounted management and organizational "weaknesses" that were exacerbating the situation. Moreover, the Chemical Weapons Working Group and other pro–alternative technology forces had begun to score some remarkable advances. Incineration might already have begun at Johnston Atoll in 1993 and at Tooele in 1996, but neutralization either had been or was on the verge of being instituted as the sole method of disposal at the sites in Maryland and Indiana, where bulk agent only—no assembled chemical weapons—was stored.

Neutralization was a much easier sell at the bulk-storage sites for a number of reasons, the obvious one being that rockets, bombs, and other explosively armed agent containers did not enter into the disposal equation. And yet, in a stunning coup by Craig Williams and other anti-incineration interests, support began to form behind a congressional bill spearheaded by McConnell in 1997 that set aside funds for the development of alternative disposal technologies like neutralization and to create a separate chain of command within the Department of Defense to isolate the program from what Williams referred to as "the incineration mentality."

The bill contained yet another landmark provision: a moratorium on the expenditure of federal funds for incineration. The intent and potential of the bill was clear: to halt the further development of the Army's incineration program pending further review. That provision, however, was not written in stone. Politics being politics, the moratorium language was offered, delegation by delegation, to the Senate and House members who represented the disposal sites in Kentucky, Colorado, Oregon, Arkansas, and Alabama. The Kentucky and Colorado delegations—those in whose districts, not coincidentally, the pro-alternative factions were strongest—accepted the provision.

The representatives from Oregon, Arkansas, and Alabama did not. Thus the final version of the bill passed by Congress established an incineration moratorium in Kentucky and Colorado only, with no restrictions in Alabama and the other remaining states.

The passage of that bill proved to be a portentous fork in the road for all concerned. Anti-incineration advocates promptly gained enormous leverage in Kentucky and Colorado. Meanwhile, in Anniston, Pine Bluff, and Umatilla, the Army moved ahead quickly. In Alabama, the Army in short order secured its long-sought building permit from the Alabama Department of Environmental Management (ADEM) and expeditiously awarded a $575 million construction contract to the Westinghouse Corporation—which essentially guaranteed that incineration would be the disposal method of choice in Anniston.

It was a huge victory for the Army. The odds were now stacked heavily in its favor. It was, concurrently, a devastating loss for Williams, Lindell, and others in the Anniston anti-incineration camp—and they knew it. Chemical weapons disposal in Anniston was headed almost irreversibly down the path of incineration—and with every additional step taken along that path, with every additional square foot of concrete poured, with every additional wall that was raised, with every additional employee hired, the challenge of stopping the process became that much greater. There was still hope, but the hill to climb had suddenly grown from the dimensions of Mount Cheaha to those of Mount Everest.

In the postmortem that followed, it seemed to Williams that convincing the Alabama delegation to agree to the moratorium had probably been a nonstarter anyway. Alabama's senators at the time were Howell Heflin and Richard Shelby, both Democrats (although Shelby, acutely attuned to the shifting political wind, would soon renounce the Democratic Party and join the GOP in midterm). The portly, suspender-swathed Heflin, a walking jowl of an elder southern statesman who had charmed a great many TV junkies during the Iran-Contra hearings, was in decline and unwilling to roil the waters. Shelby, preoccupied with self-preservation, wouldn't touch it. Congressman Glen Browder, a former political science professor at Jacksonville State, had nibbled around the edges of the anti-incineration argument but ultimately steered clear. (Browder finally grew sufficiently weary of the battering he took from incineration opponents that he staged a press conference at which he displayed four pitchers of tinted water that dramatized the amount of nerve agent in an M-55 rocket—his point being that a mere drop was deadly. The *Star* promptly praised Browder as the "most realistic and reasonable public official in the decade or more we've been having this nerve agent disposal debate.") In the final analysis, no one came close to stepping up—a predictable result, Williams figured, given the Anniston landscape, which was strewn not only with the obstacles thrown up by a populace obsessed with the military status quo, but with the spent mortar rounds left by an antagonistic newspaper hell-bent on mowing down anyone who dared disagree.

CHAPTER THIRTEEN

BE IT THEREFORE RESOLVED

By early 2003 the Anniston incinerator was built and personnel were in place and in training—some three years behind schedule. The original cost projection of $575 million had risen to nearly one billion, to the shock of mostly no one. But the job was nearly done, and the result was a towering, expansive, muscular-looking marvel that gleamed in the white winter sunshine and drew throngs of public officials, local residents, and the just curious, who streamed through on tours sponsored by the Depot and touted in the *Anniston Star*. Once past the guard station, which bristled with an electric, post-9/11 vigilance, visitors were bused down a narrow access road that provided a sweeping view of rows and rows of concrete igloos framed by the giant new edifice in the distance, the igloos jutting up like gravestones in some timeless cemetery set anachronistically next to a sparkling new crematorium of cathedralesque proportions. It was a strange vision come to life in the quiet pine forest, a scene that gave testimony to the stark reality that the weapons were not just a generations-old myth, but fact—weapons that would soon be reduced to a flinty ash at 2,700 degrees Fahrenheit, risk be hanged.

That realization was beginning to settle in among the local leadership as well. Paying special attention was the Calhoun County Commission, which by virtue of its traditional purview over the county's emergency services operations—the 911 system, disaster response, and the like—found itself in charge of making sure that the area surrounding the incinerator was adequately prepared in the event of "the unthinkable." That meant negotiating with a tangled web of governmental agencies about issues ranging from fire department upgrades to establishing zones for disaster response to installing a state-of-the-art emergency notification system.

The general feeling among the various groups that were watch-dogging the safety preparation program was that the commission had been slow on the uptake. Eli Henderson had spent most of his time in the early going trying to help the Army push ahead; he went so far as to print bumper stickers that proclaimed BUILD IT, BURN IT, FORGET IT, a slogan that was taken up by the *Star* and other supporters of incineration. The only voice on the commission that expressed consistent concern about the incinerator and whether the community was adequately prepared for the burn was Robert Downing, known universally as RD, an immensely popular Anniston figure in his late forties who grew up on the middle-class East Side and exhibited environmentalist leanings from his first race, when he upset an entrenched incumbent and gave away thousands of tomato plants to voters as a campaign gimmick. Downing had had his doubts about the Army's plans all along, and would quickly offer his support when Henderson's disillusionment with the Army flowered in full.

The problem wasn't with what the Army agreed to do. The Army and the rest of the federal government had agreed to do plenty, to the tune of $140 million—including $55 million to retrofit public buildings and, in an unprecedented concession, to over-pressurize schools in the so-called pink zone, a six-mile radius immediately surrounding the Depot. (Another pink zone perk: free gas masks for the zone's thirty-five thousand residents. It marked the first time in U.S. history that the government had issued gas masks to civilians, and proved to be a news photographer's dream. Images of children and the elderly wearing the bubblelike hoods saturated the national wires.)

The problem was that the clock was ticking, and the Pentagon brass was getting cranky. Depending upon which estimate one chose to believe, the Army stood to lose from $250,000 to a million dollars each day the incinerator sat inactive while the various agencies and contractors involved worked to satisfy the safety requirements mandated by the commission and signed off on by the Army. The Army began to push for concessions, arguing that the latest-generation incinerator that had been constructed in Anniston was more than safe enough to operate while school overpressurization and other tasks were completed. This infuriated Henderson, for one, who was beginning to feel heat about safety precautions even from his normally blasé constituents at the Depot, and besides, the Army seemed to be going back on its word. What if the commission signed off on a start-up and an accident occurred before all the safety measures were in place? Eli's district, squarely in the pink zone, would bear the brunt—and even if he were to survive, his little banty-rooster ass would be political road kill. He began to circulate a new slogan: THEY BUILT IT, WANT TO BURN IT AND FORGOT ABOUT US.

Technically, the Army did not need the commission's okay to begin the Anniston burn. But it direly needed some form of political body armor before firing up the incinerator with safety obligations left undone. It also needed a burn permit from ADEM. As far as that went, the consensus was that the Army had met the relatively modest standards required by law that were a prerequisite for the issuance of that permit. But much like the Army, ADEM director James Warr was holding off, looking for a nod from the county commission, the state congressional delegation, the governor, the dogcatcher—anybody. A classic political stalemate had developed, costing the Army a fortune at a time when defense spending was under the microscope due to President George W. Bush's aggressive military initiatives in Afghanistan and Iraq. It was a logjam that was making a lot of people look bad.

Quietly, the army—not an institution to take things lying down—played the BRAC card. Fort McClellan's closure had been traumatic enough for Calhoun County; any suggestion that the Anniston Army Depot might be targeted in the next BRAC round, slated for 2005, was enough to prompt fatalistic politicians and high-strung chamber executives to fondle revolvers gloomily in remote cabins in the woods. Except it wasn't terribly logical on its face, this whispered linkage between the incinerator and BRAC. The closure process wasn't designed to be a vengeful bludgeon wielded by the Pentagon but rather a calm, ordered, objective undertaking based on the merits of each military installation and its quantifiable contributions to the national defense. To promote just that sort of level-playing-field atmosphere, the members of the base closure commission were appointed not only by the president but by a wide range of congressional leaders to dilute the role of favoritism in the proceedings. Horse leavings, Anniston's BRAC-scarred leaders replied in unison. The list of bases to be considered for closure would be compiled and submitted to BRAC members by Secretary of Defense Donald Rumsfeld himself. Did anyone really believe that the perpetually rankled Rumsfeld was so above the politics of retribution that he would resist the urgings of his Pentagon drinking buddies to place a problem child like Anniston on the dreaded list of recommended closures? Did anyone truly buy the argument that a refusal by Anniston's political leaders to line up behind the Army—and by extension Rumsfeld—and the push to ignite the incinerator ASAP would have no bearing on whether the Depot was considered for the closure list? And if anyone believed that, what sort of mad chronic were they smoking, and could they get some for everybody?

No, too much had happened to ignore a threat, no matter how covertly or subtly conveyed, that the burn delay in Anniston might affect the very existence of the Anniston Army Depot. Those gullible souls who had ascribed to the religion of process had assured all the catastrophic thinkers in 1999 that Fort McClellan was safe. Not only did its chemical weapons school and military police training center make it indispensable to the American mission, it wasn't even *on the list* of recommended closures. But then they could only watch in *Hindenberg*-like horror as the Red River Arsenal in Texas was taken off the list and replaced with McClellan—all this orchestrated by Missouri commission members who were protecting their own backyard. So the process wasn't political? Now the talk was that the next round might come down, again, to Red River vs. Anniston—and how comfortable did everyone in Alabama feel about those odds with former Texas governor Bush in the White House? Where, exactly, was the tipping point?

The heat was pounding down in all directions. The chamber of commerce insisted that Mike Rogers, an ambitious Republican from the Saks community in north Anniston who had assumed the old Nichols congressional seat, do something. Rogers, who was also suffering the Army's lash, in turn twisted the crank on Henderson, who was now being stalked on all sides by Depot employees and legions more who were worried about either the incinerator safety issues or the Depot's survival—or both. U.S. Senator Jeff Sessions, a conservative Republican who now occupied Howell Heflin's old seat, was sympathetic to the Army's concerns but wasn't willing to get out in front of any parade to absolve the chem-demil forces of safety requirements. Sessions's fellow senator Richard Shelby was no help either—in fact, he was busy holding the Army accountable, grabbing headlines with an open letter that demanded that the Army quit stalling and "expeditiously" get to the task of fulfilling its commitments or risk his ire. It was not a threat to be taken lightly. Shelby sat on the Senate's Defense Appropriatns Subcommittee and, even more significantly, the powerful Appropriations Committee itself.

Meanwhile, Anniston was becoming the focus of an increasingly belligerent out-of-town press. "Nerve Gas Nightmare" (the *Birmingham News*) and "Alabamians Fear Chemical Disaster" (*USA Today*) were but two typical headlines above a rash of stories that detailed the growing swirl around the incinerator start-up. *Newsweek* said the situation "raises troubling health and environmental issues, and—against a backdrop of a looming war against Iraq over its alleged stockpiling of chemical weapons—Anniston offers a portrait of the United States' own worrisome handling of such weapons." The press seemed to be nearing full boil, and no one was anxious to be the wedge-buster who opened the door for the burn to begin.

Amid all this media scrutiny, the *Star* was a Prozac dispenser. Waddle, at the paper's expense, traveled with Chip Howell and a handful of others in March to Johnston Atoll to witness the dismantling of the incinerator there—an apparent happy ending to a successful chemical weapons burn. Waddle returned home and produced an extensive first-person narrative headlined "Life Triumphs in a Chemical Hell." He began,

> Doubting Thomas never traveled so far. I felt the wounds. I saw where spear points of Alabama-like chemical weapons burned away to harmless ash. I went the distance to peer ahead in time [to] when Anniston's nerve agent will be evaporated into nothingness too.
>
> Life aplenty is what I discovered—safe, secure joy. . . .

Finally a strategy was cooked up among Rogers, Sessions, and Les Brownlee, the acting secretary of the Army. It was decided that Brownlee would task a consortium of staff from the various federal regulatory agencies involved to prepare a "memorandum of agreement," the goal of which was to provide a sufficient case to get past the safety issues still outstanding in Anniston. The signatories would be Brownlee; the director of FEMA; and Alabama governor Bob Riley, a Republican who was early in his first term and who at that juncture had been a subdued voice in the incineration saga.

Riley most likely knew what he was doing, as a former congressman who had succeeded Browder and preceded Rogers as the representative for the Anniston district and well aware of the bruising incinerator debate. Besides, Riley had his hands full: To the utter apoplexy of his right-wing base, he had proposed a package of reform measures that not only would raise state taxes by some 22 percent but also gut Alabama's unconscionable constitution and effectively redistribute money from wealthy interests to the working poor. This from a politician who once was voted the most conservative member of Congress and had body-surfed that reputation into the governor's mansion. The mere whiff of a tax increase is enough to elevate pulse rates in Alabama; Riley's radical proposal was an unmitigated gasket-blower. The governor was suddenly presiding over a mutiny, and probably wasn't especially obsessed with Anniston's incinerator drama.

The memorandum was produced. The Army and FEMA happily signed on and forwarded the document to Montgomery. There was one problem: Riley, correctly deducing the obvious—that he was being set up as the fall guy—refused to sign it. Why was he the only official from Alabama whose signature would appear on the document? Where was everybody else? Riley knew he wasn't legally required to sign off on the incinerator start-up. Despite that, if he did sign it, and if the Army proceeded and then an accident occurred . . . then he was in a sling, for no practical purpose that he could discern. Still, Riley wasn't totally unsympathetic to the Army's plight, and understood as well as anyone the BRAC ramifications of the situation. He made a counteroffer: give me the power to shut down the facility at my discretion, and I'll sign it. The Army flatly refused.

And there the matter sat, coals glowing. Tim Garrett, the operations manager at the Anniston incinerator, let it be known that he was preparing a list of employees to be laid off. The message from the Army seemed clear enough: *If you don't think we'll mothball this son of a bitch, just watch.*

Watching all this from his not-so-distant remove was Chip Howell, who was growing more frustrated with every delay and dead end and debacle. There was no quibbling about the mayor's position: Let the burning begin. Sure, he was concerned about safety. He was especially concerned about the "special needs" population, the folks who were disabled, or didn't own a car, or were elderly and didn't have anyone to look after them. Efforts were being made to identify these people and deliver the masks and other safety equipment to their homes, and it was a good and noble thing to do.

Chip was for every safety measure. Who wasn't? Gas masks? Fine. Overpressurize schools? Wonderful idea. Bring it all on. But he was also a realist. In the event of an honest-to-God catastrophe at the Depot—something he viewed as virtually impossible, but let's just say—how much protection would any of these precautions really provide? If a giant toxic plume were to envelop West Anniston, the gas masks and home shelter kits and all the rest probably weren't going to save too many folks. To be brutally honest about it, the safety precautions that had been squabbled over for years and that had cost so much money . . . well, they were more or less there to make people feel better about things. According to the safety protocols that had been published ad nauseum in the *Star* and elsewhere, people would have only about eight minutes—*eight minutes*—to get out of range or don their masks or scramble to their "safe rooms" (consisting of plastic sheeting taped over the windows). How many people would be able to meet that standard? How many people would be able to properly affix their protective equipment? How many people would even know where their equipment *was*? By the time you pulled the stuff from behind the Christmas decorations out in the garage, the party would be over.

Chip also knew that only about half the people who were eligible for safety equipment had even gone to the trouble to pick it up. He had not bothered to get his. His comfort level was such that he didn't feel the trouble was worth it. These guys knew what they were doing. He had visited Tooele back in 1993, when he was president of the chamber of commerce. He had visited Johnston Atoll back in the spring. The Anniston incinerator was more advanced by half than either of those. The Army had proved to his satisfaction that the burn was a long sight safer than letting the weapons rot, although it wasn't helping matters that the Tooele facility had been shut down for several months while an investigation was conducted into a sarin exposure that had injured a worker. But the bottom line was that Chip knew that a great many people in Anniston and Calhoun County felt as he did. A recent public opinion survey had shown that 49 percent of the people queried supported incineration. He had no doubt that if people had had the opportunity to study the process as he had, support would be much higher. As it was, he didn't detect a great groundswell of fear or even concern among the people he dealt with every day. Someone had told him about an elderly woman who had appeared at the distribution center to pick up her safety equipment. She fidgeted impatiently through the presentation and confided to the woman seated next to her that the real reason she had shown up was that she heard the home shelter kit contained scissors. She needed a new pair. Otherwise, she said, she wouldn't have bothered.

To Chip, the negotiations over the safety issues and the burn permit and everything else seemed to be getting out of hand. The Army was upset. The specter of BRAC was rearing its head. A lot of bad press was radiating across the state and the country that made Anniston look like a chemical wasteland. And that was atop a wad of negative publicity surrounding the PCB litigation now in full swing, including a front-page story in the *Washington Post* and a *60 Minutes* piece that had made Anniston seem like something out of that *Erin Brockovich* movie. But the most acid insult had come in 2002 when *Forbes Magazine* and the Milken Foundation released their joint list of the "Best Places to Live," which included a separate category for the lowest-rated cities. Among smaller cities, Anniston ranked dead last in the United States—generating a series of "worst places to live" stories that circulated widely. It all added up to a very tangible battering of local morale. "Maybe this will wake some people up," Anniston resident Laron Evans was quoted as saying in a story that ran over the Associated Press wires. "I have lived in Anniston my whole life, but if someone else read that, there is no way they would want to move here. This used to be a place that people wanted to move to, but it's not anymore." *Marketplace,* the daily business program broadcast on National Public Radio, began one report this way:

> There is that old saw that any publicity is good publicity, as long as they spell your name right. Well, that might be a little hard to believe in Anniston, Alabama. That's A-N-N-I-S-T-O-N, by the way. The city's gotten plenty of bad press and a reputation to match, and that has hurt business. . . .

The frustrating thing for Chip was that the City of Anniston, due to the county commission's obligatory role as lead negotiator, didn't have a seat at the table. As the endgame progressed, the mayor had no voice in the proceedings. As the entire situation teetered at the edge of an abyss, Chip decided that the time had come to insinuate himself. If the Army needed cover, then he would do his best to provide it.

His rationale was clear. The controversy over the incinerator was threatening to have a quicksand effect on the many positive things happening in Anniston. A development strategy was coming together for the old Fort McClellan reservation. A multimillion-dollar renovation project along Noble Street had been kick-started. And in Chip's mind, an operating incinerator would be another positive in and of itself. Industry officials looking to invest in Anniston could be assured that the chemical weapons issue was being addressed, that in a few years the disposal process would be complete. He felt certain that once the incinerator flipped the switch, the debate and the media interest would drift away. But as long as this current debacle continued, Anniston would be the subject of anxious stories about nerve agent and gas masks. One photograph that ran in the *Los Angeles Times* showed a young African-American boy smiling for the camera through the transparent plastic of his protective hood. The image had an ominous, creepy, *War of the Worlds* feel to it. What parent would want to move to Anniston and place a child in a situation like that? It was killing the town.

Chip also believed that the threat of the Army pulling the plug on the incinerator if the delay continued was very real. He had developed a good working relationship with Tim Garrett, the head honcho at the plant, and Garrett had leveled with him: the Army and Westinghouse were within just a few weeks of laying people off. There was no choice in the matter. The expense of inactivity was too great to bear. The Anniston incinerator was a billion-dollar facility that due to the squabbling had basically been rendered nonfunctional. Layoffs represented a slippery slope that could precipitate an indefinite suspension of operations. The incinerators in Arkansas and Oregon were in varying stages of completion. Those operations were reaching the point of hiring their own engineers and other technical specialists, and the pool of people qualified and trained to work in chem-demil was relatively small. If Anniston were to shut down, the talent that had been recruited there would understandably be forced to examine its options elsewhere. The Anniston burn could be sidelined for many months, throwing the disposal completion into further chaos.

There were plenty of naysayers, as Chip was well aware—the Craig Williamses out there who didn't buy this worst-case scenario and contended that the Army couldn't be trusted and was crying wolf. They were the same people who didn't put much stock in the whole BRAC scare either, who dismissed it as just a convenient way for the military brass to soften community resistance. If the Pentagon was going to push for the closure of the Anniston Depot out of incinerator-related vindictiveness, the argument went, that threshold had probably been passed already. The radical extension of that line of thinking was that if the Depot was deep-sixed, so much the better; that way the town could get on with the business of growing up and no longer suckle at the teat of the military. The result would be an Anniston that would be forced to diversify its industrial base, and one that didn't have to kiss the ass of every general who wandered through. This view, however, was akin to outlawing football in the eyes of most people around town.

But Chip gave credence to the layoff threats, and he gave credence to the worries about BRAC. He would say much later that to him it was "obvious if you make life difficult and insinuate to a group of people that they are not appreciated or wanted . . . let's just say there are communities out there that will kill and die to maintain what they have." If yours is not one of those communities, then you should prepare to be left behind. And if you think logic will carry the day, then please refer to "Fort McClellan" in your real-world manuals. Chip had no doubt that the Anniston Depot was the best at what it did. More than any other Depot in the country, it had pioneered public-private partnerships to enhance its cash flow. Its tank repair operation and Stryker maintenance project promised to be indispensable as the war in Iraq evolved. But so what if your worker productivity was off the charts? So what if you had the best M1A rebuild program in the world? Chip had watched as the chemical and MP schools at McClellan, both models of efficiency and value, were snatched away like purses from defenseless old women. If that could happen, anything could.

Three or four times a year, the mayors of Calhoun County's seven municipalities met quietly to discuss common concerns. During the past year or so, the incinerator had been a dominant topic of discussion. Chip knew from these discussions that each mayor agreed with him that incineration was the right choice and that the sooner the burn started, the better. Armed with that knowledge, Chip hatched a plan and began placing calls to the mayors. His message to each was the same: It's time to do something; will you support me? And they agreed, to a man.

So Chip went home, sat down, and started preparing a resolution. He worked late, sporadically calling a friend for counsel. Shortly after midnight, he was satisfied with what he had put together. The next day, he faxed over a copy of the document to each mayor, asking for input. One mayor suggested a small change, which was incorporated. Chip then had his secretary prepare the resolution on official-looking paper with an ornate border that emanated gravitas. It read:

WHEREAS, for many decades, the Calhoun County area has enjoyed a close working relationship with the U.S. Army and the Department of Defense; and

WHEREAS, the Army has provided employment, cultural events and activities, and support for community organizations; and

WHEREAS, in exchange, the community provided dedicated workers and a willingness to live in the shadow of a chemical weapons stockpile; and

WHEREAS, these communities are in close proximity to the Anniston Army Depot, in which over 2,200 tons of chemical agent are stored; and

WHEREAS, the continued storage of these agents poses a danger to area residents that increases each day as the weapons continue to degrade; and

WHEREAS, the means to safely destroy such chemicals, a state-of-the-art third generation facility with a highly qualified and trained work force, stands ready to begin the process of eliminating the chemical stockpile through incineration; and

WHEREAS, incineration has proven a safe and efficient disposal process, having successfully destroyed over 9,000 tons of chemical agent in other communities with no loss of life, serious injury or adverse health or environmental consequences; and

BE IT THEREFORE RESOLVED that we, the Calhoun County Council of Mayors, urge any and all state, federal and local agencies, as well as private sector groups, to eliminate any impediments that would further delay the incineration of the chemical stockpile.

WITNESS our hands this 28ᵗʰ day of May 2003.

The resolution was signed by Hoyt W. Howell Jr., Mayor of Anniston; Leon Smith, Mayor of Oxford; Robert Pyles, Mayor of Hobson City; Charlie Fagan, Mayor of Piedmont; Jerry Smith, Mayor of Jacksonville; Ed Kimbrough, Mayor of Weaver; and

Joseph Roberson, Mayor of Ohatchee. Chip secured the signatures himself, driving from city hall to city hall over the course of two days. The mayors were all on the same page. Their hands were tied from participating in the negotiation process, so this was the next best move: to apply pressure by attempting to inject public opinion.

The mayors may have had no inkling of just how successful their gambit would be.

On the day after all the signatures were collected, Chip presided over a well-attended press conference. A story quickly bolted over the AP wires. The *Star* expressed its approval. And Chip placed a strategic call to Jerre Watson, the former commander of the Fort McClellan chemical school, now retired but still living in Anniston and still beautifully connected to the Army hierarchy. Word was quickly relayed up the ladder to the Washington brass. And at the Pentagon, the 233-word resolution was seen for exactly what it was: the keys to the kingdom.

The next several days for Chip constituted a head-spinning, diplomatic-style tour that took him from Anniston to the Pentagon to the office of the governor in Montgomery. After receiving the news of the resolution, Army Secretary Brownlee immediately issued an invitation for Chip to meet with him at the Pentagon. On behalf of the city and his fellow mayors, Chip expressed his appreciation to the Army for its nearly century-long commitment to the Anniston area; Brownlee expressed his appreciation for the resolution and pledged to take full advantage. Chip left the Pentagon encouraged, and soon headed for an appointment with Governor Riley. Upon arrival at the governor's office, Chip was forced to wait for a while; Riley, he was told, was with his pastor (praying, presumably, that some higher power might keep the antitax lynch mob at bay). Once the meeting began, however, Riley greeted the resolution with great interest. Like Brownlee, the governor instantly grasped the potential of the document—if handled correctly, it could be the ticket to a start-up of the incinerator and to the dispersal of a very problematic political black cloud. The topic of discussion quickly became the issue of the yet-to-be-issued ADEM permit. Armed with a burn permit and the mayors' support, the Army very likely would make the decision to move ahead with its incineration schedule.

Riley explained to Chip that, much as Chip had no official role in the emergency response program, the governor had no official role in the ADEM permitting process. Whether the Army got its burn permit was strictly up to ADEM. But if Riley could be satisfied that the state of preparedness in Calhoun County was acceptable—then perhaps he would be willing to convey the mayors' wishes personally to Jim Warr at ADEM. Chip put Riley on the phone with the appropriate friendly people in Anniston, who updated the governor on the county's readiness. Finally Riley agreed to see what he could do.

As far as Riley and ADEM were concerned, of course, this was sheer choreography. The governor and the regulatory agency were both well aware of the resolution and its import. Some days after Chip traveled to Montgomery, Riley and Warr met for lunch. During their conversation, Riley inquired about the status of the Army's burn permit. Warr replied that there was no legal reason why the permit should not be issued. All the criteria had been met. (Not that this was a feat that defied gravity; Alabama is not noted for its exacting environmental regulations.) Riley told Warr that his mind was made up once and for all, that he was not going to sign the Memorandum of Understanding prepared by the Army. Further, if

ADEM issued the burn permit, that was the agency's call and Warr certainly wouldn't hear any carping from the governor's office. If the Army then proceeded with the burn and something went south, the mayors were on the chopping block. And suddenly, for Riley and Warr, skies were blue and birds were offering songs to heaven. Lunch was over, and both men left the table with their political interests covered, as Craig Williams would describe it, "six ways from East Jesus."

That same afternoon, ADEM issued the burn permit to the Army. The Army quickly announced it would begin to burn in a matter of weeks. Chip Howell played a crisp round of golf at the country club and figured it had all been a pretty good piece of work.

"Ready to Begin?" The *Star* posed the question in large type on Tuesday, August 5, 2003, the day before the Anniston facility was scheduled to destroy its first munitions, a cache of ninety M-55 rockets armed with GB agent. The rockets would be transferred from the pregnant igloos to a high-tech conveyor that would slowly transport the weapons into the burn area—and thus would begin the end of a Cold War menace that had called Anniston home longer than its average resident had been alive.

The usual flurry of eleventh-hour lawsuits seeking injunctions had been filed, with incineration opponent David Christian sponsoring one suit that contended, accurately, that the distribution of protective gear and overpressurization of schools was not complete. It was "good law," as the attorneys like to say, but didn't appear to have a chance. In a final lunge, an appeal was filed in federal court in Washington, and the Army held off the burn as the case was considered. Judge Thomas Penfield Jackson ruled on Friday, August 8, that there was no "imminent harm" and that the plant could begin destroying weapons. The stop-the-burn groups would grouse among themselves that if Don Siegelman, the Democrat who had preceded Riley, were still governor he would have gone to federal court himself and probably would have won a stay. But Siegelman wasn't governor and Riley still was, and Bill Nichols was still dead and Fort McClellan was still gone, and the Atlanta Braves still didn't beat the Yankees in the 1996 World Series, and the sun very likely was going to rise in the morning, and everything was the way it was and the incinerator was going to start burning.

On Saturday morning, August 10, the first rocket was pierced, drained of its sarin, chopped into eight pieces, and then roasted in a furnace. A short time later, Army officials gathered under a tent to report to a throng of press and other interested parties that the deed was done, like the warden at San Quentin who finally emerges to describe the execution of a Death Row inmate. "That rocket is now history," said incinerator spokesman Michael Abrams. "This community is now one rocket safer."

Outside the gates, a lone protestor, Rufus Kinney, complained that the court order had come so unexpectedly the day before and the Army had then acted so quickly to get started that morning that his colleagues had not had time to get organized. David Christian would later tell the *New York Times,* "We're very disappointed today. They're putting poisons in the air and we may not know for years what the effects will be."

Chip Howell watched the entire scene unfurl and reflected to himself that nobody ever said that exercising leadership was easy. A decision had been needed, he had forced one, and he was willing to live with it.

CHAPTER FOURTEEN

THE COURTHOUSE STEPS

What would Andy do?

It was a query that Judge Joel Laird often posed to himself in the course of his life and work. It wasn't a totally serious question, of course—even though Laird was a legendary fan of the old *Andy Griffith Show,* had been written up about it in the *Wall Street Journal* and the *Birmingham News,* owned one of the most impressive memorabilia collections related to the program in the country, even maintained a replica of Sheriff Taylor's patrol car in his driveway—he knew you couldn't base a personal philosophy on a TV character. Still, it was tempting. Laird found that the way people dealt with things in fictional Mayberry, North Carolina, where decency and common sense always prevailed, more often than not provided a good rule of thumb for the real world.

Laird wasn't sure how Andy would have dealt with the *Abernathy* case. But he definitely knew that Sheriff Taylor would relate to his attempts to bring peace to a trying situation. Sometimes, when Donald Stewart and one of the attorneys for the Monsanto defense team were volleying over some issue or another, clawing at Laird for a ruling, the judge would flash to a mental image of an exasperated Andy standing wordlessly amid a group of townspeople—Barney, Floyd, Gomer, Goober, Aunt Bea, maybe Clara too—while they bickered among themselves about some small-town contretemps, the sheriff's eyes raised to the sky as the music swelled and the scene faded to black. Sometimes life really did imitate art.

With the trial finally under way in early 2002, Laird was the first to confess that he had had no idea what he was getting into when he decided to allow that sleeping dog of a case file to remain in his office on that innocuous morning back in 1996. It had taken six years to get the case to trial, and frankly, Laird had hoped it would never get so far. In Laird's view, one of the most vital services a judge could provide was to keep as many cases as possible *out* of the courtroom. There was no reason most cases couldn't be settled, and settlement was usually in the best interests of all concerned. Trials were expensive and time-consuming, not only for the parties involved but for the state. And they were risky. A plaintiff with a great case might wind up with nothing. A defendant with right on his side might get taken to the cleaners. Better to compromise, shake hands, and move on.

That's what had happened in the biggest case Laird had presided over to date, when a group of Toyota dealers in the South, including an Anniston dealer, had sued the Toyota Corporation over claims of unfair business practices. In that case, Laird had finally ordered all the lawyers and their clients to appear in his courtroom for a settlement conference, including the Japanese president of Toyota USA, a Mr. Togo. The Toyota executive had impressed Laird. When, during the settlement proceeding, a Toyota attorney edgily argued a point with Laird, Togo audibly admonished him: "This man is the judge, you treat him with respect." The parties ultimately settled—the plaintiffs received a substantial sum—and Togo sent Laird a letter of thanks that the judge framed and hung on his office wall. It had been a difficult case, but everyone had worked through it and found middle ground. Togo had come to understand the risks involved with going to trial, and had directed his legal team to work something out—a prudent decision, in Laird's view, the system working at its best.

God knew he had tried to get the *Abernathy* parties to settle. From where he sat as an impartial observer, it was clearly in Solutia's best interests to settle this case. It was a land mine waiting to go off. During the long years leading up to the trial, while the defense had stalled and delayed and put him through the wringer, Laird had watched as Stewart and the New York lawyers who trailed him everywhere had intricately constructed an outstanding case. They were ready to go. Laird wasn't so sure about the defense, which had made an art form of acting as if they had everything in the bag. But Laird believed the defense was in trouble, and he had tried his best to encourage them to come to the settlement table and negotiate in earnest. He even tried the tactic that had worked in the Toyota case, ordering all the parties to his courtroom for a confidential settlement conference. But in stark contrast to Mr. Togo's air of cooperation, the Solutia executives sat in pouting silence, annoyed to be there. It seemed clear to Laird that the defense had either convinced themselves that they would prevail in the courtroom, or had simply decided that settling wasn't their best strategy. There were other suits pending out there, including Johnnie Cochran's, so perhaps they feared that settling would encourage more litigation. Whatever, the defense wasn't budging.

Laird, to be sure, kept his personal opinions about the case to himself. Given his tempestuous relationship with the defense, that policy was more appropriate than ever. It was nearly impossible to see the defense's antagonism toward him as anything other than a personal attack. "I'm human," Laird would say much later. "People try not to be human and pretend that things don't bother them. But I am what I am and I'm comfortable with that. I was bothered by it. But it just made me more determined to be as fair and impartial as I could be and keep everything on track." It was difficult to keep a steady keel; it seemed as if the defense was filing a petition to the supreme court every other day, the way a spoiled child runs to Mama when he doesn't get his way on the playground. But Laird was determined to stand his ground and rule as he saw fit. What he didn't know about the subject matter and the law related to it, he would stay up late into the night to study and learn. (And for someone who took only one science class in college—astronomy—there was a lot to learn in *Abernathy*.)

Laird was also acutely aware that the national spotlight had begun to play on the case and on Anniston. On New Year's Day, days before the trial was to begin, the lead story on page one of the *Washington Post* was an extensive article that carried the headline "Monsanto Hid Decades of Pollution," with the subhead "PCBs Drenched Alabama Town, But No One Was Ever Told." The story, by Michael Grunwald, began:

ANNISTON, Ala.—On the west side of Anniston, the poor side of Anniston, the people ate dirt. They called it "Alabama clay" and cooked it for extra flavor. They also grew berries in their gardens, raised hogs in their back yards, caught bass in the murky streams where their children swam and played and were baptized. They didn't know their dirt and yards and bass and kids—

along with the acrid air they breathed—were all contaminated with chemicals. They didn't know they lived in one of the most polluted patches of America.

Now they know. They also know that for 40 years, while producing the now-banned industrial coolants known as PCBs at a local factory, Monsanto Co. routinely discharged toxic waste into a west Anniston creek and dumped millions of pounds of PCBs into oozing open-pit landfills. And thousands of pages of Monsanto documents—many emblazoned with warnings such as CONFIDENTIAL: Read and Destroy—show that for decades, the corporate giant concealed what it did and what it knew. . . .

The article was exhaustive and devastating, and made ample use of the documents Stewart had fought to obtain. The story was crisscrossed with Stewart's tracks, in fact, and Laird saw it as an opening salvo in the plaintiffs' strategy to apply pressure to the defendants both in the courtroom and on the street—especially Wall Street. (Indeed, Solutia's stock dropped sharply on the first day of trading after the *Washington Post* article appeared.) The defense was going to have a heck of a time fighting Stewart in Laird's courtroom and in the court of public opinion. If Laird had learned anything on the bench, it was that in any given case the lawyers are the supreme factor affecting the outcome. The facts help, but he had seen lawyers blow cases with the facts on their side. The defense by all appearances had neither the facts nor much of a handle on the firefight they were blundering into. The team from the prestigious firm of Lightfoot, Franklin & White, it seemed apparent, would struggle to dispute the facts that Stewart and company had marshaled against them. But it was the path they had chosen, and Laird figured he had done all he could to save them from themselves.

After six years of waiting, the *Abernathy* trial whipped by in a blur and seemed almost anticlimactic. It lasted seven weeks, with Stewart stalking Monsanto like big game. He presented a damning indictment populated with sympathetic plaintiffs, dynamic expert witnesses, and compelling visuals—lots and lots of visuals. It seemed as though he was constantly beaming onto the wall a large-scale image of one of the Monsanto memos. To Laird, the jurors seemed transfixed by the documents. Meanwhile, as expected, the defense attempted to depict the plaintiffs as overreacting, the medical evidence as inflated. "We would all rather live in a pristine world," defense attorney Jere White told the jury in his opening statement. "We are all going to be exposed to things on a daily basis. Our bodies can handle it."

But Stewart sent a relentless parade of experts to the stand to paint a picture of a community sucker-punched by chemical contamination. One witness, Dr. Ian Nisbet, a Massachusetts toxicologist, testified that the sixteen plaintiffs in the first phase of the trial had average PCB levels of 46 parts per billion—twenty-seven times the national norm. "This is by far the most contaminated community that I've ever encountered," Nisbet told the jury. Evidence was presented concerning cancer rates, children with tumors, the medical histories of people who lived near the plant. Charts and diagrams were displayed that demonstrated how discharges from the plant and landfill infiltrated the surrounding neighborhood. And peppered throughout, memos, memos, memos, strafing the defense's contention that Monsanto had acted honorably.

To Laird, who had played football in high school, Stewart resembled nothing less than a gifted quarterback at the top of his game, a vast playbook at the ready, always on the attack and prepared to respond to any adjustment by the defense. He didn't even appear to be consulting his notes during his examination of witnesses—he had everything down that cold. In one especially impressive turn, Laird watched as Stewart screened a lengthy videotaped deposition of Dr. Robert Kaley, the environmental affairs director for Solutia and the PCB expert for the American Chemistry Council. Then, in a surprising and highly unusual move, Stewart called Kaley to the stand in person and proceeded to twist him into knots along a completely different line of questioning, extracting testimony about Monsanto's monitoring and cleanup activities in Anniston that many observers viewed as some of the most crucial of the trial. Stewart would ask a technical question, Kaley would respond, and then Stewart would produce a refuting document that he would ask Kaley to examine. Kaley became so riveted on Stewart, Laird noticed, that on a couple of occasions Stewart offered Kaley totally unrelated documents to examine, which Kaley failed to notice. (Stewart would later admit he pulled the prank to amuse himself. He would also say that Kaley "wasn't that deep, and I knew he was afraid of me.") For a time it seemed as if Stewart might start extracting documents from behind Kaley's ear, the way a sleight-of-hand artist coaxes coins from a child.

Stewart also seemed to have the jury calibrated perfectly. He knew when they were tiring of a particular subject, when they wanted more questions, when to pick up the rhythm, and when to slow it down. White and the other defense attorneys, by contrast, seemed shrill and less than genuine. When the defense had the floor, it seemed as if the jury was being forced to swallow bitter medicine; Stewart always seemed to be serving strawberry shortcake with whipped cream. It was a performance that Laird had to appreciate, knowing as he did that Donald Stewart could be as disagreeable as anyone on earth when he wished to be. But the jury liked Stewart. They watched him for his every reaction when the defense had the floor, and even then he never seemed to hit a false note. It was Stewart's courtroom, by a mile.

Stewart was not above trickery to get his way in the courtroom. On one watershed day, Solutia plant manager David Cain was scheduled to testify as the final witness for the defense. Cain would help the defense finish on a strong note. He was African-American, which would help him connect with the black members of the jury, and was a formidable and charismatic presence besides. Cain was very polished and, among his many talents, could quote relevant biblical scripture at length. He was a cross-examination nightmare. Stewart fervently wished to call Cain as a hostile witness, so he could ask leading questions and defuse whatever line of testimony the defense had prepared.

Jere White came over to the plaintiff's table that morning and told Stewart, "David Cain's going up. Who's got him on your side?"

"I do," Stewart replied.

"How long are you going to take?"

"That depends on how long you take."

"We've got about twenty minutes."

"I've got about an hour and a half."

"An hour and a half?! Why do you need that much time?"

"I've got some stuff to go over with him."

"Okay," White said. He rushed back over to his table where he began conferring with his team. Dan Fedderman, a Kasowitz attorney and Stewart's second chair that day, was mystified. They didn't have an hour and a half for Cain—they barely had anything. "What are you doing?" he hissed at Stewart. "Just shut up," Stewart said. "Look straight ahead and pretend like you're preparing stuff."

In a few minutes White approached the bench. "Judge, the defense rests."

"Rests?" Laird asked. "I thought you were going to put David Cain up."

"No," White replied. "We're through."

"In that case," Stewart jumped in, "I'd like to call David Cain as a rebuttal witness."

White gazed at Stewart in disbelief, then turned to Laird: "Judge, he can't do that. He has to give us forty-eight hours notice! What about the forty-eight-hour rule?"

Laird, experiencing a Sheriff Andy Taylor moment, wearily replied, "Yeah, there's a forty-eight-hour rule, but are you going to insist that Donald abide by that with David Cain? Suit yourself, then. Donald can have him when we come back next week." Thinking better of it, White said he would agree if the defense was given the lunch hour to prepare Cain.

All had gone as Stewart had hoped. Now he had Cain on his terms. Cain took the stand and began to work his spell. He smiled warmly and made lots of eye contact with the jury—the exquisitely prepared witness. And as his testimony wound down, he was effusive in his description of Solutia as a first-rate corporate citizen and of Anniston as a perfectly safe and healthy town, a place where anyone would be well-advised to live, as opposed to what the ill-informed outsiders and craven detractors were saying about it.

Stewart moved in for the kill. "And where do *you* reside, Mr. Cain?"

Cain paused, then replied: "Jacksonville." The jury laughed out loud.

Soon the jury was dismissed. In the hallway, a juror said, "Well, guess it wasn't good enough for him to live there!" ("It's funny,"

Stewart would say later, "how little bitty things like that tick the living hell out of a jury.")

The defense was being dragged around the courtroom like a cavewoman by her hair. Still, Lightfoot, White and their colleagues radiated nothing but confidence. Even the normally disinterested court reporters thought the defense was deluded. Near the end of the trial, one of the defense attorneys was regaling a table of court reporters (four were assigned to the case to produce a daily record that would eventually run to fifteen thousand pages) about how well things were going. "How can you *think* that?" sputtered one court reporter, who was quickly silenced by a kick under the table. Court reporters were supposed to shut up, keep transcribing, and then collect their very handsome wage. But it was plain who was doing well—and who wasn't.

A few days later the jury returned its verdict. The defendants were found to be responsible for the PCB contamination alleged by the plaintiffs and would be assessed damages on the basis of a case-by-case evaluation of each plaintiff's claims, a process that the jury would begin immediately. The verdict wasn't fuzzy. It read, in part, that Monsanto's conduct was "so outrageous in character and extreme in degree as to go beyond all possible bounds of decency, so as to be regarded as atrocious and utterly intolerable in civilized society."

The defense announced plans to appeal, and within days filed a petition with the Alabama Supreme Court to have Laird removed from the case on the grounds that he was prejudiced in favor of the plaintiffs. The supreme court would reject the petition seven months later in an eighty-seven-page opinion. Donald Stewart had his outrage verdict. Now the only question was how high the damages would go.

David Baker had never understood the concept behind the institution of the U.S. Senate hearing until he, Shirley, and James Hall
entered cavernous Room SD-138 in the Dirksen Senate Office
Building on Capitol Hill a few weeks after the liability verdict
against Solutia in Judge Laird's court. The concept: intimidation.
The tables where witnesses sat and delivered their testimony, David
now saw, were sunk in a deep well in front of the battery of soaring
risers where the senators were ensconced in all their looming
authority. The whole setup was rigged to make the senators seem
like Moses upon the mountaintop with exclusive access to the Ten
Commandments and the Almighty, while the flop-sweating witnesses were relegated way down in the valley of the shadow of
death. Later, when the time arrived for David to testify, he also
came to understand why they put big pitchers of ice water on the
witness tables. His throat would be parched as desert sand, and he
wasn't even on the hot seat.

The hot seat was reserved for others on this particular morning
before the Senate Appropriations Committee's Subcommittee on
VA, HUD, and Independent Agencies. The hearing, requested by
Alabama senator Richard Shelby, had been convened to discuss PCB
contamination in Anniston and the reaction to it of various governmental agencies, particularly the EPA. Shelby was present at the
hearing, as was Democratic senator Barbara Mikulski of Maryland,
chairwoman of the subcommittee. Present to testify were four witnesses: Stanley Meiburg, Deputy Regional Administrator of Region 4
of the EPA; Dr. Henry Falk, Assistant Administrator of the Agency
for Toxic Substances and Disease Registry of the U.S. Department of
Health and Human Services; Stephen Cobb, Chief of the Hazardous

Waste Branch of the Alabama Department of Environmental Management; and David Baker.

Mikulski, one of the last of the great Senate liberals and a fierce interrogator, got right to the point, declaring that Anniston "is like so many American communities, working-class folks trying to make a living, a once-thriving, heavy industrial community. . . . These hardworking people are facing an immense public health crisis after decades of pollution from a PCB factory, and Anniston's waterways, backyards and playgrounds have been polluted. . . ."

Mikulski was in a snit, and soon explained why. She noted that an array of high-ranking EPA officials who normally would have appeared before the subcommittee on the matter of Anniston had "to be recused from this issue because of past associations with the companies involved." (Mikulski would later mention Jimmy Palmer, the regional administrator for Region 4, a lawyer who in private practice had represented companies that owned foundries in Anniston and had been implicated in potential lead contamination there; and Linda Fisher, deputy administrator of the EPA, the agency's number two official, who worked for Monsanto in the 1990s. Both were appointed after the election of President George W. Bush and despite the protests of environmentalists who claimed they were too closely bound to the industry they were charged with regulating.)

But then the senator got to the crux of her discontent, reviewing the history of Anniston's PCB contamination and the unsuccessful efforts of residents to get state and federal agencies to pursue a cleanup. Finally, she said, frustrated residents sued Monsanto, and only after the very recent liability verdict did the EPA announce a consent decree with the company that outlined a cleanup plan—one that seemed to be eminently favorable to Solutia's interests and threatened to co-opt the proceedings in Laird's court. "EPA says the timing was coincidental," Mikulski said. "I find it surprising."

Shelby would add: "Knowing what I know about the history of PCBs in Anniston, Alabama, I do not believe that everything has been done to protect [the public's] health and well-being. In fact, I am fairly certain that many of these agencies were, at the very least, complacent in their dealings with Monsanto." He then outlined the decades-long paper trail of Monsanto's early knowledge about the dangers of PCBs: "So what we have from the very beginning is a conscious decision to conceal information from the public, information that might well have protected numerous Anniston residents from exposure to harmful chemicals in these waterways.

"No one monitored EPA's activities," Shelby went on. "No one monitored ADEM's activities, and most importantly, no one monitored Monsanto's activities."

In response, Meiburg conceded that the EPA had been aware of Monsanto's PCB contamination issues in Anniston as early as the 1970s, but due to a welter of labor-sharing guidelines stipulated by Superfund regulations passed in 1980, state-level agencies in Alabama like ADEM had been given most of the oversight of the company's modest compliance and cleanup activities. Not until the EPA received a letter from David Baker and CAP in 1999, contending that PCB contamination was much more widespread than the areas that had been previously addressed—which essentially included the plant site itself and a grouping of properties immediately surrounding it—did the EPA become more aggressively involved in Anniston, Meiburg said. The EPA's interest was further fueled in 2000 by President Clinton, who inquired about Anniston's PCB situation after receiving a letter from Alabama governor Don Siegelman.

Mikulski then took her turn with Meiburg and honed the point:

"What took EPA so long?" she asked. She quoted from Meiburg's submitted testimony: " 'Over the years, EPA has attempted to work closely with ADEM and other agencies to maximize the resources the government is able to bring to bear in Anniston. EPA and ADEM followed a basic division of labor for Anniston, with the State taking the lead role in the remediation of the Solutia plant property, while EPA handled all other areas.'

"Well, when did EPA become actively involved in Anniston? . . . Why did it take all these years that—I know the community has been active, and raising concerns, and taking it to [the state]—that we do not get a consent decree until March 25, 2002?"

"Senator, I can supply a detailed chronology for the record," Meiburg replied. "But the larger question you have asked, 'Why did it take so long,' is probably the most difficult question, as I look back on it. And I think it is fair to say that if we knew—if we had known some years ago what we know now about the site, then I think the course of action might have been different."

MIKULSKI: Can you understand how I look at this?

MEIBURG: Yes.

MIKULSKI: It is that, according to this, the chronology of your own testimony says EPA was involved with the highest level of the legal community in Alabama, and the legal enforcement, in terms of the attorney general who himself asked for help on Snow Creek, and Snow Creek was both literally and metaphorically what was happening in other hot spots around Anniston. Nothing, nothing. Divisions of labor between EPA and ADEM. Nothing. Nothing.

In the meantime, this is leaking, hemorrhaging all the while into the community, into the playgrounds, into gardens, and into creeks. People had brain tumors. Children were born with defects. Young men were dying. And it is hard enough in this world for young black men to survive, let alone when EPA is still doing divisions of labor.

Well, whatever way you divided those labors did not seem to work.

Mikulski had delivered a rebuke of the first order. David couldn't believe what he was hearing. To have a mighty U.S. senator throw thunder down on the EPA in this imposing setting, to issue the same indictment that David and so many others had been clamoring about for years—it was almost unreal. David turned to look at James Hall and realized he had tears in his eyes.

Soon it was David's turn to testify. He got his money's worth.

"The people of Anniston, Alabama," he began, "have waited for more than 40 years for the federal government to step in and help us clean up the PCB contaminants in our backyards, and in our playgrounds, our rivers, our creeks, and in our bodies. Unfortunately, after 40 years of waiting, I am here today to report that the federal government has failed the people of Alabama, and left the fox guarding the henhouse."

David began to tear up again, and his voice cracked with emotion. Looking up at Mikulski and away from his prepared text, he explained that the residents of West Anniston couldn't attend the hearing, "So I cry for them."

He resettled and continued, leaving his written remarks behind:

This company that I speak about today, and this problem that I speak about today, when you find that it is a bailout, after knowing that all these years that people knew and did nothing about it, hardens my heart. . . . Just a few days ago, when the courts finally gave us justice by finding this company guilty of all these notorious crimes, the EPA *then* decided to have an enforcement order.

We knew that there was an attempt made prior to this to have these enforcement orders done, to make this enforcement order come to be, but . . . when they found them guilty, it popped up. From where I stand, and from where our community stands, if it walks like a duck, and it quacks like a duck, it has to be a duck.

Why did you wait until we had found them guilty in a court of law, and then turn around and do an enforcement order, and claim that there is no way you can get rid of it, and this is the best deal you can have? As a labor leader, I remember in negotiations, when you are negotiating, if you do not like what is being said, you just continue the negotiations. If you have been negotiating for two years, what was the hurry at that particular time?

David's head blurred with the images of his neighborhood, his town, the people he was speaking for, some of them dead and gone:

Three and a half million dollars, they keep jumping up and saying they want to give us for our special education. Sure, we need it. We need this special education money, because we have children who cannot learn, but we also have children who are handicapped; we also have children just being born who are deformed. We also have people who are 30 or 40 years old who have cancer.

Just the other day, the EPA came into the community and told the lady across the street from where I live—her son is three years old—"Do not let him go outside and play in the yard, because your yard is highly contaminated." . . . We have been living this way for the last four years. The last four years, we have had to take off our shoes when we are ready to go into the house. Our children cannot play on the grass, so they play in the streets.

Our children should wash their balls if they are playing outside, wash the dogs if they wanted to play with their own pets in their yard. We cannot plant a garden in our yard any more. . . . We have people planting collard greens in five-gallon buckets just to enjoy the land that they live on.

No one will loan us money on our property. No one wants to move into our community. . . . The landfill that caused this problem . . . it *is* the cause of this problem. It is buried. Many times today I have heard them talk about PCBs, but it is not just PCBs that are buried in that landfill. They buried lead—two lead vats that we know of. Mercury. They released it on the community. And for 40-something years, people have looked the other way.

Why is the government so interested at this point to run in as a last-minute savior to bail Monsanto out, I do not know. But I thought that when we went to court the other morning—when I was called and told that we had won the case, that we had won, and I got up in the bed and began to cry. It was the first time in four years that some relief had come.

And then there is a 180-degree turn. Monsanto ran right into court right after this decree order was signed, and said, "Throw out 3,500 complainants' cases," and asked the judge to do so. Why did [the EPA] give them leverage? I do not know. Was it done intentionally? I cannot say. But the other night when they told the community and my neighborhood that they had the best deal in the world, it did not work. And I hope that today you have heard enough, and I think that you have presented enough yourself.

You understand that Anniston is not in South Africa, Rhodesia, or some other totalitarian country, that we are Americans, and we live in Anniston, Alabama, and all we want to do is live a normal life.

Yes, we do need a health study. We do need a health assessment. We need a health clinic. We need everything that could be offered, because we have suffered so long.

I thank you.

There was abject silence, and then a great gradual swelling of applause from the audience in the chamber.

"Well, thank *you* very much, Mr. Baker," Mikulski said. "That was a pretty compelling conversation."

A few minutes later, after a round of questioning by Shelby, Mikulski wistfully recounted her own background in activism in Baltimore, how she raised money for a legal fund to fight a highway by staging bake sales—"you know, 'Bake Sale Barb' up here"— which drew an appreciative laugh from the audience. "Now," she asked David, "how have you been able to do this, and are you holding a big bill? I just want you to know, I am worried not only about your public health but about your financial health as well."

"Well," David said, "let me just say, when we first started out, we started out with what you just said, the cake sales, the fried chicken sales on Saturdays and Sundays, and many of us reaching into our own pockets. We opened an office in the community. We got a grant. . . ."

"It sounds like my old days," Mikulski said, then added: "I want to just thank you, and I want to thank all those people who cooked, and baked, and sang, and rallied, and so on, and put in their own tremendous sweat equity. I know that you put in three shifts. You put one in the marketplace, earning a living; you put in another shift with the family to make sure the living is worthwhile; and now you put in a third shift, as a community activist. And I just want to say: God bless you."

"Thank you," David said, and cried for the third time that morning.

A few weeks later, the Justice Department and the EPA withdrew the controversial consent decree with Solutia that had been lodged in federal court in Birmingham. An attorney who researched the matter said it was only the second time in the EPA's history that the agency had retracted a consent decree that had been submitted to a judge for approval.

By the summer of 2003, the grinding pressure on Solutia had become almost audible. In Gadsden, the *Abernathy* jury was still at work assessing damages stemming from the liability verdict of the previous year. The jury had made its way through about five hundred of the thirty-five hundred plaintiffs' cases and had awarded some one hundred million dollars, or an average of about two hundred thousand dollars per claim. At that rate, the damages seemed headed toward the seven-hundred-million-dollar mark—and those were just property claims. The jury would next move on to health damages. It seemed entirely plausible to project that the total *Abernathy* awards might surpass one billion dollars.

And *Abernathy* was only one of the legal challenges facing Solutia. Fast approaching was the *Tolbert* case, scheduled to begin in October in federal court in Birmingham. While the average *Tolbert*

plaintiff probably had less grievous claims than his *Abernathy* coun-
terpart, the *Tolbert* case had four times as many plaintiffs. Who could
say what the potential damages for *Tolbert* could be? Five hundred
million? One billion? *Two* billion? Combine those kinds of catastrophic numbers with the specter of Johnnie Cochran performing
rites of mass hypnotism on Court TV, and the situation for Solutia
began to look truly dire. There was also the matter of cleanup costs,
which could easily run to a hundred million dollars or more. And it
wasn't just Solutia's balance sheet on the line. Monsanto was on the
hook if Solutia couldn't pay.

Negative publicity continued to flail Monsanto, Solutia, and
Anniston itself. Particularly painful was a *60 Minutes* piece broadcast just before Thanksgiving 2002 that described Anniston as
"America's most toxic town," referred repeatedly to the memos
uncovered by Stewart, and featured correspondent Steve Kroft hammering away at Solutia CEO Hunter. "You understand the anger of
the community?" Kroft asked Hunter at one juncture. "I understand
the concerns of the Anniston community," Hunter replied. "And,
you know, if you're asking me, do I wish that things might have been
done differently in the past than they were? Sure I do." Stewart
landed his punches as well. Guiding Kroft through the Monsanto
paper trail, Stewart charged that Monsanto "lied, is basically what
they did. It would be called, I guess in our part of the country, a sin
of omission."

The bad press and mounting verdicts were causing searing
headaches for Solutia on Wall Street. In early July, the company
forecast a loss of fifteen to twenty cents per share for the second
quarter, conceding in a press release that the continuing *Abernathy*
verdicts and the ongoing delay in obtaining approval for a cleanup
consent decree had "significantly dampened" its hopes for a quick
resolution to its Anniston-related problems. The company's stock,

which in 1998 had traded as high as twenty-nine dollars a share, promptly fell nearly 25 percent the next day to a dollar seventy-three a share. Moreover, financial analysts and reporters were beginning to ask Monsanto officials if contingency plans were in place to assume liability if Solutia ran out of cash, a distinct possibility.

So when U.S. District Judge U. W. Clemon, the magistrate presiding over the pending *Tolbert* case, sent out feelers that summer about brokering a "global" settlement—that is, launching negotiations with the goal of resolving all the existing Anniston-related litigation against Solutia, which included *Tolbert, Abernathy,* and two smaller cases—Solutia finally seemed properly motivated. Publicly, the company was still attempting to keep its chin up, expressing optimism in a conference call with Wall Street analysts about the prospect of a "more level playing field" in Clemon's court than had been the case with Laird. Solutia had also made much of a lawsuit it filed in Washington against nineteen other companies, including Halliburton, Phelps Dodge Industries, and U.S. Pipe, alleging that those companies with past or present ownership ties to Anniston industry had also contributed to PCB pollution. The suit sought to recover cleanup costs from those companies, a move that even Solutia's harshest critics, including David Baker, conceded had merit. But the company was no longer able to paint the Anniston litigation as frivolous, unwarranted, or merely annoying. Stewart and *Abernathy* had exposed Anniston as Solutia's Achilles' heel. If the company was ever going to strike a deal, now was the time—not later, when the *Abernathy* damages were sure to be spiraling and Johnnie Cochran was levitating like a vampire in federal court.

Yet convincing Solutia to take a seat at the negotiating table wasn't the only challenge facing Clemon. There was the matter of Stewart and Kasowitz, Benson, who together had spent years and millions of dollars prosecuting *Abernathy,* believed that Solutia had had every conceivable opportunity to settle in the run-up to that trial, and had had to suffer the arrogance of the defense team besides. Now, after a colossal, depleting effort, the damage verdicts were rolling in like soaking thunderstorms after an extended drought. And so now the *Abernathy* attorneys were going to roll over and let Solutia bargain its way out of the trap it had constructed for itself? Not likely.

But Clemon had some substantial logic on his side. Even with the very favorable position Stewart and Kasowitz, Benson had attained, under the current process it would be years before they or their clients saw any actual money. Solutia had said it intended to appeal the *Abernathy* verdict; no appeal could be filed until the damages phase ran its course. Stewart didn't think an appeal would fly, but anything could happen. It might take five years or more to resolve everything.

In an extraordinary gesture, Clemon made a personal visit to Anniston to meet separately with Laird and Stewart to plumb their concerns about participating in settlement talks. Laird was amazed that a federal judge would visit *him* in *his* chambers—he had never heard of such a thing. Stewart was somewhat less in awe. As a U.S. senator, he had pushed Clemon's appointment to the federal bench, and the two had had at least one business dealing together. The visit spoke to Clemon's desire to avoid a lengthy and expensive trial in his court. Brokering a settlement would hinge on two factors: Solutia coming across with a respectable sum, and then getting the *Abernathy* camp to come on board. If that took some discreet politicking by a federal judge, then Clemon would do it. Stewart finally said, Look, get an offer on the table and then we'll talk.

Finally, after several weeks of jockeying about, with Cochran and Jere Beasley themselves eventually brought in during the final stages of the talks, Solutia formally offered a settlement package of seven hundred million dollars. That sum included six hundred million to settle the litigation plus another hundred million to go toward cleanup, education, and health programs, including a health clinic that would service West Anniston and serve as a national research center for PCB-related illnesses—a facility for which David and Shirley Baker had lobbied tirelessly. At last it appeared that Solutia had stepped up to the plate. If accepted, the offer would smash the previous record for a mass tort case in the United States—the three hundred million-plus obtained from Pacific Gas & Electric in the Erin Brockovich case in California.

All the attorneys were brought into the federal courthouse in downtown Birmingham to discuss the offer and the primary obstacle that stood in the way of final acceptance: how to divide the pot among their clients and themselves. On the first day, the *Tolbert* legal team shared its vision. All the plaintiffs would be combined into one group, and the money would be paid out by a single fund administrator. How much each plaintiff received would be determined by a matrix formula based on a variety of factors, including blood PCB levels. Stewart was in disbelief. People could talk all day long about how Solutia had slunk to the table out of fear of facing Cochran in court, and there might even be truth to that argument, but to his eyes the indisputable fact was that his verdicts streaming out of the Gadsden courthouse had forced the issue. His thirty-five hundred plaintiffs had sued first, had exhibited the most damages, had been in court for seven years, had begun to receive tangible awards. Now they were expected to toss all that history out and line up alongside Cochran's fifteen thousand and take whatever might come? No way. Stewart walked out of the room, left the courthouse, and drove back to Anniston.

Clemon and Laird gently nudged him back. Stewart's point had been made. His clients would have to receive far greater consideration than the others. After more negotiating, with Kasowitz and Benson playing major roles, a deal was finally struck. The money would be split equally between the two cases: three hundred million to *Abernathy,* three hundred million to *Tolbert.* Of course, there was nothing equal about it—Stewart's clients would receive an average of nearly fifty thousand dollars each, while Cochran's would average about eight thousand. Stewart, Kasowitz, and Benson saw this disparity as no disparity at all, and only fair. In the end, the *Tolbert* team was obliged to see it the same way. "The plaintiffs in the state court case had been in longer, and their people were in closer proximity to the plant site," Jere Beasley would later concede. Another factor hung over the negotiations: the fear that Solutia might go bankrupt, which would greatly complicate matters.

The offer represented much corporate brokering among Solutia, Monsanto, Pharmacia (which had previously acquired Monsanto), and Pfizer (which had subsequently acquired Phamarcia). Per agreement, Solutia was only obligated to pay a fraction of what Monsanto agreed to pay, and would do so over ten years. For each $300 million payment, the first $275 million would be paid within a week of the court order confirming the settlement. Monsanto would pay $195 million to each fund, and commercial insurance from Solutia, Monsanto, and Pharmacia would pay $80 million. The remaining $25 million would be paid by Solutia in equal installments over the ten-year period, starting in August of 2004.

The attorneys would do well in any event. With fees averaging

39 percent of the settlement total, $234 million would be distributed among the various law firms. Kasowitz, Benson was ultimately awarded a fee of $55 million after expenses, enough to help place the firm atop *American Lawyer*'s annual profits-per-partner list for 2003. ("This is Kasowitz's alpha moment," the magazine said.) Stewart received fees that topped an estimated $30 million. After years of financial difficulty, the farmer's son from Munford was a wealthy man. Under the terms of the agreement, Stewart would personally oversee the payout of the settlement money to his clients (a court-appointed claims administrator would manage the *Tolbert* funds). Several of Stewart's clients would receive some $500,000 each. (The flip side was that the meaty verdicts handed down in Gadsden were nullified by the settlement.)

Final agreement on the settlement was reached on Wednesday, August 20, 2003, less than two weeks after the first nerve gas rocket had been incinerated at the Anniston Army Depot. It was decided that a press conference would be held in Anniston the next day, after Laird had had an opportunity to convene the *Abernathy* jury and inform them of the settlement and its ramifications. Everyone—Cochran, Beasley, Clemon, and Solutia CEO Hunter included—agreed to attend, and to keep quiet until then.

Word seeped out anyway. A premature press release by a Birmingham firm associated with the *Tolbert* case made the rounds on Wednesday afternoon, and cell phones began to go off across Alabama and around the country, with reporters trying to confirm the story with the major players. David and Shirley Baker were driving from Atlanta to Anniston after a day of meetings with officials at the EPA and at Emory University about a medical study for children that was under consideration. Shirley's cell phone rang, and she listened in shock as a TV reporter gave her the highlights of the press release. "They settled," she told David as she continued to listen. David immediately pulled over to the shoulder of the interstate. "Seven hundred million," she said a few seconds later, still listening to the phone. David reeled at the number. And then: "*We got our clinic.*"

"We got our clinic?" David repeated. "We got our clinic!" But Shirley was still listening intently to her phone, trying to get more details. David felt as if he might cry, and then as if he might float from the car—he didn't know *how* to feel. He was experiencing every conceivable emotion at once: joy at the victory, relief at the resolution, anger at the fight that had been required to achieve justice, sadness at the thought of those who didn't live to see the day. It all crushed in on him at once, impossible to sort through.

The next thing he knew he was kissing Shirley full on the lips. And the next thing after that he was fumbling for his own phone . . . wait till the old man heard about *this*. "Hey Butler!" he shouted into the phone, joy having prevailed. "You sittin' down?"

The *Abernathy* jury *had* to know something big was up. For one thing, for the first time in their service, which had stretched to nearly two years, they had been called in not to their familiar assembly room in the Gadsden courthouse but to the Calhoun County Courthouse in Anniston. Then, once summoned to the jury box, it was impossible not to notice the packed courtroom and, sitting toward the rear, Johnnie Cochran. It was as unlikely an occurrence as could possibly be imagined; they quickly scanned the rest of the courtroom, just in case Jesus or Elvis had also decided to attend that Thursday morning. The odds were almost as good.

It had already been a long morning for Joel Laird. He had arrived at his office shortly after dawn to plan the day. Not only would he play the role of master of ceremonies that morning, he was scheduled to charge a jury in a capital murder case in nearby Heflin that afternoon. He would be hard-pressed to get there on time. How many times, he wondered to himself, does a humble circuit judge deal with a historic settlement and a death penalty case in the space of the same day?

Laird had decided that the press conference would be held on the original front steps of the century-old courthouse, on the south-facing side. A recent refurbishing of the facility had sealed off the original entrance and switched entry to the north side of the building, complete with metal detector. That area was shaded in the morning, not very cinematic for the cameras, plus a large gathering in front of the new entrance would disrupt normal courthouse traffic. Laird had hustled out a side door and around the building to the south steps to check things out. The first thing he noticed was that the old marble steps were covered in droppings from the pigeons that roosted in the eaves above. He went back to his office and called the county jail to dispatch a crew of inmates to scrub the steps.

Later, before summoning the jury to the courtroom, Laird sat on the bench and listened as the lawyers fought about what to tell the jury. The defense was adamant that the jurors be told as little as possible about the settlement agreement. After all, the jurors were not being officially released; the settlement was binding only if 97 percent of the plaintiffs approved of the agreement in writing within ninety days. If the settlement fell through, then the

Abernathy jurors would have to return to the task of determining damage awards in their Gadsden jury room. The terms of the settlement might prejudice their deliberations, the defense argued. But Laird was unconvinced. He respected his jurors, felt close to them, believed they had worked hard, they had sacrificed. He recalled the day when a juror phoned to say she couldn't attend the proceedings that morning because her child had suddenly taken ill and she couldn't find a babysitter on short notice. Laird had sent a courthouse employee to watch the child so the juror could come in and the critical day would not be lost. (It had been a solution that Andy would have approved of, Laird figured.) He felt his jury deserved to know what everybody else knew. They would probably hear about it anyway—it would be unavoidable—and he wanted to shape the information as he saw fit. The settlement agreement was the logical extension of the jury's verdict. They could handle the truth, and he would give it to them. One last time, he ruled against the defense.

Laird's voice broke as he informed the jury of the settlement. Some of the jurors wiped at tears. Laird thanked them for their service and told them that their dedication was what made feasible the very concept of a court of law. He asked the jurors to be part of the press conference on the steps outside, and then gaveled an end to the session. The jurors flocked to Cochran, who spent the next few minutes patiently signing autographs.

Outside, a crowd of about two hundred people had gathered as news of the settlement began to circulate in earnest. Reporters sifted through the throng, seeking comment from plaintiffs. One *Abernathy* plaintiff, Williams Lumsford, likened the settlement to a gift from God. "I think it's a blessing to this community," he told the

Star. "For so long, people have suffered. I know good things come
to those who wait. We've certainly been waiting long enough."
Shirley Baker told anyone who would listen that she had been
"jumping for joy since yesterday." Finally the steps began to fill with
the cast of this odd drama, which slowly made its way from the
courtroom. Applause broke out as the crowd glimpsed Cochran,
who stood next to David Baker. One by one, Laird ushered the principals to the microphone.

Beasley told the crowd that "corporate America has got to learn
when you do things to hurt people you have to stand up and take
the blame for it." Cochran said that Anniston "is going to be a better community, all because the citizens had the courage to stand
up." The most enthusiastic reception was for Stewart, who in what
may have been one last dig at the defense, praised Laird for steering
the case through uncharted waters. "He knew better than all the
rest of us what needed to be done," Stewart said. Even Solutia's
John Hunter received a nice round of applause. "We never produced PCBs," Hunter said, "but we are proud to be a part of this
resolution."

The parade of speakers finally exhausted itself. As Laird
approached the mike, it occurred to him that a closing prayer might
be appropriate. He drew breath to offer one himself, but suddenly
spotted Chip Howell in the crowd. He asked the mayor to come forward, if he would, and give a benediction.

Chip slowly made his way to the microphone, scanning the
steps and thinking of all the stars above that had aligned themselves just so over so many years to bring such a disparate group
together in this unlikely place and time. He reached the dais and
turned to the crowd, searching the congregation of faces for inspiration. For a moment he gazed out toward the west, toward the
foundries and the old Monsanto stacks, toward the Depot and the

great furnace that had risen there, toward the west where the past, present, and future of a flawed and great town still smoked and rumbled and heaved. Chip bowed his head, thought fleetingly of Hoyt, and then delivered up a prayer for Anniston's future, and its soul.

EPILOGUE

Suddenly it is time to come home. You frantically shovel clothes, maps, shoes, toiletries, cold-weather gear, the laptop, the five books you're reading right now, and various other provisions into the car, and then you are under way, picking your way through the late-afternoon rush-hour thicket of Sacramento, the freeway a swollen river of red taillights glowing in the listless fog.

You finally wriggle free, and soon you're plunging down I-5 through the darkening moonscape of the San Joaquin Valley toward Los Angeles, riding fast and low in the passing lane, ticking off the first hundred miles before the engine is barely warm.

A good start. Driving cross country, alone, in the shortest time possible, is easy. All you do is draw back the big slingshot, back-back-back, further, *fur*ther, until the stress is nearly unbearable and the whole thing threatens to snap in two, and then *pow ziiiiiing*— you are a two-door, heat-seeking, tailwind-riding projectile acceler-ating through time and space and nine states, burrowing into the soupy darkness like a three-stage rocket, face flapping from the Gs, hurtling past the rapid-fire slow-lane visuals of exhaust-snorting 18-wheelers and tarted-up imports and wobbling U-Haul trailers and hulking Hummers and bumper-sticker slogans (SOMEWHERE IN TEXAS A VILLAGE IDIOT IS MISSING), not to mention Maw-Maw and Paw-Paw doing thirty-five, maybe, in an ancient smoking hay truck that may or may not make the next hill.

Nothing to it. All you do is drive or die, and don't even think about slowing down until, oh, Graceland.

You're driving a 1974 BMW 2002, pure Inca orange in color, a classic. It's a car you derided as a yuppie affectation not so long ago—you remember a treasured colleague at the *Star* back in the day who drove a *green* one, for God's sake, with a sweater tied around his neck, even, a virtual Ivy League engraving plate. But you've since grown to appreciate the brilliant simplicity of the German engineering, and you've nursed this 2002 back to peak performance. So you let her rip and the odometer spins merrily, like a slot machine on New Year's Eve.

There are drawbacks. An orange BMW with California plates may not be the most, um, *unobtrusive* vehicle in which to tour George W. Bush's America at 82 mph. At about the Texas panhandle you begin to imagine an extravagant, pulsating neon sign mounted on the hood that says DETAIN THIS BLUE-STATE COMMIE IMMEDIATELY. Plus the heater is a rumor and, worse, there is no stereo. None. No radio, no CDs, tapes, nothing. So it's just you, the engine snarl, icy air whistling through the less-than-airtight windows, and the thoughts combusting in your head like popping corn.

Soon enough you enter The Zone. The Zone is where Man melds with Machine and becomes Machine Man. There is no stopping Machine Man. Machine Man lives to drive, and drives to live. There is no outside world, no reality, no dimension other than Machine Man's relentless, eastward surge. Eat? Machine Man no eat; kill food with bare hands later. Sleep? Machine Man no sleep; sleep for humans, Machine Man no relate. Restroom? Well . . . Machine Man not as young as he used to be. But Machine Man digress.

Your mission is noble and just. You are coming home.

You drive from Sacramento to Bakersfield to Barstow and hit I-40 at full bore. Between Barstow and Needles is the Mojave Desert, and you blaze across it like an orange comet on a night when you see more shooting stars flit across the sky than you've seen in a lifetime. On to Arizona and the climb into Flagstaff, where the snow-draped San Francisco Peaks shimmer in the morning light and state troopers lurk in the craggy rocks like sharks in a reef. On to New Mexico, where Albuquerque is the only blip in an endless stretch of mystical nothingness. On to Texas, where you see the Largest Cross in the Western Hemisphere outside of Amarillo, but Machine Man no stop to gawk. On to Oklahoma, where you are drafting like vintage Richard Petty behind a line of truckers, your newfound blood brothers of the road. You are rolling, bulletproof, invincible, longing for a CB and an IT'S HARD TO BE HUMBLE WHEN YOU DRIVE A PETE T-shirt, *Looks like we got us a con—*

"Mr. Love, I stopped you for following that truck too closely," Officer Hyde of the Oklahoma State Police informs you. His SUV is toasty inside and features a supernaturally focused German shepard in the rear that eyes you as if you were the neighbor's cat. "How does an Alabama boy get all the way out to California?" Officer Hyde asks. "Sometimes," you reply truthfully, "I have no idea." Officer Hyde smiles and hands you a warning ticket. "Drive careful, all right?"

And you do, as carefully as you can drive at 82 mph on an interstate that seems to crumble the farther east and south you go. Time-traveling through Arkansas you are battered by a road that has devolved into something more suitable for oxen. Tennessee isn't much better, Mississippi is worse, and Alabama—let's be honest, Alabama has never been famous for its pristine blacktop. But as you sail down U.S. 78 into Birmingham, onto I-20, and work free from the rush-hour briar patch yet again, the blue hills in the failing winter light take on the old familiar shapes . . . and the road rides like velvet.

The sun evaporates into dusk. You float into the driveway, weightless. Sacramento, California, to Anniston, Alabama, in three days flat. That, ladies and gentlemen, is how you get it done.

You leave Machine Man in the car and walk inside. You are greeted by a fire on the hearth, football murmuring on the television, and family happy to see you. California already seems like a half-dream. You are home, and you are glad you came.

People by the hundreds streamed into the Cobb Center on the West Side as the sun was setting over Coldwater Mountain where a forest fire, the flames visibly licking upward, was sending big cascading plumes of purple smoke into the sky. It was an apt backdrop for the meeting on this night, called by David Baker to address gathering unrest in the community over developments in the Solutia settlement. Some six months after the settlement was announced, a great many people were unhappy. Back up—a great many people were *angry*. One of those people, as it turned out, was David Baker, although you wouldn't have known it from the way he greeted people at the door of the auditorium. David wasn't angry about the settlement; he was angry about the people who were angry about the settlement. Weary of taking flak, he meant to have his say. "We're gonna straighten some things *out* tonight," he told one attendee conspiratorially, then swept into the gymnasium, where nearly a thousand people, almost all of them African-American, were milling about, waiting for things to begin.

Reality had hit home with people on the West Side, many of whom had interpreted the Solutia settlement announcement to mean that they were going to become wealthy. It was exactly this type of mentality that Judge Clemon had warned against at the press conference on the scrubbed-clean courthouse steps, back when peace and love were in the air. "In a case like this," Clemon had said that day, "the aim is to compensate those who have been injured. If you have not been injured, you are not entitled to compensation. Keep in mind, this case was not brought to make anybody rich." But as people, especially the plaintiffs in the *Tolbert* case, continued to hear about the large attorney fees and the gap between their awards and those made to the *Abernathy* plaintiffs, discontent and rumors began to abound. A popular one was that Baker had received a big finder's fee from Johnnie Cochran. The rumor had attained enough currency and generated enough animosity that Baker had received anonymous death threats over the telephone at his home. It was, he thought, like New York all over again.

Some of Donald Stewart's plaintiffs were unhappy as well, charging that Stewart had unfairly reimbursed himself for expenses out of the *Abernathy* kitty. Some people had taken to picketing Stewart's office, although it was later determined that the picketers weren't even *Abernathy* plaintiffs. But none of that concerned David Baker on this evening. He had invited the community to come and listen— again—to a breakdown of how the money was to be distributed, how the matrix worked, how people with the most property damage and highest PCB concentrations in their blood were to receive the most money. He had invited the various attorneys who had been involved in the cases to appear and answer questions. Only one,

David Byrne of the Beasley firm, had the gumption to show up, red meat for the lions.

The meeting finally convened amid much swirling emotion and a great venting of West Side spleen, and only episodic flashes of coherence. The low-key Byrne, sweating through his white dress shirt, turned in a heroic and surprisingly effective performance, standing firm and managing to explain in some detail the reasoning behind the decision not to take the *Tolbert* case to trial. (Bottom line: Stewart would have gotten all the money for his clients and Solutia would have gone bankrupt.) But the meeting was most remarkable for the sad spectacle of David Baker defending himself against the rumors. About half the room was with him, half against. It was an uncomfortable, even astonishing thing to see: the man who personified the rebellion of the downtrodden against the rapacious legacy of the corporate status quo, who had taken the fight from Sweet Valley and Cobbtown to the halls of the U.S. Senate, who had recruited the most feared attorney in the world to their cause, now being reduced to itemizing what he did with his lousy twenty-two-thousand-dollar settlement from the *Abernathy* case. "I don't have a dime that belongs to anybody in this room," he said, with considerable heat. As for those who would call his house with dark intentions, Baker had this to say, in a voice that seemed to ring into Georgia: *"Don't mess with me, and don't mess with my family."* At that David stepped away from the podium and the crowd erupted into a great, noisy, chaotic churn, menace fulminating everywhere. Cobb vs. County Training back in the day had nothing on this.

The ignominy was not yet over for the Bakers. The West Anniston Medical Clinic, first visualized by David Baker and funded by the *Tolbert* portion of the settlement after David had lobbied the attorneys to fight for it, ultimately had no role to offer him or Shirley—not even a slot on its board. In early 2005, Baker would walk out of a meeting in which the organizational chart for the clinic was announced, saying that the exclusion had "ripped my heart out and the heart of my staff." As the year wore on, funding for CAP was flagging and the Bakers were reevaluating not only its mission but its very existence. As "Bake Sale Barb" likely would agree, chicken dinner sales take a movement only so far.

Chip Howell was reelected mayor in the 2004 municipal elections, easily defeating his main challenger, Gene Robinson, owner of the Western Auto store on Noble Street. Robinson started running campaign ads on local cable TV almost a year in advance of the election, an unheard-of extravagance, charging that Chip's initiative to refurbish Noble Street was wrong-headed and caused undue hardship to merchants during construction. The voters clearly disagreed. By early 2005 the project was complete, and Noble Street looked more polished and welcoming than it had in decades. Many of the distinctive nineteenth-century facades had been restored. A discernable trend toward new restaurants and other businesses opening on Noble was under way. It was even possible to buy an espresso drink at the bar at Belladonna, and the Classic on Noble featured not only white linen tablecloths but some of the best cuisine in the state. To be sure, all was not well along Noble. The ten-story, fire-damaged bank building at Tenth Street, once the pride of Anniston's modest skyline, remained vacant; the old Calhoun Theater was a boarded-up eyesore, its flaking marquee a tattered reminder of another time for anyone old enough to have patronized the place before it shut down in the 1980s. But Noble Street's prospects seemed to be waxing, not waning. There was even talk of a new federal bankruptcy court going in downtown, which promised more nourishing lifeblood.

But Chip had much larger concerns than Noble Street as he continued to wrestle with events during what now could indisputably be described as one of the most pivotal periods in Anniston's history. As the incinerator proceeded with its indefatigable burn—the Army in February 2005 announced the destruction of the fifty thousandth agent-armed rocket, news that was broadcast across the top of page one of the *Star*—Chip and other business and political leaders turned their attention to the 2005 base realignment and closure process (i.e., the survival of the Anniston Army Depot). With the Pentagon's list of recommended base closures due in the fall, a flurry of lobbying efforts had been launched toward Washington from around the country as states and individual communities alike tried to muster every conceivable influence on the BRAC process. In mid-February 2005, Chip and a delegation of community leaders, including *Star* managing editor Troy Turner, traveled to Washington to tout the "indispensability" of the Anniston Depot. They met with, among others, Anniston congressman Mike Rogers, who had just been named chairman of an important Homeland Security subcommittee. Not only was the Depot the region's largest employer, with an all-time high of 6,200 people on its payroll, went the pitch to Rogers, but its productivity had been doubled in recent years. But informing Rogers of the Depot's deserving qualities was merely preaching to the converted. The reality was that there probably was little anyone could do to influence the BRAC closure list. The 2005 process was being referred to by insiders as "the mother of all BRACs," with nearly 25 percent of the U.S. military infrastructure due for elimination. And while stacks of money were being thrown at the process—Florida hired a fifty-thousand-dollar-a-month lobbyist, for example, while California governor Arnold Schwarzenegger earmarked five hundred thousand dollars to assist that state's BRAC effort—no one could be sure it made a difference. "It's a waste of money," a Heritage Foundation policy analyst told the *Fort Worth Star-Telegram*. "A community would be far better off in spending that money to hire someone to develop a plan in case the base is closed." But community leaders like Chip Howell felt they had no choice but to try.

Whether Anniston would receive any BRAC brownie points as a result of greasing the skids for the startup of the incinerator was an open question and, in all likelihood, an unanswerable one. As the BRAC decisions loomed, Chip sincerely believed that the Anniston Depot had proved its value to the American military effort and felt that he and the city had done everything possible to protect the facility from closure. He sensed the matter had been assigned to a higher power. All that could be done now was to remember Fort McClellan, hope for the best, and prepare for the worst.

In January 2005, a fascinating memo was leaked from the Pentagon to Craig Williams and his Chemical Weapons Working Group. The Army "decision memorandum" essentially said this: Due to budget cutbacks associated with the war in Iraq, the construction of the chemical agent demilitarization sites in Kentucky and Colorado might be delayed. As a result, the memo continued, the Army should consider ways to safeguard the stockpiles at those two sites, including "relocation if necessary among sites."

The implication was unmistakable. The Anniston Army Depot's chem-demil incinerator was the nearest facility to the Kentucky stockpile equipped to process weapons filled with nerve and blister agent. Despite a blizzard of assurances that it would never happen, Anniston was back on the table as a potential regional burn site—

a development that conjured images of boxcars bearing skull-and-crossbones markings, clacking and swaying in an infinite stream into northeast Alabama.

Williams, ever the Army's nemesis, promptly gave the memo to the *Star*, which splashed the story across its front page with a bitter vengeance. "Officials Look to Block Munitions" was the throbbing second-day headline, with the accompanying story featuring a pitchfork mob of elected leaders vowing to fight to the death any such importation of weapons. "Over my dead body," said Congressman Rogers. State Representative Lea Fite said, "It is outright lying to this community if they do this."

The Army made no comment. A few months later, it was quietly announced that the Army was no longer considering transferring chemical weapons between storage sites. But the notion that the Army could be trusted not to play bait-and-switch with the Anniston incinerator had taken on considerable water.

In late 2004, Judge Joel Laird finally blew.

And things had been going so well. For one thing, he had fulfilled his longtime dream of opening a restaurant, the Courthouse Café, a long-dormant landmark in Anniston that, as the name implied, sat in the shadow of the county courthouse, just a few paces from the old marble steps where the most remarkable press conference in Anniston history had transpired. True to his romantic notions of how a small town should operate, Laird believed that Anniston needed an eatery where the courthouse crowd and politicians and reporters and anyone else circling in those orbits could rub elbows and grab a meal. Laird had decorated the place with his Mayberry memorabilia, and felt he had done his part to contribute to the downtown renaissance.

Secondly, he had actually received some feelers from Hollywood. The same people who produced *Fear Factor* were contemplating a show starring a yet-to-be-cast judge who employed commonsense solutions to resolve disputes between parties. (For example, if two neighbors were fighting about a tree that sat on the boundary line between their houses, the judge might get an ax and go chop down the tree himself.) The producers had gotten in touch with Laird and asked if he had "a tape." He didn't—neither did most Alabama circuit judges—so he asked the guys at the local TV station to compile some footage they had shot of him over the years and send it to L.A. He hadn't heard back, and it had been a while, but who knew? Plus, an executive at a Christian network had called him about possibly appearing in yet another judge show. Laird had no idea how any of these people had heard of him or why they believed he might be TV material, but he would be a liar if he didn't admit it was flattering.

Mostly, however, Laird wanted life to return to normal—but the *Abernathy* case simply wouldn't go away. Now he had been forced to hold a hearing on a lawsuit that a group of *Abernathy* plaintiffs wanted to file against Donald Stewart, who was being accused of inflating his expenses in the case by as much as six million dollars. It seemed like a transparently frivolous attempt to spirit away some of Stewart's earnings from the case, the latest in what had been a series of demands by *Abernathy* and *Tolbert* plaintiffs that the attorneys involved give back substantial portions of their fees so the plaintiffs could have more. Laird had no intention of allowing the lawsuit to be filed, but would have to hold a hearing to expedite the whole business.

The hearing ultimately disintegrated into something akin to pay-per-view wrestling, with attorneys shouting at attorneys, plaintiffs and attorneys being admonished by Laird, attorneys being removed from the courtroom, plaintiffs hurling accusations at Laird, and plaintiffs being led away in handcuffs. Laird finally snapped: "This is the most ungrateful community I've ever seen. If it wasn't for that man over there," meaning Stewart, "no one in the room would have received a penny."

The courtroom at last was emptied, and Laird was left to stew alone with his thoughts. *What would Andy have done?* Andy probably would have sent the case file back to Judge Monk in the first place, that's what.

After a little time had gone by, Donald Stewart, who had won the verdict of a thousand lifetimes, decided to treat himself to a new car. He and Lulu had already decided that they would give most of the money away, but that didn't mean he couldn't splurge. He drove down to Sunny King Ford on South Quintard and found a year-old Crown Victoria sedan with only a few thousand miles on it. Stewart told the salesman, his old friend Tommy Pitts, that he would take it.

In November 2003, a few short months after the Solutia settlement was reached, the Jere Beasley law firm was one of two firms that won a mind-bending $11.9 billion verdict against Exxon Mobil Corporation on behalf of the State of Alabama, which had accused Exxon of cheating the state out of natural gas royalties.

Representing Exxon was the prestigious Birmingham defense firm of Lightfoot, Franklin & White.

To the victor goes the spoils. That cruel old saw kept echoing in David Baker's head as events continued to play out in the wake of the *Abernathy-Tolbert* settlement. Once, David had believed that when the war against Monsanto was done he would be able to relax a bit, to lead a slightly less stressful life, to finally enjoy his retirement, his marriage, his family and friends. But fate is nothing if not stubborn.

In the fall of 2005, his mother and his old union mentor, James Butler, died within weeks of one another. Mama's funeral drew a huge crowd, and a distraught David repeatedly told anyone who would listen that his mother had been his "jewel." David also spoke at Butler's memorial service in New York, which was attended by the Reverend Al Sharpton and a who's who list of New York labor. Later in 2005, David was hospitalized due to an onset of the terrible boils that have periodically tormented him since childhood, a condition that his doctors suspect is connected to the toxic levels of PCBs in his system. When he was released from the hospital he ran into ailing old friend and West Side stalwart Andrew Bowie, who was checking in. Bowie, who had made the first phone call to Donald Stewart on behalf of the Mars Hill church, died a few days later.

At year's end David took pen in hand and signed the papers that finalized divorce proceedings that Shirley had instigated. Life here on earth is crazy, David thought. Just when you think you've won a championship fight for the ages, things happen to help you understand that you're still just trying to survive the middle rounds.

In May 2005, the Department of Defense released its list of military bases recommended for closure. Under the DOD's plan, the Anniston Army Depot would remain open and be awarded an additional two thousand jobs.

It is a soft, gorgeous, unseasonably warm autumn Thursday evening in Anniston, Alabama, a full moon bathing the town in yellow, the kind of night that makes you feel young again and even tempts you to believe you might live forever. I've had a wonderful dinner with my folks, in their mid-seventies now, retired and doing well. We lingered over dessert and talked endlessly about a great many things—"chasing rabbits," my father calls it, going wherever the conversation leads us through the meandering fields and thickets of observation, opinion, and recollection. Now I'm driving down the mountain to attend a civic meeting at Anniston High School, thinking along the way about what a common yet rare pleasure it is to share time around a table with the people who brought you into the world, in the town in which you grew up and came of age. There was a time when it seemed as if I couldn't get away from this place far enough and fast enough; now, time spent here is a sparkling treasure, one that will drain through my fingers all too soon.

I have a few minutes to spare, so I decide to take a swing around the city. It doesn't take long. I roll down Tenth past Noble Street through downtown, past the railroad tracks and the old *Star* building, now vacant. I think of how I loved that gritty, awful, windowless, nicotine-encrusted old place, loved the people who worked there, even loved the bitter, corrosive vending-machine coffee that kept so many of us alive during so many late nights pounding out so many meeting stories. I loved that the building sat barely west of the tracks—circumstantial evidence, it seemed to me, that the paper had cast its lot with the less fortunate who lived on that side of town. The *Star* is now housed in a new, glassy, sixteen-million-dollar edifice on a wooded hilltop on the old Fort McClellan property. It must be a pleasure to work there—George Smith, the great and enduring *Star* columnist from whose cold, dead fingers they will no doubt have to pry the keyboard, says that deer occasionally laze up to his office window and peer inside, as if peeking over his shoulder at tomorrow's column. But it can't be the same, nor, I suppose, should it be. Everyone says Anniston's future is all about the old McClellan reservation, where college campuses, big-box stores, and the like are envisioned. The *Star*, as every viable enterprise must, looks to have thrown in with the future, and that probably is the brave and mature thing to do. I, on the other hand, am an ever-willing prisoner in that beautiful jail of nostalgia, content for the moment to hold on to the dear past.

I drift through the West Side, where there is little sign of the revolution that has taken place there, no indicator of the historic legal uprising against an industrial legacy that reaches back into the very womb of Anniston's birth. Nor would an unknowing person suspect that a giant oven of fearsome power is cremating weapons of mass destruction, real ones, in the hidden woods nearby. Every now and then I spy a yard that is bordered with orange tape, where soil decontamination by Solutia is under way. There are reports in the news that the EPA is investigating the possibility of lead contamination across the breadth and width of West Anniston down into Hobson City, the by-product, it is said, of free foundry sand used as fill dirt for generations. The talk now is of "identifying responsible parties." The courtroom wars may not be over even yet. But the lead and PCBs and whatever else percolates here are invisible to the eye. For now, tonight, things mostly look the way they've looked for many years, and it's easy to pretend that things remain the way they've always been.

The illusion holds steady as I double back across Noble Street and cruise past the Anniston High football field, which to my surprise is all aglow from the big stadium lights. The stands are empty, but in the west end zone the Anniston football team is on one knee in an attentive circle around its coach, who obviously is in mid-inspirational speech. The old Thursday pep talk for Friday night's game. I pull over on a bluff above the field to absorb the scene.

Through the open car windows, on cue, come the distant, fuzzy strains of a marching band drilling on some unseen practice field, the pounding drums and prancing horns bouncing off the hills. Nothing carries on a stone-still southern evening like the sound of a marching band, unless it is the sharp, punctuating *tweet* of a coach's whistle, sounds that live and breathe and bring with them the promise that some things truly never change.

But Anniston did change. I turned my back for only a moment—or maybe it was twenty years—and a great reckoning came to pass. People like Chip Howell and David Baker left town and went to college or the big city and came home to lead armies and make decisions and write history, so that childhoods like theirs and mine could be replicated on floodlit football fields and all the other places where young people grow up and learn about life and the living of it. Maybe they even did it so that knights-errant like me could wander to the ends of the earth and then return, if only to make sure that the old home place still stands in the mist, like Tara. And Anniston persists, by God, having nearly died and the stronger for it, different and the same, a place where an old ghost can sit on a hill on a timeless night and gaze down on what is gone forever and still there.

ACKNOWLEDGMENTS

An awful burden settles upon the writer who undertakes a book about his hometown. As with any work of nonfiction, he is obligated to report the truth as it grudgingly reveals itself to him, with as much vigor as he can muster onto the page. But an even higher standard is in play when the subject is *home* and the people who live there. It is inevitable that the writer will prevail upon people who know him, or think they know him because of the old days, and they will trust him. Because if they can't trust someone who is "one of our own," then who can they trust? And so the good people of Anniston, Alabama—perhaps against their better judgment—gave me the benefit of the doubt. They talked to me, welcomed me into their offices, their homes, and their lives, and allowed this book to happen. I am in their debt, and I hope that I have honored the trust they placed in me.

I thought I knew everyone in Anniston, but David Baker was a stranger to me until his name began to appear in connection with the grassroots movement against Monsanto. I had never met him until I arrived in Anniston in the fall of 2003 to begin work on what would become *My City Was Gone*. Even before our first conversation, I had an inkling that he might be a prominent player in this narrative; that suspicion was quickly confirmed when we sat down for an initial meeting that stretched to almost three hours. David not only had a story to tell, he *needed* to tell it—a blessing for a writer searching for voices to explain the tectonic shift that had occurred in the town that had raised both of us. In the ensuing months David was unfailingly generous with his time and provided me with the essential framework of this book, and for that I am incredibly grateful. David's mother, the late Imogene Baker, also shared her time and memories even as her health was failing. Shirley Baker also moved a few mountains on my behalf, as did the staff at Community Against Pollution.

Donald Stewart, the gifted and canny Anniston attorney who waged and won the epic legal battle against Monsanto, had no reason to indulge my requests for his time and assistance other than, perhaps, my persistence in asking for them. But still he gallantly worked me into his calendar where he could and provided me with the perspective that was absolutely crucial to the "Monsanto arc" of this story. His staff, especially Gail Ashley, also cheerfully tolerated my intrusions.

Joel Laird, the judge who watched over the *Abernathy* case with the patience of a saint, could easily have hidden behind his judicial robes and ignored my pleas for his cooperation. But he, like so many others, felt that it was important that people understand what happened and what had been at stake. He was relentlessly candid, never once mincing an opinion—again, writer's gold. I was particularly appreciative of a rainy holiday morning he spent with me in his office, and of a Sunday afternoon on which he invited me into his home. Both were occasions that he undoubtedly would have preferred to spend with his family. The judge always came through, and I thank him.

In Montgomery, the attorney David Byrne of the powerhouse firm of Beasley, Allen, Crow, Methvin, Portis & Miles did his best to accommodate my requests, as did his associate Rhon Jones and the firm's founding partner, Jere Beasley. In Tuskegee, the legendary Jock Smith of the Johnnie Cochran law firm provided a mesmerizing virtual tour of the Monsanto case and the endgame that resulted in its astonishing settlement. I also appreciate the efforts of Jere White of the Birmingham defense firm of Lightfoot, Franklin & White to make inroads with Monsanto and Solutia on my behalf, although continuing litigation effectively blocked their participation. Continuing litigation also blocked White's ability to talk to me about his firm's role in the case. It was Anniston's story I set out to tell anyway, not Monsanto's, but there may be some who complain that the corporation's side of things wasn't fully represented. To them I say: We eagerly await your version of what Monsanto did in Anniston, and why.

Thanks also to James Hall, Barbara Boyd, Shirley McCord, Pam Scully of the EPA, Dr. Howard Frumkin of the Rollins School of Health at Emory University, Janice Nodvin of May South, Inc., the late Andrew Bowie, George Murphy, the late Russell "Tombstone" Williams, the family of the late Manuel Washington, and the many others who contributed to my understanding of PCB contamination and its impact on Anniston and its people.

The "incinerator arc" of this book was another challenge altogether, dense with technicality and politics, and in dire need of a medium through which that part of the story could be told. Mayor Chip Howell became that channel for the recounting of the series of events that led to Anniston's prominent role in the chemical weapons universe, and he graciously submitted to a series of interviews that brought those events into clear view for the author. In the spirit of disclosure, it should be noted that Chip and I have known each other since the beginning of time and have been friendly over the years, but neither one of us would describe our relationship as close. We probably had not spoken in more than twenty years when I first approached him during my research for this book, and he surely must have been wary of my intentions. Still he was willing to help, and I thank him.

Craig Williams and Brenda Lindell led the fight against incineration in Anniston. Both were generous with their time and analysis, and impressive with their passion and commitment to their cause. Brenda also loaned me her extensive collection of newspaper clippings and other materials relating to incineration in Anniston and elsewhere, which proved to be of incalculable value. Calhoun County Commissioners Robert Downing and Eli Henderson illuminated the county's role in the incineration fight, and treated me to an enjoyable thrashing at the billiards table at the Eagles Lodge while they were at it. At Anniston Army Depot, Mike Abrams argued the merits of incineration and was among the many who testified to the role of the military in the evolutionary history of Anniston. At the Anniston incinerator itself, Tim Garrett and Robert Love (no relation to the author) provided a tour of the facility—no easy ticket—and tirelessly explained the efforts of the Army and Westinghouse to safely destroy the lethal weapons housed there. Pete Conroy, who always sees the big picture, connected the dots for me on several occasions. Saye Atkinson shared his expertise on the vagaries of chem-demil installations. Thanks also to those who helped me piece together the final political maneuverings that surrounded the start of the Anniston "burn" but who asked not to be identified.

In Tooele, Mayor Charlie Roberts was happy to discuss that city's long association with the Army, chemical weapons, and incineration, as were Chuck Sprague and Clint Warby at the Deseret Chemical

Depot. Dayne Applegate was among many in Tooele who served up a citizen's context with black humor on the side.

Throughout this book, and especially regarding the issue of chemical weapons incineration, I am indebted to the efforts of the staff of the *Anniston Star*, which remains one of the finest newspapers of any size in America. I have attempted to credit specific writers and articles where credit seemed appropriate and necessary, but rest assured that the totality of the paper's reportage significantly influenced my work here, through sheer osmosis from reading it for nearly fifty years if nothing else. Brandy and Josie Ayers extended their hospitality, Chris Waddle attempted to set me straight, and the impregnable George Smith offered kind words. I am grateful for every gesture.

Any exploration like mine of Anniston's unusual history owes much to the late historian Grace Gates, whose book, *The Model City of the New South*, documented Anniston's not-so-humble origins. Grace encouraged me long ago to write my own book about Anniston, and I wish she had lived to see it. I also am grateful to the Anniston–Calhoun County Public Library, particularly the staff in the Alabama Room, which houses an invaluable cache of historical Anniston documents that were of great use.

The late Randy Henderson was instrumental in helping me think through the proposal phase of this book, just as he guided my work at the *Anniston Star* and the *Birmingham News*. I still can't believe he's gone.

Anniston provided a solid infrastructure for me during the several months I spent there researching and writing. Pam Frame offered her encouragement and insight, as did Fred Burger, Basil Penny, Alice Donald, Roger Couch, Sue Vondracek, Sherry Kughn, Martha Patrick, Donna Klabnik, Ric and Lynn Jones, Steve Mullendore, Tom Sawyer, John and Becky Hollingsworth, and Danny Craft. My go-to guy regarding all things Anniston was the unsinkable Tubby Bass, whose institutional memory of the town he loves so dearly is outshined only by the esteem in which he is held by his fellow citizens. Chip Howell may be mayor, but Tubby is king.

Others in California and elsewhere offered their vitally needed encouragement at various points along the way, including Clint Williams, Teresa Rafael, Stacy Brown, DD Despard, Dorothy Korber, Tom Kunkel and, especially, Rex Babin, who knew it would happen even as I lost faith.

My agent, the steadfast Flip Brophy of Sterling Lord Literistic, believed in this book from my first halting attempts to describe it and found a wonderfully supportive editor in Henry Ferris, who artfully navigated *My City Was Gone* to publication. My thanks to Henry, Peter Hubbard, and everyone else at William Morrow and HarperCollins for making this book a reality.

Bill and Virginia Love, my unswerving parents, sporadically housed and fed me during the course of this project and offered their unconditional moral support when I needed it most. I can never repay them for the sustaining love they have invested in me for so long—a lifetime—but I can keep trying.

And, finally, thanks to my wife, the amazing Terri Hardy, who helped with the heavy lifting early on, provided inspiration throughout, and literally made this book possible with her selflessness and sacrifice. She continues to light the way.

INDEX